# Benjamin Franklin, Jonathan Edwards, and the Representation of American Culture

# BENJAMIN FRANKLIN, JONATHAN EDWARDS, AND THE REPRESENTATION OF AMERICAN CULTURE

Edited by

BARBARA B. OBERG

HARRY S. STOUT

New York   Oxford
OXFORD UNIVERSITY PRESS
1993

## Oxford University Press

Oxford   New York   Toronto
Delhi   Bombay   Calcutta   Madras   Karachi
Kuala Lumpur   Singapore   Hong Kong   Tokyo
Nairobi   Dar es Salaam   Cape Town
Melbourne   Auckland   Madrid

and associated companies in
Berlin   Ibadan

## Copyright © 1993 by Oxford University Press, Inc.

Published by Oxford University Press, Inc.
200 Madison Avenue, New York, New York 10016

Library of Congress Cataloging-in-Publication Data
Benjamin Franklin, Jonathan Edwards, and the
representation of American culture /
edited by Barbara B. Oberg and Harry S. Stout.
p. cm.   ISBN 0-19-507775-X
1. American prose literature—18th century—History and criticism.
2. Franklin, Benjamin, 1706–1790—Criticism and interpretation.
3. Edwards, Jonathan, 1703–1758—Criticism and interpretation.
4. Language and culture—United States—History—18th century.
5. National characteristics, American, in literature.
6. United States—Intellectual life—18th century.
I. Oberg, Barbara.
II. Stout, Harry S.
PS367.B46   1993   810.9'001—dc20   92-34327

2 4 6 8 9 7 5 3 1

Printed in the United States of America
on acid-free paper

# Acknowledgments

Several individuals have helped contribute to this work. We express our thanks to Lewis J. Nescott and John H. Edwards, who organized the conference out of which this book emerged. We are also deeply appreciative of the insights offered by the commentators at the conference: Patricia Bonomi, David D. Hall, John M. Murrin, and Gordon S. Wood. Their perceptions have enriched several of the essays published here. Support for the conference was provided by the Pew Charitable Trusts, the Ellis L. Phillips Foundation, the Connecticut Humanities Council, and the Whitney Humanities Center at Yale University. We are deeply appreciative of their support. Finally, we are grateful to Ava Chamberlain and especially Kenneth P. Minkema for their assistance in preparing this manuscript for the press. Their help has been invaluable.

# Contents

# LANGUAGE

## *Abbreviations Used in Citations*

*PBF*  *The Papers of Benjamin Franklin* (New Haven, Yale Univ. Press, 1959–    )

*WJE*  *The Works of Jonathan Edwards* (New Haven, Yale Univ. Press, 1957–    )

# Contributors

A. OWEN ALDRIDGE
University of Illinois
Champaign-Urbana, Illinois

RUTH H. BLOCH
University of California
Los Angeles, California

WILLIAM BREITENBACH
University of Puget Sound
Tacoma, Washington

R. C. DE PROSPO
Washington College
Chestertown, Maryland

ELIZABETH E. DUNN
Auburn University
Montgomery, Alabama

EDWIN S. GAUSTAD
University of California
Riverside, California

DANIEL WALKER HOWE
Oxford University
Oxford, England

BRUCE KUKLICK
University of Pennsylvania
Philadelphia, Pennsylvania

J. A. LEO LEMAY
University of Delaware
Newark, Delaware

DAVID LEVIN
University of Virginia
Charlottesville, Virginia

LEONARD I. SWEET
United Theological Seminary
Dayton, Ohio

MICHAEL ZUCKERMAN
University of Pennsylvania
Philadelphia, Pennsylvania

Benjamin Franklin,
Jonathan Edwards, and the Representation of
American Culture

# 1

# Introduction

BARBARA B. OBERG AND HARRY S. STOUT

It is difficult, if not impossible, to think of two more widely studied colonial figures than Benjamin Franklin and Jonathan Edwards. On Edwards alone there have been more than 1,500 books, articles, and dissertations published in the last century. Scholarship on Franklin is no less impressive: historians of politics, science, literature, and culture have produced close to 4,000 works—scholarly and popular—on Franklin.[1] Most recently, two collections of essays have appeared detailing the present "state of the art" in Franklin and Edwards scholarship.[2] Nor have their own writings been ignored. Modern editions housed at Yale University have been providing a steady volume of their work in critical editions designed to preserve their words into the twenty-first century.[3]

As Franklin and Edwards have been studied individually over the generations, so also have they been looked at together in comparative exercises dating back at least as far as George Bancroft in the 1840s.[4] In all of those studies the two emerge as quintessential "representative men." Like all representative figures, Franklin and Edwards considered together have not been studied for their own sake or simply to cast light on their age. Rather, they are selected because in some profound sense they prefigure or anticipate a subsequent era. In this case, while other colonial figures exerted comparable, or even greater, influence on their age, none so completely anticipated the subsequent shape of an American culture, at once material and spiritual, piously secular and pragmatically sacred, as did Edwards and Franklin. It is thus in the intersection of Franklin's and Edwards's colonial times with an ever changing American "present"

3

and in the endlessly renewing creative tensions fostered by the meeting of their ideas that the two enjoy a unique representative status.

In identifying exactly what Franklin and Edwards typify in American culture, the two most frequently invoked labels are "Puritan" and "Yankee." Puritan values, signified by Edwards and sustained in American "evangelicalism," have as their organizing terms and values "God," communal "faith," and "self-denial." Yankee attributes, signified by Franklin and sustained in American liberal republicanism, coalesce around the trinity of hard work, independent "virtue," and utilitarian "self-happiness." For two and a half centuries these alternative emphases and orientations have coexisted in uneasy tension both individually and in American society at large. In their intersection we see both the contrasts and the fusions, the conflict and the confluence, that create what Michael Kammen terms a "people of paradox."[5]

As representative men, Franklin and Edwards have been tied as much to an ever changing present as to their own completed past. Even as scholars in each generation rehearse the legacies of the two, they do so in ways that reflect their own distinctive times and issues. For the longest period, historians and literary scholars were more concerned with the contrasts between Franklin and Edwards than with the connections or larger unities. Often these contrasts coincided with thinly veiled sentiments of admiration or disdain. Writing in the 1930s, for example, Vernon Parrington, contrasted the forward-looking, "free soul" Franklin with the "Great Anachronism" Edwards.[6] Like others in the Progressive Era, Parrington reflected the liberal optimism of the age both in his secular repudiation of religion as a "backward" force and in his confidence that American liberal democracy could create a better world. Without ever deprecating Edwards's prodigious intellect and promise, Parrington nevertheless saw in Edwards the regressive and pessimistic qualities holding back America's march to progress, while Franklin embodied the hope of an ever more liberal, enlightened American order.

Twenty years later, writing in the aftermath of World War II and in the midst of the Cold War, Perry Miller reassessed the legacies of Franklin and Edwards in ways that passed the torch of progress to Edwards. In an age of holocaust and nuclear terror, Miller affirmed, it was Edwards, the "child of genius," whose realistic vision was "modern," and it was Franklin (and by extension the Progressives) whose faith in reason and technology represented an old-fashioned and naïve social faith.[7]

In virtually all of the studies completed through the 1950s, Franklin and Edwards acquired the characteristics of mutually exclusive "ideal types"—figures abstracted from their historical context and set into categories as different (and opposed) as "traditional" and "modern." In all of them, the polemical edge was never far beneath the surface, so that, by implication, the contrasts took on the moral quality of "good" and "bad," "right" and "wrong." Whatever commonalities the two had were stripped away in the face of irreconcilable differences. Not only were their world views polar opposites, they seemed to compete for adherents.

Now, in the 1990s, it is clear that many of the old historiographical categories have broken down. The historical profession is more inclined than ever before to take religion seriously and on its own terms. At the same time, "church historians" have moved out of their defensive polemics and institutional apologetics to understand and join with the larger professional enterprise of which they are a part. Inevitably, this accommodation casts any exercise in comparative representation between Edwards and Franklin in a new light. What do joint studies of Franklin and Edwards have to tell us today?

It is this question that prompted the editions of Benjamin Franklin and Jonathan Edwards to host a 1990 conference at Yale University looking at Edwards and Franklin in comparative contexts.[8] Despite the numbers of individuals who have examined Franklin and Edwards together over the centuries, this was, we believed, the first time a major conference, consisting of prominent scholars from both the Franklin and the Edwards camps, convened to look at the two in a comparative framework. The exercise was old, but the altered context and changing times created entirely new insights and arguments. In the following essays, published from that conference, it is clear just how far scholarship—and American society—has moved from the 1840s or the 1950s, and how much more complex is our understanding of Franklin and Edwards in relation to each other and in relation to the society.

This book differs from earlier treatments of Edwards and Franklin in several ways. Most dramatic is the virtual disappearance of mutually exclusive, polemical contrasts. That change was signaled in David Levin's keynote address, in which questions of good and bad, right and wrong, were subordinated to the larger question of commonality on the level of "reason, rhythm, and style."[9] Levin's keynote sounded quite literally a note or refrain that sounds throughout the essays. Instead of mutually exclusive types, Edwards and Franklin emerge in these essays together as contrapuntal themes in a larger unity. Neither their legacies nor their inner selves admit of simple, self-contained compartments that set one off against the other. Any contrast between the two can, as Bruce Kuklick points out in his essay, be "widened" into a larger shared universe. In this sense, it is fruitless to ask whether the similarities or differences are "more important." What is instructive is the similarities *and* the differences existing in creative tension. And in the tension of widening and contracting, comparison and contrast, the unique contribution—and spirit—of these essays becomes clear.

Necessarily, any comparative exercise using Franklin and Edwards produces less a complete biography or assessment of the two as men of their age than would emerge if they were considered individually. Significant aspects of each of their careers fail to appear. Franklin the statesman and diplomat is largely hidden, as is Edwards the pastor and preacher. But there are corresponding gains that surface as we see each in the context of what American culture has become. Two "American" dimensions in particular emerge that were common to Franklin and

Edwards and that serve as the organizing sections for this volume. These might be labeled "Mind" and "Culture." Bridging the two is a third rubric that both links and transcends mind and culture: language, or rhetoric.

Under "mind" we group those essays concerned broadly with what the eighteenth century termed "moral philosophy" and what we would call social thought and ethics. Franklin and Edwards were profound philosophers who never called themselves philosophers. Both came to the ethical task of defining the values of a nation by other routes, especially journalism (Franklin) and theology (Edwards). Yet in their common concern with mind, character, and virtue, they shaped a legacy that would define much of American character for generations to come. As moral philosophers, the recurring problem they faced was the problem of human nature. This problem, Daniel Walker Howe points out, was in fact the "central problem of eighteenth-century moral philosophy." How does one do the right thing or, for that matter, know what the right thing is? Can virtue be taught? What are the respective roles of the "faculties" of reason and the passions in regulating conscience and behavior? Those questions lay at the heart of issues shaping American society in a dawning age of revolution, and they have continued to shape issues of public policy and corporate identity in American society ever since.

Besides sharing the concerns of the eighteenth-century British moral philosophers, Franklin and Edwards were products of a colonial New England culture that shaped them as much as they shaped it. By "culture," we have in mind what Elizabeth Dunn terms the "clusters of beliefs and values" that function on a symbolic or pretheoretical level to provide meaning and direction to individuals within any particular society. Many essays examine Franklin and Edwards together in what might be termed a cultural context. Here the concern is less with philosophy and public policy than with more personal qualities of language and style, family and gender roles, or humor and promotional strategies. The cultural essays are necessarily more diffuse and look less at their minds than at the nonpublic, nonofficial sides of Franklin's and Edwards's lives. To be sure, Franklin and, to a lesser extent, Edwards did not have much of a private life. Yet, as Michael Zuckerman points out in his essay, this itself is symptomatic of an emerging public culture of autonomous individuals.

The organization of the essays follows the sequence from mind to culture. *Benjamin Franklin, Jonathan Edwards, and the Representation of American Culture* begins with William Breitenbach's consideration of the ways in which Franklin's *Autobiography* and Edwards's *Treatise on the Affections* stand within the wider context of "cautionary tales." He explores ways in which both classics "are about ways to salvation and success. In short, both books are about conversion." Four essays follow on the intellectual world in which Franklin and Edwards addressed the pressing issues of their age. Owen Aldridge asks a question similar to Breitenbach's but looks at a different text. Focusing especially on Edwards's *History of Redemption*, Aldridge demonstrates both the "enlightened" foundation of Edwards's ethics and the "awakened" religious sensibilities of Franklin's theology. Using yet a third text, Edwin Gaustad examines Edwards's *Two Dissertations* and "Charity sermons" to show how Edwards's sense of virtue as "universal love" related to his larger cosmology—a world view shared by Franklin in its affirmation of a "superintending providence in a moral universe." It is this shared cosmology, Gaustad argues, that accounts for the fact that even as the two travel in separate orbits, they "inhabit the same moral universe." That universe, in brief, was the moral fabric of the eighteenth century.

As intellectuals, Edwards and Franklin were natural philosophers as much as they were moral philosophers; they saw in nature analogues for virtue and piety. Although most of the essays dealing with mind have concentrated on moral philosophy, Elizabeth Dunn's essay contrasts the "essentialist" focus of Edwards, which drove him to theoretical science and cosmology, with the "functionalist" orientation of Franklin, which drove him to practical science and technological innovation. The two ways Edwards and Franklin approached mind, Dunn continues, account not only for the common interests and diverse paths in science, but, more generally, for their opposite tendencies to organize and express belief in public *virtue* (Franklin) or public *faith* (Edwards). The first section concludes with Daniel Walker Howe's overview of the intellectual context that framed eighteenth-century Americans' preoccupation with the problem of human nature. Both Edwards and Franklin absorbed a "faculty psychology" that functioned both descriptively, as a model of the self, and prescriptively, as a guide to the proper mixture of reason, passion, and conscience in human behavior. Yet within this "social science," Edwards and Franklin would offer opposed solutions, and in the end both would transcend the conventional primacy of the reason with, respectively, virtuous "habits" (Franklin) and pious "affections" (Edwards).

In moving beyond mind to culture, we see the complex ways in which they were similar to and different from one another and, in turn, how each was attuned to but simultaneously at odds with his society. In a rapidly changing eighteenth-century milieu, both Franklin and Edwards operated, as Bruce Kuklick shows, on the fringes of their society. In fact, Kuklick argues, the two were not "representative men," if by that term is meant figures typical of their age and recognized as such in their own lifetime. Only after the Revolution could Franklin be seen as the "progenitor" of the American Yankee, and only after the collapse of Calvinism in New England could Edwards be seen as Puritanism's "final representative."

As humorists and lovers, Franklin and Edwards were apparently as far apart as two men could possibly be. In pathbreaking essays, Leonard Sweet and Ruth Bloch pursue these two dimensions of Edwards's and

Franklin's private life in the context of a changing eighteenth-century culture. Sweet concedes that Edwards was often melancholic in mood and shy in company, but nevertheless documents extensive instances of light, joy, and "high" humor that in an aristocratic culture was every bit as humorous as the more bawdy "folk" humor for which Franklin was famous. In her essay, Bloch notes that as husbands and lovers, Edwards and Franklin evidenced very different attitudes toward gender, love, and marriage. Yet, again, there were similarities in the ways both "helped set the stage for the transformed gender ideology of the late eighteenth century."

The essay on Franklin and P. T. Barnum by Michael Zuckerman concentrates on the "selling of self" so apparent throughout Franklin's career. Yet, at the same time, Zuckerman points out, the line between self-help and public virtue was often blurred. In fact, Zuckerman would argue, Franklin had no inner self, so that his life in fact was given over to the public. Although Edwards never showed the promotional skills seen in Franklin, other eighteenth-century "Awakeners" did. And here, Zuckerman's essay fits well with Daniel Walker Howe's suggestion that in George Whitefield, Edwards the pietist and Franklin the promoter came together in a potent combination that would come to define modern "evangelicalism."

Besides publicity, humor, and romance, culture is, above all, language. In Levin's keynote, together with essays by J. A. Leo Lemay and R. C. De Prospo, Edwards and Franklin are compared less on *what* they said than on *how* they said it. Both Lemay and Levin invite readers to open their *ears* to Franklin and Edwards as well as their eyes. Levin shows how Edwards and Franklin manifested a sense of clarity in language and an instinct for proportion and balance that were persuasive and that constituted, in Lemay's terms, an implicit "rhetorical strategy," which can be reconstructed quite clearly in Edwards's *Sinners in the Hands of an Angry God* and Franklin's *Massacre in Lancaster County*. De Prospo's essay moves beyond the rhetorical analysis of texts to what he terms a "modern humanist, poststructuralist" attempt to recover the context in which key documents were composed and, in De Prospo's words, "save the texts of early American literature."

If these essays show anything, it is how closely connected Franklin and Edwards remain to their ever changing American presents. How long they will continue to be American icons in a postmodern world is unclear. But surely in 1993, as in 1840, they remain America's most resonant colonial "representatives."

## Notes

1. Works on JE through 1981 are catalogued in M. X. Lesser, *Jonathan Edwards: A Reference Guide* (Boston, 1981). Works on BF through 1983 can be located in Melvin H. Buxbaum, *Benjamin Franklin: A Reference Guide*, 2 vols. (Boston, 1988).

2. See Nathan O. Hatch and Harry S. Stout, eds., *Jonathan Edwards and the American Experience* (New York, 1988), and J. A. Leo Lemay, ed., *Reappraising Franklin: A Bicentennial Perspective* (Newark, Del., 1993).

3. The Yale edition of *The Works of Jonathan Edwards* began at Yale in 1954, publishing its first volume in 1957. To date, ten volumes have been published, with twenty scheduled to follow. The Yale edition of *The Papers of Benjamin Franklin* began at Yale in 1954, publishing its first volume in 1959. Twenty-nine volumes have been published, with some seventeen more coming to complete the edition.

4. See David Levin, "Reason, Rhythm, and Style," selection 11 herein.

5. Michael Kammen, *People of Paradox: An Inquiry Concerning the Origins of American Civilization* (New York, 1972). Kammen links Franklin and Edwards three times in his discussion: pp. 93, 111, and 196.

6. Vernon Louis Parrington, *Main Currents in American Thought* (New York, 1927, 1930), 148–78.

7. Perry Miller, *Jonathan Edwards* (New York, 1949; reprinted Amherst, Mass., 1981), xxxii.

8. The event was named "The National Conference on Edwards and Franklin." Participants from across the country and abroad met for three days, February 22–24, 1990.

9. See also David Levin's earlier comparative essay, *The Puritan in the Enlightenment: Franklin and Edwards* (Chicago, 1963).

# MIND

# 2

# Religious Affections and Religious Affectations: Antinomianism and Hypocrisy in the Writings of Edwards and Franklin

WILLIAM BREITENBACH

When I received the letter inviting me to participate in a conference on Benjamin Franklin and Jonathan Edwards, I was somewhat startled to read in it the assertion that "there has been little serious effort to bring the thought and intellectual legacy of these figures into a scholarly dialogue."[1] If it startled me, this statement would have stunned my students, who for years have struggled with paper assignments and examination questions asking them to compare the ideas of these two great thinkers. Perhaps the key phrase in the letter was "serious effort," for I cannot swear that my students always undertook their task with the appropriate solemnity. In any event, I'm sure they would be pleased to know that their doctor has finally been dosed with his own medicine.

Let me begin with the same broad questions that I pose to my students. Here we have two men, both born in New England at the beginning of the eighteenth century, both sharing a common Puritan heritage and a common commitment to the values of the Enlightenment, and yet they developed quite different intellectual systems. Or did they? Should one be struck more by the similarities or the dissimilarities in their ideas? I shall attempt to answer the questions by examining the theme of morality and true virtue in the two men's masterpieces— Franklin's *Autobiography* and Edwards's *Religious Affections.*

At first glance it is hard to imagine two moralists less alike. The one was an austere Calvinist, a supernaturalist and biblicist, a subtle theologian and formidable polemicist, who spent each Lord's Day preaching from the pulpit. The other was a genial Deist, a naturalist, a despiser of all dogmatism and sectarianism, who preferred to spend his Sunday as a "Studying-Day."[2] The most famous work of the one is governed by the ominous image of "slipping." In it he spoke of human depravity and said that sinners' wickedness made them as odious and loathsome as spiders. The most famous work of the other is governed by the buoyant image of "swimming."[3] In it he spoke not of sin nor even of sins but of "errata," and he concluded that "a benevolent Man should allow a few Faults in himself, to keep his Friends in Countenance."[4] The one found the way to salvation in an instantaneous and disjunctive moment of regeneration, during which the Holy Spirit came to dwell in him as a principle of new nature, infusing supernatural habits of holiness in his heart. When the other set out to achieve moral perfection, he steadily and gradually built up his own habits of virtue by working on them one at a time in a series of thirteen-week courses. The one believed that his sins could be washed clean only by the blood of Christ. He was a God-made man. The other—the self-made man—found it convenient to record his faults in a memorandum book with ivory leaves so that he "could easily wipe out" his own blots "with a wet Sponge."[5] The one devised an elaborate doctrinal system about which it was said, "You can if you will and you can't if you won't; you're damned if you do and you're damned if you don't." The other published a profitable almanac in which he wrote, "God helps them that help themselves." The one sought to save men's souls. The other sought to improve their characters. The one considered religion to be a matter of piety and defined it as "a love to divine things for the beauty and sweetness of their moral excellency."[6] The other considered religion to be a matter of ethics and concluded "that the most acceptable Service of God was the doing Good to Man."[7] Both centered their creeds on the concept of virtue. But the one meant by that something so pure and refined and selfless that only the regenerate could display it, for it was none other than the "true *grace* and real *holiness*" of converted saints.[8] The other thought that virtuous service to others was not incompatible with the alert pursuit of self-interest; that an imperfectly virtuous person was preferable to a perfectly vicious one; and that if one could not achieve the reality of virtue, the semblance of it was an acceptable substitute. So there you have it— Edwards and Franklin, The Preacher and the Printer: A Tale of Religious Affections and Religious Affectations.

There is, of course, much more to it than this quick catalogue of contrasts would suggest. For in many respects, *Religious Affections* and the *Autobiography* are remarkably similar works. Both books answer in their own ways the questions that Edwards asks at the outset of his: "What are the distinguishing qualifications of those that are in favor with God, and entitled to his eternal [Franklin would substitute "earthly"] rewards? . . . and wherein do lie the distinguishing notes of that virtue and holiness, that is acceptable in the sight of God?"[9] Both books are about the ways to salvation and success. Both are guidebooks that instruct readers how to recognize and secure the qualifications that will entitle them to the rewards dispensed by a just God. In short, both books are about conversion.[10] Perhaps equally important, both are cautionary tales— as much about ways to fail as about ways to succeed.[11] Both detail the dangers of false conversions and describe the false hopes and false appearances on which those delusory conversions so precariously perch. Both warn, as Edwards put it in his preface, of the "inexpressibly dreadful" consequences of failing "to distinguish between true and false religion, between saving affections and experiences, and those manifold fair shows, and glistering appearances, by which they are counterfeited."[12] In effect, both are handbooks of signs and no-signs that enable their readers to penetrate hypocrisy and decipher the hearts of others and themselves.

This purpose is more evident in *Religious Affections,* an analysis of the nature and evidences of conversion. Edwards wrote the book in the aftermath of the Great Awakening, when true religion was being counterfeited by two sets of forgers.[13] The first kind of bogus divinity was being disseminated by "legal hypocrites," who tried (as he says it) to buy their way into heaven with mere outward morality and external religion. According to Edwards, the legal hypocrites mistakenly thought that conversion involved just an improvement in behavior and not an internal transformation of the heart. The more dangerous threat, however, and the one against which *Religious Affections* was mainly directed, came from the group that Edwards termed "evangelical hypocrites." These were the enthusiasts and antinomians who made up the radical wing of the New Light camp. They supposed themselves the special favorites of God, a conviction they based on the imaginary impulses and revelations they claimed to have received about their own salvation. Such internal visions and impressions—"that their sins are forgiven them, that their names are written in the *Book of Life,* that they are in high favor with God, etc."—they took as the surest and most glorious evidence of their justification, assuming these things to be the witness of the Spirit.[14] Naturally, those supposed revelations made evangelical hypocrites supremely confident; indeed, they assumed that an unwavering assurance of their election was itself the highest virtue. Such assurance they refused to doubt or question even when they fell into lifeless frames and corrupt, wicked ways. Theirs was a boldness, a certainty, not to be shaken by sin.

Edwards noted that these false Christians tended to give sound Cal-vinist doctrines an antinomian twist. Emphasizing the sufficiency of Christ's imputed righteousness above any human qualification for justi-fication, they incautiously preached that saints should live by faith, not by sight; that they should live upon Christ and not upon experiences; and that they should not make their good frames the foundation of their faith. These were excellent doctrines when rightly expounded, but the evangelical hypocrites distorted them by defining justifying faith as the faith of assurance; that is, their certain belief that Christ's righteousness is applied particularly to them to satisfy the debt of sin. Edwards spelled out the antinomian implications:

> Hence they count it a dreadful sin for them to doubt of their state, whatever frames they are in, and whatever wicked things they do, because 'tis the great and heinous sin of unbelief; and he is the best man, and puts most honor upon God, that maintains his hope of his good estate the most confidently and immovably, when he has the least light or experience; that is to say, when he is in the worst and wickedest frame and way; because, forsooth, that is a sign that he is strong in faith, giving glory to God, and against hope believes in hope.[15]

Masking their immorality with perfervid talk and boastful pretensions, the antinomians preached a kind of religion that made good bad and bad good. The concepts of vice and virtue, like all customary notions of morality, became, for the evangelical hypocrites, mere empty distinctions, heeded only by the weak in faith.

Such a creed had, of course, a great appeal for conceited, proud sin-ners. Edwards censured the evangelical hypocrites particularly for the selfishness of their religion. Indeed, he suggested that their delusive visions and impulses were nothing more than wishful fantasies. It was striking, he noted, and easily explained, that their revelations always revealed "such things as they are desirous and fond of."[16] Evangelical hypocrites were like people

> . . . that have had a fond desire of something of a temporal nature, through a violent passion that has possessed them, and they have been earnestly pur-suing the thing they have desired should come to pass, and have met with great difficulty and many discouragements in it, but at last have had an im-pression or supposed revelation that they should obtain what they sought; and they have looked upon it as a sure promise from the Most High, which has made them most ridiculously confident, against all manner of reason to convince them to the contrary, and all events working against them.[17]

What these pretenders sought, and what they found in their self-centered imaginations, was a short cut to salvation—a way to be saved without ceasing to be a sinner and without the hard work and ongoing struggle of becoming a saint.

Edwards called this kind of evangelical hypocrisy more abominable "than the gross immoralities of those who make no pretenses to religion."[18] These hypocrites were worse offenders because they injured the cause of true religion. For not only did they delude themselves, they also deceived all those who credulously assumed that this spurious brand of piety was the real thing. With their bluster and boldness, their self-vaunting pretensions, their high claims of Christ's favor, their seeming zeal and fluent fervor, they often *appeared* to be better Christians than the real ones. That appearance might fatally mislead those eager and earnest seekers who could be tempted by the promise of an effortless and certain salvation without the bothersome demands of virtue and morality. Hence, in *Religious Affections*, Edwards devoted himself chiefly to unmasking the evangelical hypocrites. Not that he expected to undeceive the antinomian enthusiasts themselves, for they were like madmen, insensible to all argument or proof, but he did at least hope to disabuse those simple and gullible souls who might otherwise be duped by the fair performances and boastful speeches of these masters of deceit. Perhaps vulnerable and unsuspecting people could find in his arsenal of signs and no-signs the weapons they needed to protect themselves in a false and deceptive world.

Franklin's world too was full of hypocrites, deluders, and pretenders, amidst whom a naïve young man had to work out his salvation. In the *Autobiography*, Franklin offers a story of regeneration that conveys a doctrinal message quite similar to the one found in *Religious Affections*.[19] The young Franklin enters Philadelphia a pilgrim. Without any prospects or promises, he must settle his fate. Always in the back of his mind is a sort of original sin, a Vernon's debt, a liability that was originally another's, but one that has been imputed to him and that he has made his own by wrongfully partaking in it. This debt he must satisfy at a day of judgment or he will be doomed, but he does not know when that day will come or whether he will then possess the assets essential for his redemption.

Like those, to requote Edwards, "that have a fond desire of something . . . and have met with great difficulty and many discouragements" in pursuing it, Franklin received "an impression or supposed revelation that [he] should obtain what [he] sought."[20] That vision comes in the hypocritical form of Governor William Keith, a "finely dress'd" gentleman of fluent speech and prepossessing manner who appears to be "one of the best Men in the World."[21] Promising to impute his interest and apply his influence in Franklin's behalf, Governor Keith proposes to make the young man's fortune—to save him. This appeal to selfish appetite triumphs over principle, and Franklin eagerly accepts the proffered short cut to salvation. In fact, he soon begins to play the hypocrite, proudly and confidently acting as if he were already saved. He returns to Boston, seemingly successful, sporting "a genteel new Suit from Head to foot, a Watch, and . . . Pockets lin'd with near Five Pounds Sterling in Silver," some of which he disburses with great magnanimity and condescension among his old printshop cronies.[22]

Of course, it all comes a cropper. Franklin's rebirth is a false one, because the Governor is a false savior. His fair pledges and fine visions are hollow. The letter of credit on which Franklin relies is always promised but never delivered; even if it had come, it would have been worthless, for the Governor had "no Credit to give."[23] Franklin's errors were the same ones committed by Edwards's evangelical hypocrites. Like them, he surrendered to his pride, his conceit, and his selfishness. Like them, he sought an easy way to salvation—one that relied entirely on the imputed merit and credit of another and that ignored the necessity of his own works and righteousness.[24] Like them, he wanted to be saved without the trouble of changing his ways. Like them, he continued to cling confidently to his audacious assurance even when reason and evidence pointed the other way.

The antinomian tendency of Franklin's false conversion is yet more pointedly suggested in the story of his relationship with James Ralph.[25] Ralph appears repeatedly in the *Autobiography* as Franklin's alter ego, on two occasions actually exchanging identities with him. A plausible young man of genteel appearance and great eloquence—Franklin thought he "never knew a prettier Talker"—James Ralph was in life, as he once sought to be in profession, an actor—all show and no substance. He hoped to "make his Fortune" by poetry, relying, like an enthusiast, on his imagination and scorning the diligent industry that his more sensible friends recommended as the path to success. Despite all evidence of his deficiencies, despite his literary sins and the "many Faults" in his poetic performances, he refused to abandon his assurance that he possessed the poet's afflatus.[26]

Time and time again, Franklin was drawn into Ralph's amoral way of life. The two first traded identities when Franklin, who had himself aspired to be a poet, posed as the author of Ralph's versification of the 18th Psalm, which, appropriately enough, is about redemption. ("The Lord rewardeth me according to my righteousness; according to the cleanness of my hands hath he recompensed me. For I have kept the ways of the Lord, and have not wickedly departed from my God.") But Franklin and Ralph did not keep the ways of the Lord. Indeed, at the same time that Franklin was being deceived by Governor Keith's hypocritical promises of favor, he and Ralph were treating others with a similar disregard for morality. They both selfishly broke promises with the women to whom they were pledged. As "inseparable Companions," they haunted London's theaters and places of amusement, in the process augmenting the debt that hung over them.[27] Franklin wrote a metaphysical piece on *Liberty and Necessity*, dedicated to Ralph, which, much like the antinomians, advanced the argument "that nothing could possibly be wrong in the World, and that Vice and Virtue were empty Distinctions, no such Things existing."[28] Living by this creed, Franklin in effect became one with his immoral alter-ego. While James Ralph, still "confident of future better Fortune," took Franklin's name, Franklin, "being at this time under no Religious Restraints," attempted to seduce Ralph's mistress.[29] The episode is powerful in the telling, marking in its indulgence of selfish and licentious appetite the very nadir of Franklin's unregenerate condition.

Yet out of that moment of debasement, Franklin was reborn. Freed from Ralph, though now even deeper in debt, he immediately entered two sanctuaries—the "Chapel" of Watts's printing house and the secular "Nunnery" of his lodgings with a Roman Catholic landlady.[30] In those holy places he learned to curb his greedy appetites and selfish desires. He also learned to attend to business and to work diligently at his calling. His salvation now rested on a new principle, the very one preached by his Puritan father at the time of Governor Keith's offer of patronage.[31] Franklin would no longer attempt to rise by relying on the vicarious and imputed credit of another. Instead, he would work out his fortune in a continuing daily struggle to exercise industry and frugality. His new model and savior was not the glib and serpentine Governor Keith but the Christ-like Mr. Denham, who had once in an act of supererogation repaid a great debt, already discharged through bankruptcy, by assembling the creditors at a last supper and serving them, not food for their carnal appetites, but the entire obligation due them plus interest.[32]

Franklin emerged from his conversion with a new theology. Concluding that the distinction between good and evil was not arbitrary or meaningless, he abandoned the antinomian-like tenets of his freethinking treatise, which, he remarked, "appear'd now not so clever a Performance as I once thought it."[33] His new doctrines inspired a corresponding alteration in his conduct. He "grew convinc'd that *Truth, Sincerity and Integrity* in Dealings between Man and Man, were of the utmost Importance to the Felicity of Life," and his behavior toward others became less unscrupulously self-serving.[34] He began to transact his affairs with unwearied industry and undeviating frugality, eventually acquiring enough capital to pay off his debt, principal and interest.[35] Finally, he attempted, in his quest for moral perfection, to conquer the self-gratifying impulses, inclinations, and appetites that had threatened to damn him.[36] Though Franklin never achieved perfection, he remained convinced that the habitude of his thirteen virtues was the mark of his salvation, and he enjoined his audience to "follow the Example and reap the Benefit."[37]

Franklin's point—that one must stake one's fate on the practice of virtue in the course of one's daily business—is much like that made by Edwards in *Religious Affections*, where he identified "Christian practice or a holy life" as "the chief of all the signs of grace."[38] Even Edwards's language resembles Franklin's. The regenerate man, said Edwards, "makes a business of such a holy practice above all things; that it be a business which he is chiefly engaged in, and devoted to, and pursues with highest earnestness and diligence: so that he may be said to make this practice of religion eminently his work and business."[39] A holy life offered an assurance of salvation more substantial than the sudden, extraordinary, and easy promises of personal redemption received in enthusiasts' visions. Holy practice was a standard that did not imply, as did the antinomians' faith of assurance, that redeemed saints were exempt from the moral law. Indeed, it was, as Edwards noted, "exceeding absurd, and even ridiculous, for any to pretend that they have a good heart, while they live a wicked life."[40] Finally, holy practice meant a kind of religion grounded on "the transcendently excellent and amiable nature of divine things, as they are in themselves, and not any conceived relation they bear to self, or self-interest."[41] True religion was more than the excuse for the display of mercenary self-aggrandizement or the indulgence of selfish inclinations and appetites. In sum, Edwards, like Franklin, found the signs of salvation in the evidence of sanctification. There could be no faith without works. True godliness was "effectual in practice."[42] Grace issued in action, "for 'tis the very nature and notion of grace, that 'tis a principle of holy action or practice."[43] Conversion was the beginning and not the end of one's redemption. There were no short cuts to heaven.[44]

Both Edwards and Franklin tried to anchor salvation in the real world. Both warned of the specious lures of antinomianism and urged their audiences instead to rest their hopes on the objective ground of holy practice. Yet both recognized the difficulty involved. The problem was precisely how to judge the inner state of the soul from the outward evidence. How was one to read the authenticity of the heart when counterfeit religion presented such a plausible appearance? The problem was compounded for Edwards and Franklin because each had himself once been taken in by beguiling hypocrites—Franklin by Governor Keith, and Edwards by the New Light enthusiasts during the early stages of the Great Awakening. These twice-born men were both once-burned. But their wariness went even deeper: both men realized that they had been duped because they themselves had succumbed to the temptations of antinomianism. Both had eagerly seized on the bright promises of an easy and effortless redemption. So it was not just the deception of others that worried them; they were equally conscious of the potency of self-deception.

It was this awareness of their own capacity for self-delusion that made both Franklin and Edwards such astute psychologists. Both were remarkably conscious of the subtle ways that the mind worked to rationalize wickedness. Both knew firsthand the devious workings of pride. Edwards wrote in *Some Thoughts Concerning the Revival* that

> . . . spiritual pride is the most secret of all sins. The heart is so deceitful and unsearchable in nothing in the world, as it is in this matter. . . . It takes occasion to arise from everything; it perverts and abuses everything, and even the exercises of real grace and real humility, as an occasion to exert itself. It is a sin that has, as it were, many lives; if you kill it, it will live still; if you mortify and suppress it in one shape, it rises in another; if you think it is all gone, yet it is there still. There are a great many kinds of it, that lie in differ-

ent forms and shapes, one under another, and encompass the heart like the coats of an onion; if you pull off one there is another underneath.[45]

Franklin knew this, too: "In reality there is perhaps no one of our natural Passions so hard to subdue as *Pride*. Disguise it, struggle with it, beat it down, stifle it, mortify it as much as one pleases, it is still alive, and will every now and then peep out and show itself. You will see it perhaps often in this History. For even if I could conceive that I had compleatly overcome it, I should probably [be] proud of my Humility."[46]

How, then, was one to accomplish the tricky and treacherous business of reading the secrets of the heart? Only through examining the conduct of life—action, not talk; sustained practice over time. This was not certain evidence, but it was the best available. As Edwards put it, "words are cheap; and godliness is more easily feigned in words than in actions. Christian practice is a costly laborious thing. Hypocrites may much more easily be brought to talk like saints, than to act like saints."[47] Thus, Edwards and Franklin looked for reliable signs of the state of the soul in the visibility of external performance. Both of them, ultimately, called upon people to build up a record of themselves in the world. Life became an ongoing process of fabricating and sustaining an identity that could be taken as evidence of spiritual authenticity both by others and by oneself. Indeed, in his treatise on the will, Edwards insisted that the acts of will—the choices made in life—are the only expressions of the prevailing inclination of soul, "so that in every act, or going forth of the will, there is some preponderation of the mind or inclination, one way rather than another; and the soul had rather have or do one thing than another, or than not to have or do that thing; and that there, where there is absolutely no preferring or choosing, but a perfect continuing equilibrium, there is no volition."[48] In a sense, living properly was an exhibition of the inner self, an act of persuasion, a playing out of roles.[49] When Franklin suggested that his readers should cultivate the appearance of virtue by dressing plainly, keeping the lights on late in the shop, and not being seen in "Places of idle Diversion," he was not advocating hypocrisy; rather, he was proposing a way to avoid the uncertainty that hypocrisy represented.[50] Reality was not to be at odds with appearances; instead, appearances were to be the manifestation of the reality: "In order to secure my Credit and Character as a Tradesman," Franklin wrote, "I took care not only to be in *Reality* Industrious and frugal, but to avoid all *Appearances* of the Contrary."[51] Or, as Edwards put it, "To speak of Christian experience and practice, as if they were two things, properly and entirely distinct, is to make a distinction without consideration in reason."[52] Edwards called this approach "experimental religion" (a term Franklin would surely have applauded) because it brought religious affections and intentions "to the test of fact," giving saints the "opportunity to see, by actual *experience* and *trial*, whether they have a heart to do the will of God."[53]

There were good reasons why these men should want an experimental religion. They lived at a time when identities were increasingly unfixed and when the reading of other people's signs was growing more difficult. Franklin found in Philadelphia a relatively anonymous urban setting where hypocrites could practice deceit with impunity and where young men could try on different identities like disguises.[54] Similarly Edwards discovered that revivals could be the rural equivalent of city life. In the mass conversions of the Great Awakening, people could ostentatiously drop old identities and instantly take up new ones, misrepresenting themselves as the greatest of saints while remaining selfish sinners still. In their responses to the attenuation of identity, both men anticipated nineteenth-century solutions. Both attempted to create voluntary associations—the Junto and the restricted-communion church—in which the pure were sifted out from the hypocritical and fraudulent.[55] In organizing their institutions, both relied on public opinion and public reputation as the mechanisms for enforcing authenticity. But the criterion of visibility was always problematical, for it depended, in the end, on the presentation of the self. And, as Edwards noted, "no external manifestations and outward appearances whatsoever, that are visible to the world, are infallible evidences of grace. . . . Nothing that appears to them in their neighbor, can be sufficient to beget an absolute certainty concerning the state of his soul: for they see not his heart, nor can they see all his external behavior; for much of it is in secret, and hid from the eye of the world: and 'tis impossible certainly to determine, how far a man may go in many external appearances and imitations of grace, from other principles."[56]

It was this recognition of the unavoidable artificiality of the visible character, of the need to construct a version of the self in the world, that accounts, I think, for the peculiarities of these two men's personalities. They were both, though in different ways, detached, reserved, and remote. They were both impenetrable men; it seems impossible truly to know them, to get beneath their onion-skin surfaces. Though both Franklin and Edwards became great models and even heroes, much admired by posterity, in their own times they lacked warm personal relationships. They were very private public men. They had disciples, but not friends. They distanced themselves from others. Edwards described himself as possessing "a low tide of spirits; often occasioning a kind of childish weakness and contemptibleness of speech, presence, and demeanor, with a disagreeable dulness and stiffness, much unfitting me for conversation."[57] His writings are full of double negatives and argument by indirection. The elaborate heaps of things that are "no signs one way or the other" stand as barricades through which the reader must fight his way to reach the inner truth.[58] Similarly, Franklin's use of the Socratic method, his policy of hiding his opinions by being undogmatic, his efforts to obscure his role in originating public improvements, even his ingratiating and jovial tone—all made him an elusive, aloof, and inaccessible man.[59] Both Edwards and Franklin recognized that the heart can't be worn on the sleeve. Their isolation was perhaps the price they paid for resisting the glistering attractions and easy assurance of antinomianism. It was the unavoidable cost of insisting that salvation be worked out in the world, where religious affections could be known only through religious affectations.

## Notes

1. Barbara B. Oberg and Harry S. Stout to William K. Breitenbach, April 4, 1989. My own efforts have been more at monologue than dialogue, for though I have a scholar's knowledge of Edwards, I confess to only a teacher's familiarity with Franklin. When I speak of Edwards in the pages to come, I speak for myself, but when I speak of Franklin, I echo others. Of the many scholars who understand Franklin better than I, I have relied most on R. Jackson Wilson, Kenneth Silverman, and especially Michael T. Gilmore, all of whose works are frequently cited below.

2. *The Autobiography of Benjamin Franklin*, ed. Leonard W. Labaree *et al.* (New Haven, 1964), pp. 145–46.

3. Michael T. Gilmore has noted the importance of images of swimming in the *Autobiography*. See Gilmore, "Franklin and the Shaping of American Ideology," in Brian M. Barbour, ed., *Benjamin Franklin: A Collection of Critical Essays* (Englewood Cliffs, N.J., 1979), p. 108; also Kenneth Silverman, "Introduction," in BF, *Autobiography and Other Writings* (New York, 1986), p. xx.

4. *Autobiography*, ed. Labaree, p. 156.

5. *Ibid.*, p. 155.

6. *WJE, 2*, pp. 253–54.

7. *Autobiography*, ed. Labaree, p. 146.

8. JE, *The Nature of True Virtue*, ed. William K. Frankena (Ann Arbor, Mich., 1960), pp. 25–26. In this and in all other quotations, I have retained the original italics.

9. *WJE, 2*, p. 84.

10. Many scholars have noted the resemblances between BF's *Autobiography* and Puritan conversion narratives. See, for examples, Philip D. Beidler, "The 'Author' of Franklin's *Autobiography*," *Early American Literature* 16 (1981–82): 257–69; Gilmore, "Franklin and the Shaping of American Ideology," pp. 111–12; John Griffith, "The Rhetoric of Franklin's *Autobiography*," *Criticism 13* (1971): 89–93; David Levin, "The *Autobiography* of Benjamin Franklin: The Puritan Experimenter in Life and Art," *Yale Review 53* (1964): 261–63; David L. Parker, "From Sound Believer to Practical Preparationist: Some Puritan Harmonics in Franklin's *Autobiography*," in *The Oldest Revolutionary: Essays on Benjamin Franklin*, ed. J. A. Leo Lemay (Philadelphia, 1976), pp. 67–75; William C. Spengemann, *The Forms of Autobiography: Episodes in the History of a Literary Genre* (New Haven, 1980), pp. 51–61; Charles L. Sanford, "An American Pilgrim's Progress," in *Benjamin Franklin's Autobiography: An Authoritative Text, Backgrounds, Criticism*, ed. J. A. Leo Lemay and P. M. Zall (New York, 1986), pp. 300–313; Daniel B. Shea, Jr., *Spiritual Autobiography in Early America* (Princeton, N.J., 1968), 234–48; Silverman, "Introduction," pp. x–xi; Karl J.

Weintraub, "The Puritan Ethic and Benjamin Franklin," *The Journal of Religion* 56 (1976): 231–34; and R. Jackson Wilson, *Figures of Speech: American Writers and the Literary Marketplace, from Benjamin Franklin to Emily Dickinson* (New York, 1989), pp. 31–39.

11. James A. Sappenfield, *A Sweet Instruction: Franklin's Journalism as a Literary Apprenticeship* (Carbondale, Ill., 1973), pp. 198, 203; Gilmore, "Franklin and the Shaping of American Ideology," p. 108.

12. *WJE,* 2: 88.

13. *Ibid.,* p. 173.

14. *Ibid.*

15. *Ibid.,* p. 177.

16. *Ibid.,* p. 173.

17. *Ibid.,* p. 174.

18. *Ibid.,* p. 181.

19. My interpretation accepts the argument, advanced by many, that BF's *Autobiography* is a carefully crafted work of literary art. See Gilmore, "Franklin and the Shaping of American Ideology," pp. 105–24; Griffith, "Rhetoric," pp. 77–80; Levin, "The *Autobiography*," pp. 259–61; John F. Lynen, *The Design of the Present: Essays on Time and Form in American Literature* (New Haven, 1969), pp. 146–48; Sappenfield, *Sweet Instruction,* p. 201; Robert Freeman Sayre, "The Worldly Franklin and the Provincial Critics," *Benjamin Franklin's Autobiography,* ed. Lemay and Zall, pp. 313–14; Wilson, *Figures of Speech,* pp. 23–29; and P. M. Zall, "A Portrait of the Autobiographer as an Old Artificer," in *Oldest Revolutionary,* ed. Lemay, pp. 53–65.

20. *WJE,* 2: 174.

21. *Autobiography,* ed. Labaree, pp. 80, 87.

22. *Ibid.,* p. 81.

23. *Ibid.,* p. 94.

24. R. Jackson Wilson argues persuasively that BF's *Autobiography* describes a struggle to break out of a system of patronage and to establish independence and autonomy. See Wilson, *Figures of Speech,* pp. 42–51; see also in this regard, Hugh J. Dawson, "Fathers and Sons: Franklin's 'Memoirs' as Myth and Metaphor," *Early American Literature* 14 (1979–80): 269–78. It is perhaps worth noting that JE and his New Divinity followers, in their discussions of original sin and the atonement, moved away from the older interpretations of imputation and convenantal status that were, in a sense, theological versions of a patronage system. See William Breitenbach, "The Consistent Calvinism of the New Divinity Movement," *William and Mary Quarterly* 41 (1984): 247–55.

25. An excellent discussion of BF's use of alter-egos and doubles in the *Autobiography* can be found in Gilmore, "Franklin and the Shaping of American Ideology," pp. 108–13; see also Sappenfield, *Sweet Instruction,* pp. 203–4, and Dawson, "Fathers and Sons," p. 271. In describing BF as "antinomian," I am using the term loosely to signify a challenge to the concepts of virtue and vice. I do not mean to suggest that BF at any time adopted the tenets of the radical New Lights. It is interesting to note, however, that Samuel Keimer, one of the cautionary figures from whom the young BF must break if he is to be saved, was a genuine enthusiast. He was a French Prophet, or Camisard, a group much condemned for their antinomian beliefs.

26. *Autobiography,* ed. Labaree, p. 90.

27. *Ibid.,* pp. 95–96.

28. *Ibid.*, p. 114.

29. *Ibid.*, pp. 98, 99.

30. *Ibid.*, pp. 100–3; Gilmore, "Franklin and the Shaping of American Ideology," pp. 110–11; Wilson, *Figures of Speech*, pp. 49–51.

31. Several scholars have noted perceptively that BF's "conversion" reconciled him to the values of his Puritan father. See Gilmore, "Franklin and the Shaping of American Ideology," pp. 106–7, 111; R. Jackson Wilson, "Introduction," in Benjamin Franklin, *The Autobiography* (New York, 1981), pp. xxiv–xxv; and Dawson, "Fathers and Sons," pp. 269–78.

32. *Autobiography*, ed. Labaree, pp. 104–5. On the role of Thomas Denham as BF's "savior," see Gilmore, "Franklin and the Shaping of American Ideology," p. 111, and Zall, "A Portrait," pp. 61–62.

33. *Autobiography*, ed. Labaree, p. 114.

34. *Ibid.*

35. *Ibid.*, pp. 118–19, 125–26, 143–44.

36. *Ibid.*, pp. 148–60.

37. *Ibid.*, p. 157.

38. *WJE, 2*: 406.

39. *Ibid.*, p. 383.

40. *Ibid.*, p. 428.

41. *Ibid.*, p. 394.

42. *Ibid.*, p. 393.

43 *Ibid.*, p. 398.

44. I want to insist that I am not trying to transform BF into a Calvinist or JE into an Arminian. My aim is simply to show similarities in the two men's approaches to the general issue of morality. For a fuller discussion of my interpretation of JE's theology, see William Breitenbach, "Piety and Moralism: Edwards and the New Divinity," in *Jonathan Edwards and the American Experience*, ed. Nathan O. Hatch and Harry S. Stout (New York, 1988), pp. 179–90.

45. *WJE, 4*: 416–17; see also *2*: 319–20.

46. *Autobiography*, ed. Labaree, p. 160.

47. *WJE, 2*: 411.

48. *WJE, 1*: 140.

49. Many scholars have noted BF's careful presentation of self to his audiences. See especially John Griffith, "Franklin's Sanity and the Man behind the Masks," in *Oldest Revolutionary*, ed. Lemay, pp. 123–38; Levin, "*Autobiography*," pp. 259–61, 272–74; Lynen, *Design of the Present*, pp. 136–37; Robert F. Sayre, *The Examined Self: Benjamin Franklin, Henry Adams, Henry James* (Princeton, N.J., 1964), pp. 15–23; John William Ward, "Who Was Benjamin Franklin?" in Lemay and Zall, eds., *Benjamin Franklin's Autobiography*, pp. 330–31; and Wilson, *Figures of Speech*, 26–29.

50. *Autobiography*, ed. Labaree, pp. 125–26, 119.

51. *Ibid.*, p. 125.

52. *WJE, 2*: 450.

53. *Ibid.*, p. 452.

54. Gary B. Nash describes the disintegration of Philadelphia as a corporate community in *The Urban Crucible: Social Change, Political Consciousness, and the Origins of the American Revolution* (Cambridge, Mass., 1979); see also Sayre, *Examined Self*, p. 23, and Ward, "Who Was Benjamin Franklin?" pp. 329, 335.

55. Wilson, *Figures*, pp. 53–54; Gilmore, "Franklin and the Shaping of American Ideology," p. 113.

56. *WJE*, 2: 420.

57. *Jonathan Edwards: Representative Selections*, ed. Clarence H. Faust and Thomas H. Johnson (New York, 1962), p. 410.

58. *WJE*, 2: 127.

59. On BF's detachment, see Carl Becker, "Franklin's Character," in *Benjamin Franklin*, ed. Barbour, pp. 11–12; Ralph Lerner, *The Thinking Revolutionary: Principle and Practice in the New Republic* (Ithaca, N.Y., 1987), pp. 57–59; Silverman, "Introduction," pp. xiv–xx; Ward, "Who Was Benjamin Franklin?" pp. 332–33.

# 3

# Enlightenment and Awakening in Edwards and Franklin

## A. OWEN ALDRIDGE

The contrary perspectives of the religious movement known in America as the Great Awakening and the intellectual movement embracing most of Europe and America known as the Enlightenment may be seen in the attitudes of a representative of each movement, Jonathan Edwards and Benjamin Franklin, respectively. Illustrating basic attitudes toward life, Edwards reflected that "Christ recommended rising early in the morning, by his rising from the grave very early,"[1] and Franklin in the guise of Poor Richard assured his readers that activity in the prime of the morning makes a man healthy, wealthy, and wise. Here spiritual and secular values and motives are clearly separate but, nevertheless, not completely opposed. Likewise the Awakening and the Enlightenment seem by definition to be antithetical, but they are not necessarily incompatible. In historical terms, the Great Awakening was a religious revival that swept the American colonies from New England to Georgia, according to some scholars between 1739 and 1744, and, according to others, between 1734 and 1749. In theological terms, the Great Awakening was the process by which God was presumably establishing Christ's kingdom in America. Edwards described the movement as "a great and wonderful event, a strange revolution, an unexpected surprising overturning of things, suddenly brought to pass. . . . It is the work of new creation which is infinitely more glorious than the old. . . . The New Jerusalem in this respect has begun to come down from heaven, and perhaps never were more of the prelibations of heaven's glory given upon earth."[2]

Franklin offered no parallel definition of the Enlightenment, but a superb one is to be found in the works of one of his French admirers, the abbé André Morellet:

> It is this ardor for knowledge, this activity of mind which does not wish to leave an effect without seeking the cause, a phenomenon without explanation, an assertion without proof, an objection without a reply, an error without combating it, an evil without seeking the remedy, a possible good without seeking to obtain it; it is this general movement of minds which has marked the eighteenth century and which will constitute its glory forever.[3]

Franklin had almost as much faith that the goals of the Enlightenment would flourish upon the earth as Edwards had concerning those of the Awakening. "God grant," Franklin wrote in 1789, "that not only the Love of Liberty, but a thorough Knowledge of the Rights of Man, may pervade all the Nations of the Earth, so that a Philosopher may set his Foot anywhere on its Surface and say 'This is my Country.'"[4]

In the broadest sense, Edwards may be considered an exponent of a philosophical concept associated with European writers prior to the Great Awakening. The ontology of his essay "Of Being," affirming that everything in the universe has existence only in God's mind, coheres with the notion in Shakespeare and Calderón that life is a dream. Franklin on the Enlightenment side reflects the notion that existence is "a mighty maze! but not without a plan," as Pope had said, and Franklin's personal history embodied his effort to fix "a regular design" in his own life.[5]

Paradoxically, Edwards expressed an Enlightenment goal that seems to belong instead to Franklin, that of thinking big or comprehending in a single system the entire universe of knowledge. Edwards proposed but never brought to completion the writing of an encyclopedic work comprising the history of three worlds, heaven, earth, and hell, "considering the connected successive events and alterations in each." His projected *History of the Work of the Redemption* would be a spiritual parallel to the *Universal History* that was actually published in England. He also at one time proposed to discover and write about a "thousand things" in natural philosophy "by nice observations of the spheroid of the world."[6] Franklin never conceived of a grand synthesis of any kind, but in actual life he became involved in almost every intellectual occupation of the age and wrote about most of them. Franklin represented a related Enlightenment attitude, cosmopolitanism, that was completely alien to Edwards. Even on the Awakening side, Edwards was provincial. He may be contrasted with the evangelist George Whitefield, called the "Grand Itinerant," who proclaimed that "the world is my parish," as Thomas Paine was later to boast, "My country is the world, and my religion is to do good." Franklin made four round trips across the Atlantic, and Whitefield made even more, but Edwards hesitated to cross a single time, even though offered a pastorate in Scotland. Edwards condemned Jews, Pharisees, Papists, and Mohammedans as wicked men who compounded with God in their forms of worship,[7] while Franklin complacently affirmed ecumenical principles. Franklin had favored erecting a meeting house in Philadelphia, which most of the city associated with the Great Awakening, but he had supported the building not "to accommodate any particular Sect, but the Inhabitants in general, so that even if the Mufti of Constantinople were to send a Missionary to preach Mahometanism to us, he would find a pulpit at his Service."[8] Edwards's view of geography divided the world into two spheres, the old and the new, that is, America and Europe.[9] He argued that the people of his own land were "more committed to our care than the people of China, and we ought to pray more for them."[10] China he described as "wild Tartary."[11] Franklin, on the other hand, wanted the *Rights of Man* to be known in all the nations of the earth; he admired the works of Confucius and told his friend Benjamin Vaughan that he was "very fond of reading about China" and "that if he were a young man he should like to go to China."[12]

In essence, the Awakening accepted Biblical authority, and its partisans were swayed by emotion. The Enlightenment rejected all authority, and its exponents followed reason, experiment, and history. Yet adherence to one of these movements did not automatically eliminate influence by the other. Edwards was touched by the Enlightenment without embracing it fully, and Franklin encountered the Awakening in personal relations with his family and close associates. Although each man's principal commitment to life was in a different sphere, both possessed a number of common interests. On the Enlightenment side, Edwards became familiar with the science of Newton in his college years, and as a philosopher he attempted to resolve problems raised by John Locke and the deists Anthony Collins and Mathew Tindal. Franklin absorbed deistical thinking long before becoming familiar with Newtonian science. He and Edwards were introduced to electricity about the same time; Franklin by the public experiments of Archibald Spencer, and Edwards by those of Ebenezer Kinnersley.[13] Franklin preceded Edwards, however, in publishing thoughts on the freedom of the will. On the Awakening side, the movement literally represented for Edwards not only an extraordinary work of the creator, but the great end of all God's other works.[14] For Franklin, the Awakening was merely the intensified expression of a religious system with which he had been familiar since boyhood, but one that he had experienced primarily as a spectator.

Edwards and Franklin would have responded in quite contrary ways to the injunction of Poor Richard in 1755, "Think of three Things, whence you came, where you are going, and to whom you must account." The Awakening and the Enlightenment were most sharply divided over "whence you came"—involving the nature of man's past. Edwards and his fellow theologians found the answer in the doctrine of original sin, defined by Edwards as "the *innate sinful depravity of the heart*," deriving from the first sin of Adam together with "the liableness or exposedness of Adam's posterity, in the divine judgment, to partake of the punishment of that Sin."[15] Franklin, in company with such Enlightenment figures as Rousseau, Voltaire, and Hume, maintained to the contrary that man was by nature good or at least not prepossessed by evil. He found this comfortable doctrine in Lord Shaftesbury, whom he frequently quoted or paraphrased. He specifically opposed Calvinist theology, affirming that the concept of "*our lost and undone State by Nature*" is an absurdity used "to fright and scare an unthinking Populace out of their Senses, and inspire them with Terror, to answer the little selfish Ends of the Inventors and Propagators."[16] Franklin also portrayed the universe itself as reflecting benevolence rather than depravity. "Most happy are we," he wrote, "the sons of men, above all other creatures, who are born to behold the glorious rays of the sun, and to enjoy the pleasant fruits of the earth." He believed that after a life of using reason in doing good, we are rewarded with "the sweet sleep of death, pleasant as a bed to a weary traveller after a long journey."[17] In regard to man's future, the two movements were also far apart. Edwards at the height of the Great Awakening felt that the dawn of the New Age or Christ's kingdom on earth was not only at hand, but that the earliest stages would take place in America.[18] In his best-known sermon, he observed that "God seems now to be hastily gathering in his elect in all parts of the land; and probably the greatest part of adult persons that ever shall be saved, will be brought in now in a little time." Even after the Great Awakening had run its course, Edwards's vision remained fixed upon the kingdom of heaven and a delayed rather than an imminent millennium. Although he believed that loving God required doing good to man, he felt that this earthly service was a subordinate duty. Franklin believed, to the contrary, that doing good to man was the most effective means of serving God. His prospect of the future both for himself and for mankind pertained to the terrestrial, not the heavenly, world. Although he expressed no formal utopian dream, he believed that what he called "true science" was making extraordinary progress. Specifically placing the concept of millennium in a secular framework, he wrote to Joseph Priestley late in life:

> It is impossible to imagine the Height to which may be carried, in a thousand years, the Power of Man over Matter. We may perhaps learn to deprive large Masses of their Gravity, and give them absolute Levity, for the sake of easy Transport. Agriculture may diminish its Labour and double its Produce; all Diseases may by sure means be prevented or cured, not excepting even that of Old Age, and our Lives lengthened at pleasure even beyond the antediluvian Standard.[19]

How Edwards reacted to the question of "to whom you must account" is a rather complex matter. From the standpoint of the Scriptures, he obviously believed that he must answer directly and personally to Christ and that on the day of redemption he would appear among either the saints or the sinners.[20] But awareness of the plan of redemption gave him little help in managing his day-to-day conduct. The Bible offered strong motives to virtue but no universal rule for deciding which actions are virtuous and which not. Edwards affirmed that men must act out of a sense of duty. In his miscellanies he seemed to accept the "dictates of the natural, common and universal moral sense of mankind in all nations and ages."[21] While maintaining that "devotion and not mutual love, charity, justice, beneficence, etc. is the highest end of man,"[22] he also insists on the paramount obligation of works of charity. Although he speaks of those things that are our duty as "being required by moral rules, or absolute positive commands of God,[23] nowhere does he declare whether rules of conduct are based upon Scriptures, rational decision, or conscience. In his philosophical system, he placed conscience on a lower level than what he called true virtue and attributed moral goodness only to "a sense and relish of the essential beauty of virtue."[24] But this metaphysical virtue provided no practical guidelines for conduct. Edwards was forced, therefore, to fall back upon his own notions of behavior even though his ultimate accounting was to God. In a set of "Resolutions" composed in his twentieth year, he determined to do whatsoever "I think to be most to the glory of God and my own good, profit and pleasure" and "to do whatever I think to be my *duty*, and most for the good and advantage of mankind in general." He was accountable to God but followed his own notions of right and wrong.

For Franklin, the problem of accountability is not in the least complex. Although he believed in a deistical God throughout his life, there is no evidence that he ever acknowledged a personal relationship with Christ. Indeed, in a statement in his private "Articles of Belief and Acts of Religion" at the age of twenty-two, he specifically denied the possibility of personal communication with the supreme being. In his words, "I imagine it great Vanity in me to suppose, that the *Supremely Perfect*, does in the least regard such an inconsiderable Nothing as Man . . . I cannot conceive otherwise, than that He *the Infinite Father*, expects or requires no Worship or Praise from us, but that he is even INFINITELY ABOVE IT."[25]

At that time, Franklin conjectured that each of the planets had its own god, and he granted a measure of communication between this inferior god and his created beings. "Let me then not fail to praise my God continually," Franklin proposed, "for it is his Due, and it is all I can return for his many Favours and great Goodness to me; and let me resolve to be virtuous, that I may be happy, that I may please Him, who is delighted to see me happy." Shortly after setting forth his articles of belief, Franklin conceived of "the bold and arduous project of arriving at moral perfection." As he explains at length in his *Autobiography*, he decided what he considered to be the thirteen principal virtues, defined them, entered them into a notebook with spaces for marking infractions against them, and gave a week's attention to each one successively, hoping eventually to go through a period of thirteen weeks without a single infraction. He even carried the project to his discussion group or Junto as a question to be debated: "Can a man arrive at Perfection in this Life as some Believe?"[26]—and he later envisioned calling the scheme his "Art of Virtue." Although he recognized the "blessing of God" in his quest for moral perfection, he considered himself accountable only to himself. In comments on his thirteen virtues, he tried to show the means and manner of obtaining each one, thereby distinguishing his method "from the mere Exhortation to be good, that does not instruct and indicate the Means, but is like the Apostle's Man of verbal Charity, who only, without showing to the Naked and the Hungry *how* or where they might get Clothes or Victuals, exhorted them to be fed and clothed.—James ii. 15, 16."[27] This is an implied criticism of the type of charity preached by Edwards and other adherents to the Great Awakening—noble and sublime in sentiment, but deficient in practical application. One can only imagine, on the other hand, how Edwards and his fellow divines would have reacted to Franklin's footnote, "Nothing so likely to make a man's fortune as virtue." Franklin elsewhere, however, as a good Shaftesburian, affirmed the beauty of virtue—although not at all in Edwards's sense of love "to being in general" as expounded in his *Nature of True Virtue*. Franklin considered his own Art of Virtue to be of universal utility and an alternative to religious-based ethics for those who do not accept Christianity.[28] His view that it could lead to moral perfection was compatible with the perfectionist doctrine of the Wesleys, completely rejected by Edwards, that man could be completely cleansed of sin.

Edwards also discussed the possibility of several different gods having created the several stars in the sky, but he rejected the notion on the grounds that "the parts of these different systems are not only communicated to and diffused through one another, but act upon one another; and this is a mutual action and reaction between their different blended parts by the same laws of matter and motion." It would, therefore, be unreasonable to suppose anything "other than that this action and reaction are both by the laws and influence of the same God."[29] Edwards did not, however, examine a hypothesis, like Franklin's, that there might be one supremely perfect god, father of the subordinate gods of each individual star. At the time he made his comments on polytheism, Edwards knew considerably more about Newtonian philosophy than Franklin did. As early as 1716, he had access to the Yale copy of the *Principia*, and his youthful essay "Of Being" indicates that he made full use of it. Franklin as late as 1746 does not seem to have read, or at least digested, any of Newton, for in a letter to one of his friends in that year, he affirmed that he was not able to comprehend "the concept of *Vis Inertiae essential to Matter*."[30]

The intricacy and sublimity of the cosmos or the far reaches of the universe represented for Franklin, as for many other minds of the Enlightenment, deists and Christians alike, a proof of the existence of a divine creator. Franklin in his youth derived his belief in a supremely perfect being when, in his words, he stretched his "Imagination thro' and beyond our System of Planets, beyond the visible fix'd Stars themselves, into that Space that is every Way infinite." Later in life Franklin does not seem to have taken seriously this mode of reasoning or imagining that in the eighteenth century was called physico-theology. During his sojourn in France, he parodied the related notion of discerning purpose in the universe through the life cycle of plants and animals and the structure of the human body. In a private letter he complimented the benevolent wisdom of the creator for adjusting the human elbow so that the wine glass could be raised precisely to the mouth.[31] Caustically he reported in his *Memoirs* the explanation offered by an Indian chief that the great Spirit, who made everything in the universe for some use, pronounced that rum should be used for Indians to get drunk with. Franklin added, "indeed if it be the Desire of Providence to extirpate these Savages in order to make room for Cultivators of the Earth, it seems not improbable that Rum may be the appointed Means."[32] Edwards was aware of this kind of natural theology, which he adopted in his early letter on spiders.[33] He traced back to John Locke the related notion that recognition of the wonders of nature leads to knowledge of the existence of god, but rejected it entirely. "If we look over all the accounts we have of the several nations of the earth, and consider everything that has been advanced by any or all of the philosophers," he affirmed, "we can meet with nothing to induce us to think that the first religion of the world was introduced by the use and direction of mere natural reason."[34] To the contrary, man's reason and speculations lead to "false and ill-grounded notions" of the creator. In Edwards's view, divine revelation alone has provided man with the correct notion of the "true nature and the true worship of the deity."[35] He even suggested that the imagination interferes with human perception of the universe and the divine workmanship it reflects. In somewhat rhapsodical terms, he affirmed that "the universe is created out of nothing every moment and if it were not for our imaginations, which hinder us, we might see that wonderful work performed continually which was seen by the morning stars when they sang together."[36] Yet Edwards also used teleological arguments in one of his proofs of God's existence. "The being of God," he affirmed, "may be argued from the desirability and need of it,"[37] a remarkable declaration that comes close to prefiguring Voltaire's famous pronouncement, "If there were no God, it would be necessary to invent him." Edwards argued that we have the moon and stars to keep us from being miserable in the darkness of night, that in Greenland where the sun's rays are oblique, the sun stays longer above the horizon as compensation, and that since camels are forced to go for a long time without water in desert areas, they have a large vessel within them to carry water.[38] Edwards also treated at some length "the wisdom of God" in contriving the mechanism of the human eye, the roundness of the earth, the position of the planets, and the motion of the comets.[39]

Despite Edwards's placing of revelation above reason, he was as a philosopher a confirmed rationalist. It is a paradox, therefore, for Vernon L. Parrington to call him an "anachronism" in the Age of Reason. Rationalism, another scholar has said, "is not the whole of Edwards's philosophy, but it is the basis of it."[40] His *Freedom of the Will* is a masterly exercise in logic that seldom refers to Scripture, and his *Nature of True Virtue* is based entirely on reason. In defining reason, Edwards combines ratiocination with intuition or self-evidence, and he argues that the reasoning process comprises the experience of mankind, including history, tradition, and memory together with the testimony of our senses.[41] In his treatise on the religious affections he affirms that in matters of religion intuition may supersede reason, that "a soul may have a kind of intuitive knowledge of the divinity of the things exhibited in the gospel; not that he judges the doctrines of the gospel to be from God, without any argument or deduction at all; but it is without any long chain of arguments; the argument is but one, and the evidence direct; the mind ascends to the truth of the gospel by but one step."[42] This is as close as he ever came to asserting, as Franklin did more than once, "the great uncertainty . . . in metaphysical reasonings."[43] Edwards did not, however, accept special revelation that is not directly related to the Scriptures. In his remarks on the Awakening, he vigorously repudiated the notion that anything may be made known by inspiration or immediate revelation "that is not taught in the scripture as the words lie in the *Bible*."[44] There is nothing paradoxical in characterizing Franklin as an exponent of the notion of the Age of Reason, even though he was more of an experimenter than a rationalist. He seems not to have clung to an early affirmation "that no Authority is more convincing to Men of Reason than the Authority of Reason itself."[45] In later years, he contrasted reason with "a good sensible Instinct" and suggested that the latter is to be preferred. He also wrote to a friend in France that reason must be fallible "since two people like you and me can draw from the same principles conclusions diametrically opposite. This reason seems to me a guide quite blind. A good and certain instinct would be worth much more to us."[46] In both of these references, instinct applies to all matters, not only to religion, and Franklin says merely that it would be desirable to have, not that it actually exists. Edwards, on the other hand, firmly believed in the existence of his intuition in religious matters. He based his philosophical treatises upon the principles of reason while at the same time asserting that revelation is a superior source of knowledge. Franklin carried out experiments in many scientific areas, rejected supernatural revelation, and used reason primarily in practical affairs. Edwards was America's greatest artisan of metaphysical reasoning or "dialectical pyrotechnics," as one scholar has it.[47] Franklin distrusted the process and inveighed extensively against it.

Both Edwards and Franklin, in company with several other writers of the Enlightenment and the Awakening, denied freedom of the will, but they did so from opposing principles and propositions. In a sense, their two discourses are not comparable, as Franklin's was written when he was a mere teenager, and he soon after repudiated its principal doctrine; Edwards's treatise was in some ways the crowning intellectual achievement of his life, and he never wavered from the principles it comprises. Franklin's discussion was limited to a slight pamphlet of twenty-nine pages, although given the title of a *Dissertation*, and Edwards's amounted to a book of more than three hundred pages. The principles in both works are, nevertheless, respectively representative of the two historical currents we are considering, Enlightenment and Awakening. I obviously cannot at this time summarize all of Edwards's arguments against free will, but I can state the major ones. He argues that all of our actions are based upon the strongest motive at each apparent exercise of choice; that every action is determined by our mental volitions even though there may be no physical requirement for that action; and that every action of every individual is part of a chain of cause and effect operating within that individual and at the same time interconnected with every other activity in the universe. Franklin's argument is essentially a variation of the last of those three, with greater emphasis on the role of god as the interconnecting principle. Indeed, in Franklin's pamphlet, god and the universe are absolutely equivalent, and his system is a purely mechanistic one. He affirms as the foundation of his argument that people of "every Sect and Opinion" admit "a first Mover, who is called GOD, Maker of the Universe," and who is "all-wise, all-good, all powerful." God is, therefore, directly and uniquely responsible for every action in the universe, including everything to which we give the name evil. And if man "is thus limited in his Actions, being able to do only such Things as God would have done; then he can have no such Thing as Liberty, Free-will or Power to do or refrain an Action." In Edwards's thought, god, the universe, and man are separate entities, but are interconnected by the spirit of god. His system is spiritual rather than mechanical. Edwards disposes of the problem of evil by means of a distinction between mental volition (required action) and lack of physical restraint (or freedom), a distinction he characterizes as between moral and natural necessity. He thereby makes man responsible for evil since man is physically free to refrain from any immoral action. Franklin, however, does not allow responsibility for actions that are considered evil to be transferred from God to man. He insists that since all actions depend

upon God, all are equally good. In other words, he completely removes
the distinction between virtue and vice. In Franklin's words, "we must
allow that all Things exist now in a Manner agreeable to His Will,
and in consequence of that are all equally Good, and therefore equally
esteem'd by Him." To buttress this proposition, Franklin adds an argument that all creatures on earth experience an exact balance of pleasure
and pain. Men may have different quantities and qualities of sensation,
but since each man's total experience of either pleasure or pain is
exactly in proportion to the opposite feeling, the result is perfect equal-
ity for all mankind.

Soon after publishing his pamphlet, Franklin had second thoughts
about his mechanistic universe, bordering as it does on atheism, and he
therefore wrote a lecture "On the Providence of God in the Government of the World," which he delivered to his fellow tradesmen in Philadelphia. He later summarized it as based upon the proposition "'That
almost all men in all ages and countries have at times made use of prayer.'
Thence I reasoned, that if all things are ordained, prayer must among
the rest be ordained. But as prayer can produce no change in things that
are ordained, praying must then be useless and an absurdity. God would
therefore not ordain praying if everything else was ordained. But praying exists, therefore all things are not ordained."[48] Edwards knew nothing about Franklin's dissertation or his lecture, but about the same time
that Franklin was delivering the latter, he wrote in his "Miscellanies" an
explanation of how God could intervene in the system of creation without upsetting his predetermined chain of cause and effect. The explanation depends upon foreknowledge. In Edwards's words, "God decrees
all things harmoniously and in excellent order, one decree harmonizes
with another, and there is such a relation between all the decrees as makes
the most excellent order. Thus, God decrees rain in drought because
He decrees the earnest prayers of His people, or thus, He decrees the
prayers of His people because He decrees rain . . . God decrees the
latter event because of the former no more than he decrees the former
because of the latter."[49] Somewhat later (April 1753), Edwards wrote to
his son Timothy in terms surprisingly similar to Franklin's: "Whatever
your circumstances are, it is your duty not to despair, but to hope in
infinite mercy, through a Redeemer. For God makes it your duty to pray
to him for mercy; which would not be your duty, if it was allowable for
you to despair." Edwards's argument of foreknowledge may take care
of the harmony of prayer and predetermined events, but it hardly recon-
ciles God's interfering by special providence in a scheme of predetermined events without changing the course of these events. If God's
interference or providence is part of the pre-established pattern, it cannot be considered as an authentic interposition. The law of cause and
effect is obviously incompatible with divine intervention. Edwards's sermons are no more satisfactory. In his *The Most High a Prayer Hearing
God* (1735–36), he affirms that God hears the prayers of men and that

he exercises his mercy, but Edwards still does not put the two statements together in an assertion that individual prayers are responded to. He merely cites examples from the Old Testament that affirm a direct relationship.[50] Indeed, Edwards specifically declares that "the mercy of God is not moved or drawn by any thing in the creature; but the spring of God's beneficence is within himself only; he is self moved; and whatsoever mercy he bestows, the reason and ground of it is not to be sought for in the creature, but in God's own good pleasure."[51] Even on the affirmative side, Edwards says merely that "God can answer prayer, though he bestow not the very thing for which we pray. He can sometimes better answer the lawful desires and good end we have in prayer another way."[52] He also declares unequivocally that "God is pleased sometimes to answer the prayers of unbelievers" by granting their requests, but he immediately reduces the force of this statement by adding that "God may, and sometimes does, hear the cries of wicked men, as he hears the hungry ravens, when they cry."[53] Essentially the relationship in Edwards's system of prayers, God, and subsequent events related to these prayers is the same as that between the individual's moral conduct and his eventual salvation or damnation. These relationships have all been determined by God in a pattern of pre-established harmony. In his "Miscellanies," Edwards explains that decrees of our everlasting state as well as our prayers and strivings have been present with God from all eternity. In his metaphysical system of idealism, all creation is nothing but an idea of God, and therefore no chronological succession or pattern of sequence exists. This theory, however, applies to God and not to ordinary mortals, who do reside in a system of chronological relationships as well as in one of cause and effect.

Edwards believed that God could intervene in the system of nature for other purposes besides the answering of prayer. On one occasion he cited the Old Testament narrative in which "God changed the course of nature, and caused the sun to go from the West to the East."[54] Here Scripture certainly supersedes Newton, the theology of the Awakening outranking the science of the Enlightenment. Franklin in his lecture on divine providence less dramatically reached the same conclusion concerning God's intervention. In his words, "the Deity sometimes . . . sets aside the Events which would otherwise have been produc'd in the Course of Nature, or by the Free Agency of Man."[55] In *Poor Richard*, Franklin appealed to Newton to refute a common Enlightenment notion, "the opinion of all the modern philosophers and mathematicians that the planets are habitable worlds. If so," Franklin asked, "what sort of constitutions must those people have who live in the planet Mercury? where, says Sir Isaac Newton, the heat of the sun is seven times as great as it is with us; and would make our Water boil away."[56]

Franklin did not long retain the confidence expressed in his youthful lecture that a benevolent providence is the foundation of all religion. In a letter in 1769 to the star of the Great Awakening, George Whitefield, he expressed doubt that divine providence attends regularly to human affairs. "I rather suspect, from certain circumstances," he wrote, "that though the general government of the universe is well administered, our particular little affairs are perhaps below notice, and left to take the chance of prudence or imprudence, as either may happen to be uppermost. It is, however, an uncomfortable thought, and I leave it."[57] One wonders whether Franklin really changed his mind back again during the War for Independence when he attributed military successes to the "Interposition of Providence" or when in his *Memoirs*, he acknowledged "that I owe the mention'd Happiness of my past Life to his kind Providence, which led me to the Means I us'd and gave them success."[58] Franklin's indecision concerning the workings of providence obviously has relevance to his opinion concerning the efficacy of prayer. His early articles of belief assume that the creator of the world is a good being who is pleased with the praise and thanksgiving of his subjects, but nothing is said about personal petitions to God or to the possibility of their being answered. Throughout the rest of his life Franklin had a great deal to say about the utility of prayer—the psychological comfort it provides to the individual and the sense of order and common purpose it gives to the community, but he never expressed an opinion that particular prayers are answered. In 1773 he published in collaboration with an English nobleman an abridgment of the Anglican *Book of Common Prayer*, to which he contributed an explanatory preface, and soon after he prepared a revision of the Lord's Prayer for his own use. These experiments or exercises support his conviction, previously expressed to his daughter, that a ritual of prayer and praise is more important in the divine service than a sermon or other discourse.[59] One of the most drastic changes Franklin made in his abridgment of the *Book of Common Prayer* was the elimination of those psalms that "imprecate, in the most bitter terms, the vengeance of God on our adversaries, contrary to the spirit of Christianity, which commands us to love our enemies, and to pray for those that hate us and despitefully use us." He also omitted as objectionable the Commination and "all cursing of mankind." It is conceivable, although never previously suggested in print, that Franklin may have had in mind the sinner psychology of New England theology as well as Anglican formal prayers in his opposition to the attributing of imprecations to God and the portraying of God as vengeful. Although Edwards was skilled, as we all know, in portraying the punishment meted out by an angry god, he nevertheless also took a stand against pulpit prayers that joined "a sort of imprecation with their petition for others" or, as he expressed it, "a sort of cursing men in our prayer, adding a curse with our blessing."[60] At the Constitutional Convention, Franklin made a speech advocating daily prayers during its deliberations. In this speech he affirmed his conviction "*that GOD governs in the Affairs of Men*," a reversal of his skeptical opinion expressed to Whitefield. But even here he did not hold out the hope that specific prayers or petitions would be answered.

Although prayer is commonly considered by Edwards and others to be an emotional experience or, in Edwards's terms, an outpouring of the religious affections, Franklin did not indicate emotion as an aspect of prayer—and in his writings he paid little attention to emotion in general, except for warning against the harmful passions, especially avarice, the love of money; ambition, the love of power; and pride, the hardest to subdue. Both Edwards and Franklin came under the influence of Lord Shaftesbury's *Inquiry concerning Virtue*, which, among other things, made the passions respectable in British moral philosophy, but while Edwards looked upon virtue as a type of affection, Franklin considered it in purely rational terms. Edwards throughout his works makes a distinction between head and heart, which does not exist anywhere in Franklin's thought, even though it is paramount in another Enlightenment model, Thomas Jefferson. The workings of heart or the emotions may be traced in the lives of both Edwards and Franklin, however, in the area of social welfare, one of the illustrations of the confluence of Enlightenment and Awakening.

On one occasion, Franklin's sister had admonished him from the perspective of her "New England Doctrines" for slighting the duties of worship and for believing that good works alone are sufficient to gain entry into heaven. After absolving himself of the first charge by reminding her of his private book of devotions and of the second by affirming in somewhat equivocal terms that "there are few, if any, in the World so weake as to imagine that the little Good we can do here, can *merit* so vast a Reward hereafter," he urged her to read Edwards's more tolerant view in his *Thoughts* concerning the revival.[61] Here Edwards considers "the Expressions of our Love to GOD, by obeying his moral commands of Self-denial, Righteousness, Meekness, and Christian Love, in our Behavior among Men" of much greater importance than ceremonial acts of worship such as praying, hearing, singing, and attending religious meetings.[62] In a later passage Edwards insists that a religion of deeds is more important than a religion of words, contrary to the usual disparaging of good works among those preaching justification by faith. Edwards further conjectured that "the remarkable Hearing that God has given Mr. Whitefield, and the great success with which he has crowned him, may well be thought to be very much owing to his laying out himself so abundantly in charitable designs."[63] Franklin also respected Whitefield for his charitable designs, particularly for his project of erecting an orphanage at Savannah. In a long passage in his *Memoirs*, he explains how in advance of hearing Whitefield speak he had resolved not to respond at all to fundraising appeals, but that under the spell of Whitefield's admirable oratory he decided successively to donate his coppers, his silver, and finally all the money on his person, including five pistoles in gold. This is a rare instance of Franklin's succumbing to an emotional appeal. It is also a prime example of the overlapping of the Enlightenment and the Awakening, the good works of the first merging with the acts of charity of the second.

## Notes

1. A. Owen Aldridge, *Benjamin Franklin and Nature's God* (Durham, N.C., 1967), p. 19.
2. *Works of President Edwards,* 8 vols. (Worcester, Mass., 1808–9), 3: 145–46.
3. Aldridge, *Benjamin Franklin and Nature's God,* p. 5.
4. *Writings of Benjamin Franklin,* 10 vols. ed. Albert Henry Smyth (New York, 1905–7), 10: 172.
5. *PBF, 1*: 100.
6. *WJE, 6*: 230.
7. *Works of President Edwards, 8*: 345.
8. *Benjamin Franklin's Autobiography,* ed. J. A. Leo Lemay and P. M. Zall (New York, 1986), p. 88.
9. *Works of President Edwards, 3*: 154.
10. *Ibid., 3*: 287.
11. *The Philosophy of Jonathan Edwards from His Private Notebooks,* ed. Harvey G. Townsend (Eugene, Ore., 1955), p. 207.
12. *Works of Benjamin Franklin,* 10 vols., ed. Jared Sparks (Boston, 1836–40), 2: 241.
13. Ola E. Winslow, *Jonathan Edwards, 1703–1758* (1940; rep. New York, 1961), p. 117.
14. *Works of President Edwards, 3*: 144.
15. *WJE, 3*: 107. Emphasis in original.
16. *PBF, 2*: 114. Emphasis in original.
17. *Writings of Benjamin Franklin,* ed. J. A. Leo Lemay (New York, 1987), pp. 232–33.
18. *Works of President Edwards, 3*: 153.
19. *Writings of Benjamin Franklin,* ed. Smyth, 9: 10.
20. *Works of President Edwards, 2*: 362.
21. *Philosophy of Jonathan Edwards,* ed. Townsend, pp. 71, 161, 225.
22. *Ibid.,* p. 237.
23. *Works of President Edwards, 3*: 257.
24. Norman Fiering, *Jonathan Edwards's Moral Thought and Its British Context* (Chapel Hill, N.C., 1981), p. 358.
25. *PBF, 1*: 102. Emphasis in original.
26. *Ibid., 1*: 261. Emphasis in original.
27. *Benjamin Franklin's Autobiography,* ed. Lemay and Zall, p. 74.
28. *PBF, 7*: 105.
29. *Philosophy of Jonathan Edwards,* ed. Townsend, pp. 108–9.
30. *PBF, 3*: 85. Emphasis in original.
31. *Writings of Benjamin Franklin,* ed. Smyth, pp. 7, 436–37.
32. *Benjamin Franklin's Autobiography,* ed. Lemay and Zall, p. 102.
33. *WJE, 6*: 168.
34. *Philosophy of Jonathan Edwards,* ed. Townsend, pp. 212–13.
35. *Ibid.,* p. 213.
36. *Ibid.,* p. 17.
37. *Ibid.,* p. 79.
38. *Ibid.,* p. 179.
39. *WJE, 6*: 307–10.
40. *Philosophy of Jonathan Edwards,* ed. Townsend, p. viii.

41. *Ibid.*, p. 221.
42. *WJE*, 2: 298–99.
43. *Writings of Benjamin Franklin*, ed. Lemay, pp. 435, 1016, 1359.
44. *Works of President Edwards*, 3: 243.
45. *PBF*, 1: 265.
46. Aldridge, *Benjamin Franklin and Nature's God*, p. 74.
47. *WJE*, 3: 96.
48. *Writings of Benjamin Franklin*, ed. Lemay, p. 1016.
49. *Philosophy of Jonathan Edwards*, ed. Townsend, p. 134.
50. *Works of President Edwards*, 8: 57.
51. *Ibid.*, 8: 55.
52. *Ibid.*, 8: 69.
53. *Ibid.*, 8: 64.
54. *Ibid.*, 3: 158.
55. *PBF*, 1: 268.
56. *Ibid.*, 3: 345.
57. *Writings of Benjamin Franklin*, ed. Lemay, p. 845.
58. *Writings of Benjamin Franklin*, ed. Smyth, 9: 261.
59. *PBF*, 11: 450.
60. *Works of President Edwards*, 3: 298.
61. *PBF*, 2: 385. Emphasis is in original.
62. *Works of President Edwards*, 3: 343.
63. *Ibid.*, 3: 349.

# 4

# The Nature of True—
# and Useful—Virtue:
# From Edwards to Franklin

### EDWIN S. GAUSTAD

Perry Miller's unhappiness over the misinterpretation of his "From
Edwards to Emerson" essay (as though he had argued "in some mystical pretension . . . for a direct line of intellectual descent") should warn
one against the particular grammatical construction of the subtitle. Miller
at least had the advantage of a good deal more "from-ness," one century to another, in moving between Edwards and Emerson than between
Edwards (b. 1703) and Franklin (b. 1706). Yet Franklin's longevity does
allow for some chronological movement, though of course the interest
here is more than temporal tracing or pigeonholing, more—to quote
Miller once more—than treating the history of ideas as some sort of
"mail-order catalogue."

So let it be said that I do not argue for a direct line of intellectual
descent but will attempt, rather, to enter the differing intellectual worlds
of our two figures. However distinct these separate worlds were, it will
also be argued that the orbits of those worlds moved in a common cosmos, sometimes in a parallel or overlapping rotation. And both men
hoped to prevent wild eccentricity of orbital motion. If a New Order of
the Ages was envisioned at all, the emphasis for both men might well
be more on the "order" than on the "new."

First, to those separate worlds. Edwards wrote and thought within an explicit, consciously embraced, elaborately constructed theological frame. Nowhere is this more evident than in the *Two Dissertations*, with which we shall be immediately concerned, but those treatises cannot be divorced from his other major philosophical works or from his sermons or from his jotted notes and reflections. In the world of Calvinist divinity, Edwards lived, moved, and had his being. The nature of virtue, the reality of virtue, the reason for being of virtue are essentially and inextricably theological. Violence is done, and has been done, to Edwards's ethical theory when the fundamental foundations are regarded as anything less than that: built in, built on.

So, let me briefly enter that Edwardsean world, taking the *Two Dissertations* as the widest path of entrance and taking Paul Ramsey's posthumous volume, with enormous gratitude, as the principal vehicle. For Edwards, as for Thomas Aquinas, "the truths of faith and reason are *one.*"[1] Edwards's philosophy cannot be divorced from his theology, nor his commitment of faith from his exercise of reason. That remains true even though Edwards, for reasons of rhetoric and apologia, does distinguish between the grounds of appeal or the avenues by which the conviction might come to others. With respect to his own conviction, however, Edwards found faith and reason mutually reinforcing, not antagonistic; he found the truest virtue, like the truest knowledge, a gift of grace—all of a piece with the miracle of redemption. "If any man be in Christ," the Apostle Paul noted long ago, "he is a new creature." That newness, that re-creation, that second birth infused all; it did not permit separation of functions or faculties, of hearts or minds, of morals or metaphysics.

That oneness, infusing all and connecting all, comes through clearly in Edwards's 1738 series of sermons on the thirteenth chapter of First Corinthians. This extended meditation of fifteen sermons has a single theme: love—Christian love, divine love, all-embracing, all-radiating love. Love is "the sum of all virtue," Edwards proclaimed from the pulpit, and "it is all from the same Spirit influencing the heart." Whether love is expressed toward God or toward one's fellow creatures," it is from the breathings of the same Spirt that the Christian's love arises."[2] There is not one kind of love directed toward the Creator, and another toward that which has been created: it is all one and the same, and it is all a consequence of the redemptive act. "The Spirit of God in the work of conversion renews the heart by giving it a divine temper."[3] We are disposed to render honor and all duties to those whom we love, whether God or man; therefore, "it follows that love is a root and spring and, as it were, a comprehension of all virtues."[4] Both Scripture and reason lead to the same conclusion, agreeable to the insight of the Apostle that without love we are nothing.

Love has an intrinsic priority, Edwards declared in the twelfth sermon of this series, but that should not obscure the remarkable fact that it never stands in isolation. Rather, Christian love is connected to all other Christian graces (notably, faith and hope): "the graces of Christianity are all linked together or united one to another and within one another, as the links of a chain." Where there is one grace, "there are all; and when one is wanting, all are wanting." There is, in short, "a concatenation of the graces of Christianity," a mutual dependence, an enfolding and meshing that does not allow for separation or insulation one from the other.[5] While this might seem quite surprising or perhaps even incredible, further reflection, Edwards argued, demonstrates why this must be so. All Christian graces, for example, come from the same Spirit; all are involved in the one work of conversion, the one change of heart. Furthermore, all the graces have the same purpose: "they are all directed to the same end, viz. God, his glory, and our own happiness in him; which shows that they must be nearly related, and very much linked together."[6]

Love is so central, so supreme, that we cannot find a better understanding of heaven, Edwards noted, than to call it a "world of love." There love is undiluted, uninterrupted; there love is always requited, always fulfilled, always total in its trust and satisfaction and assurance. "As the saints will love God with an inconceivable ardor of heart, and to the utmost of their capacity; so they will know that he has loved them from eternity, and that he still loves them, and will love them to eternity."[7] The harmony there is like some great musical accord, yet even sweeter since no "intermediate expression" will in heaven be required. "If heaven be such a blessed world," Edwards concluded, "then let this be our chosen country, and the inheritance we seek."[8] This was, after all, a sermon, and Edwards never forgot the primary purpose of pulpit oratory: to bring men and women into a right relationship with God, here on earth to be sure, but even more critically in the eternity beyond.

This 1738 series of sermons on *Charity and Its Fruits*, along with many of his "Miscellanies" recorded even earlier, demonstrate Edwards's abiding concern with virtue, true virtue. It is, of course, in the *Two Dissertations*, published posthumously in 1765, that one finds Edwards's most sustained and systematic treatment of the matter. His world view, however, has not shifted; the Augustinian restlessness that finds rest only in God remains evident. The *Dissertations*, intimately joined, explain first "The End for Which God Created the World" in order then to explicate "The Nature of True Virtue." God created the world, let it be bluntly said, for his own glory, for the manifestation of his own "glorious attributes," out of a "supreme respect to himself."[9]

But some will object that such a view implies that God lacked something, that he needed to create a world to fill some void in his own nature. Not so, said Edwards; it is in the very nature of God to communicate, to emanate, to bestow. God does not create in order to find fulfillment, for he is already fulfilled: "As the sun receives nothing from the jewel that receives its light, and shines only by a participation in its brightness."[10] God creates, not out of paucity or need, but out of fullness and boundless love. If he finds pleasure in his creation, it is due not to some great quality found there and not previously known, but only to the fact that his nature is now more fully revealed. His happiness in creation "is the necessary consequence of his delighting in the glory of his nature, that he delights in the emanation and effulgence of it."[11] Surely, Edwards noted, "'tis no argument of indigence in God that he is inclined to communicate of his infinite fullness. 'Tis no argument of the emptiness or deficiency of a fountain that it is inclined to overflow."[12]

Another may object that God's creating the world out of a supreme respect to himself is basically an act of consummate selfishness. But this, Edwards points out, is to mistake and misunderstand the situation totally. For one cannot equate the nature of God ("infinitely the most valuable Being") with the nature of the private individual. To reason in this fashion is to allow our tendencies toward anthropomorphism to run wild. We think thus: we should not do things out of a "supreme respect" to ourselves; therefore, God should not behave this way. But in God, you see, Edwards patiently explained, there is no conflict between the private and the public good, for he is the source of all good. He is "the Author and Head of the whole system: on whom all absolutely depend; who is the fountain of being and good to the whole. It is more absurd to suppose that his interest should be opposite to the interest of the universal system, than that the welfare of the head, heart and vitals of the natural body should be opposite to the welfare of the body."[13]

Or, by following a similarly flawed anthropomorphic path, one might object that God delighting in his own glory is like some mere mortal who wants nothing more than the approval and applause of his fellows. It is all a matter of proportion, Edwards points out: a proportion of excellence, of knowledge, of Being. On all these counts and more, God does well to delight in his own glory; similarly, he does well to delight in those who perceive and praise that glory as an excellence beyond all other excellencies. This, Edwards wrote, far from being blameworthy, is but a "necessary consequence." If we love a friend for his virtues, so then we esteem and approve of all others who, in recognition of those true virtues, also acclaim and honor that friend.[14] This is obvious; this is reasonable. But if reason be not enough, we have the eloquent testimony of Scripture as well that "The Lord hath made all things for himself" (Prov. 16:4). When God explained that he was the alpha and the omega, the beginning and the end, he was, said Edwards, declaring that he was the first cause, the formal cause, the efficient cause, and the final cause of all creation.[15]

Once one comprehends the end for which God created the world, then one is ready to see clearly what constitutes true virtue. And if Edwards has just used Aristotelian language in speaking of origins and purpose, he sets out on a kind of Platonic pilgrimage in order to determine what that eternal idea or form of virtue is, by which all else is to be judged in order to claim the attribute, in which all else must in some degree participate in order to be recognized as true. We must take Edwards, at first, densely packed. "True virtue most essentially consists in benevolence to Being in general. Or perhaps to speak more accurately, it is that consent, propensity, and union of heart to Being in general, that is immediately exercised in a general good will."[16] A hundred pages follow (in Edwards, not here) to explicate those two sentences. We shall return to some of those pages later in making comparisons with Franklin, or in expounding Edwards further on specific virtues. Here it may be necessary only to underline the fact that God and his creation, God and the end for which he created the world, stand as the determining structure of genuine virtue.

Virtue most essentially consists in love, Edwards repeated, taking us back to the 1738 sermon series. This is declared to be the case in Scripture; most Christian divines acknowledge it to be true, and even "the more considerable Deists" will concede this point. Now, one must become clear about the object of that love: namely, "Being in general, or the great system of universal existence."[17] From a universal love or benevolence, a disposition of love to particular beings may be derived—though not the other way around. Private love, love of family or country or humanity, falls short of the measure of true virtue, for these particular loves bear "no proportion to the great all-comprehending system." True virtue can be found only where the proportions are right: only where all creaturely affection is "subordinate to a propensity or union of the heart to God, the Supreme and Infinite Being."[18]

Once that union is achieved, the immediate effect is the exercising of a general good will to all—the *immediate* effect, just like emanation with respect to the fullness of God's own nature. Now his creatures, with a fullness all their own, communicate or perhaps reflect the virtue and love that they find in God. Even as God seeks the good of his creation, so those who worship and praise him seek the good of the creature in all things. "And that temper or disposition of the heart, that consent, union, or propensity of mind to Being in general, which appears chiefly in such exercises, is virtue, truly so called; or in other words, true grace and real holiness."[19] Much more deserves to be said by way of general orientation and cosmic point of view, but this, I trust, is sufficient to show that the underpinnings of Edwards' moral philosophy are unarguably theological.

In contrast, Benjamin Franklin begins more with anthropology than with theology, more with works than with faith, more with consequences than with presuppositions. Not only does Franklin reject explicit theological systems as the appropriate starting point, he rejects certain tenets as injurious or fatal to the whole moral undertaking. The doctrine of Original Sin, for example, was for him, as for so many other "considerable Deists," a stumbling block of major magnitude. It was an "Opinion every whit as ridiculous as that of imputed Righteousness," Franklin wrote, an invention of "Priests (whether Popish or Presbyterian I know not) to fright and scare an unthinking Populace out of their Senses."[20] Like John Adams, Thomas Jefferson, and a host of earlier critics of Calvinist orthodoxy, Franklin saw this notion of original sin as no spur to moral conduct but a convenient evasion of all moral responsibility.

Franklin was even more exercised about the priority that faith had over works, believing that these priorities were tragically wrong. Men allow themselves to be hypnotized by good words instead of by works; they prefer "pious Discourses" to "Humane Benevolent Actions." Good actions are dismissed by theologians, Franklin said, who call "Morality, rotten morality, Righteousness, ragged Righteousness and even filthy Rags; and when you mention Virtue, they pucker up their Noses as if they smelt a Stink." The old proverb, Franklin noted, used to go like this:

> A Man of Words and not of Deeds,
> Is like a Garden full of Weeds.

The Calvinist theologians prefer a revised version:

> A Man of Deeds and not of Words
> Is like a Garden full of _____.

I've forgotten the rhyme, Franklin adds disingenuously, but "'tis something the very Reverse of Perfume."[21]

In 1753 Franklin wrote to a correspondent that faith "has doubtless its use in the World." But, Franklin quickly added, "I wish it were more productive of Good Works than I have generally seen it: I mean real good Works, Works of Kindness, Charity, Mercy, and Publick Spirit; not Holiday-keeping, Sermon-Reading or Hearing, performing Church Ceremonies, nor making long Prayers, fill'd with Flatteries and Compliments, despis'd even by wise Men, and much less capable of pleasing the Deity."[22] And a decade earlier, Franklin tried to reassure his sister that he did not intend to throw faith out the window or to suggest that God ought not to be worshiped or to suppose that good works gained one an automatic entry into heaven. But good deeds do count, Franklin insisted, and to support his case he turned to none other than Jonathan Edwards, urging his sister to read Edwards's latest book, *Some Thoughts Concerning the Present Revival of Religion in New England* (1742), where she would discover that even the Northampton divine himself concluded that acts of righteousness and moral duties counted for more than the mere externals of religious worship.[23]

Of course, like other men of the American Enlightenment, Franklin did have a faith. At least he had one after recovering from the youthful skepticism and cynicism reflected in his *Dissertation on Liberty and Necessity*, published when he was a mere eighteen years of age. In his maturity he, like his fellow deists, believed in a superintending providence, in a moral universe, in a rational order, and in the necessity of both public and private virtue. In an age of virtue where nearly everyone had something to say on the subject, Franklin said even more. "Virtue alone is sufficient to make a Man Great, Glorious and Happy," Franklin wrote in the pages of *The American Weekly Mercury* in 1729. The ancient Persians, he noted, taught virtue as a liberal art, and so they should, since "it is certainly of more Consequence to a Man that he has learnt to govern his Passions; in spite of Temptation[,] to be just in his Dealings, to be Temperate in his Pleasures, to support himself with Fortitude under his Misfortunes, to behave with Prudence in all Affairs and in every Circumstance of Life." This, Franklin concluded, was worth more than all the degrees that might be bestowed upon a human being. Though we fear the rich and applaud the learned, we reserve (said Franklin) our highest adoration for those who are virtuous.[24]

Franklin thought that the noblest service he might render would be to promote virtue: promote it by organization, by precept, and to some modest degree by example. His Philadelphia Junto seized upon Cotton Mather's suggestion that voluntary organizations be created to promote religion and morality. The morality part caught Franklin's attention and directed his energies. Points of morals were explicitly laid on the table for discussion and for the preparation of meetings. Among the ritual questions to be asked, moreover, were these: "What unhappy effect of intemperance have you lately observed or heard? of imprudence? of passion? or of any other vice or folly?" A similar question on the positive side called for reports of the "happy effects" arising from any observed practice of virtue. Junto members, moreover, were asked to consider what contributions might be made on behalf of mankind, of country, of friends, and only lastly of themselves.[25] Franklin even thought of creating what he called the United Party for Virtue, in anticipation of which he kept jotting notes to himself with regard to both principles of organization and practical agenda.

With respect to precept, we have of course the often tongue-in-cheek moral advice of Poor Richard, but in addition Franklin's more serious intent to write a book with the title *The Art of Virtue*. The book was never written, though often discussed. "Many People lead bad Lives," he wrote in 1760, "that would gladly lead good ones, but know not how to make the Change." His little book would show them how, for virtue can be an acquired taste, or better an acquired art. "It is as properly an Art, as Painting, Navigation, or Architecture," Franklin noted. And in all those arts, it is not enough to advise a person to be a painter, or even urge them to do so. One must be shown *how*; one must learn how to use the proper instruments, and "My *Art of Virtue* has also its Instruments, and teaches the Manner of Using them." Though the book was never written, some elements of what was projected may be preserved in the *Autobiography*. What gives Franklin's moral counsel special force was this effort to offer a method, a program of training, that would make virtue the more likely consequence. Virtue comes not by happenstance, certainly not by inertia. "If we were as industrious to become Good, as to make ourselves Great," Franklin wrote, "we should become really Great by being Good, and the Number of valuable Men would be much increased."[26]

But Franklin, perhaps more than most women and men, thought words cheap if not reinforced, if not authenticated, by deeds: his own words by his own deeds. So, while it is easy to poke fun at Franklin's efforts at a moral calculus, those efforts should be understood as his own sustained endeavor to demonstrate that words without deeds simply do not count. So for Franklin himself virtue was an art, to be worked at as diligently and as self-consciously as any other, learning the principles, practicing the methods, perfecting the techniques. In one of Franklin's Socratic dialogues, Socrates avers that a man of sense might slip in his effort to practice virtue, but he is still a man of sense provided he is aware "of his Failing and diligently applys himself to rectify what is done amiss, and to prevent the like for the future." A mathematician does not cease to be such because he makes a mistake "in casting up a long Account," but he does cease to be such if he has no idea how to correct his mistake or makes no effort to do so.[27] We shall be judged at that Last Day, Franklin wrote his parents in 1738, not by "what we thought, but what we did."[28] Franklin was prepared so to judge himself.

Jonathan Edwards and Benjamin Franklin proceed, therefore, from sharply different cosmologies and theologies. Space and time for the two men seem to be charted on totally different grids. Their paths across the skies inscribe separate orbits, and yet we see evidence that they do revolve around the same sun, that they do inhabit the same moral universe. Both men engaged in what Norman Fiering calls "moral preaching"; both men, fired by a sense of mission, "were caught up in the same colloquy."[29] Three areas of overlap or of mutual concern will be considered.

First, for both men virtue had to be something more than mere outward conformity or memorization of some rules. Virtue had to be an inner disposition, a natural (or supernatural) tendency, a regular and predictable propensity or response. Edwards spoke of true virtue, Franklin of truly virtuous habits. Edwards spoke of a new nature, Franklin of a new disposition. For Edwards, true virtue came through a redemptive act that gave men and women a new sense of the heart and a new will. The Holy Spirit, Edwards noted, causes "some motion, or affection, or apprehension to be in the soul, that at the same time would not be there without him."[30] With this new principle dwelling within, with virtues now infused, one proceeded steadily to manifest the consequences of true virtue.

Franklin wrote often of the "habits of virtue," implying a kind of moral behavior that became so much a part of one's nature as to be, in effect, built in. He noted that "long Habits of Virtue" might even have an effect upon one's countenance and total demeanor.[31] One of the values that Franklin found in religion is that it often served as a useful device to help develop just such habits. In one's youth or in one's ignorance, religion helped restrain persons from vice and offered support in their practice of virtue. This it would do until virtue "becomes habitual, which is the great Point for its Security."[32] At that point, one pursues the moral life for its own sake, no longer dependent upon promises of punishment or reward.

Edwards also used the word "habit," habit being "only a law that God has fixed, that such actions on such occasions should be exerted."[33] Like Franklin, Edwards maintained that if a man acted virtuously over and over, such action would eventually become habitual to him. Unlike Franklin, however, he saw that first truly virtuous action as impossible without the Holy Spirit dwelling within the redeemed man. A man cannot begin to act virtuously until true virtue is planted in him. "Tell me [how]," Edwards urged, "a man that has no true grace within him shall begin to exercise it: before he begins to exercise it, he must have some of it."[34] For Franklin, it was enough that the exercise began, and continued, and at last became, as we say, "second nature." On the source of that "second nature," the two men would keep to their separate orbits. Though neither used Tocqueville's happy phrase, "habits of the heart," each would (I believe) have readily adopted it to describe that condition wherein the practice of virtue is more reflex than reflection. Though neither employed Kantian language to the effect that nothing in the world is good in and of itself except a good will, each would (I believe) have found that formulation congenial to his own understanding of *both* true and useful virtue.[35]

Second, both of our moral philosophers saw behavior as the ultimate test of one's redeemed or altered nature. The title of Edwards's tenth charity sermon, "Grace Tends to Holy Practice," made his position explicit. Grace is not the reward for virtue, it is the means to virtue. "Good practice is not the ground of election," Edwards declared, "as the Arminians suppose who imagine that God elects men upon a foresight of their good works. But Christian practice is the scope and end of election." God converts individuals "and infuses grace into them for that end, that they might exercise themselves in holy practice." Employing one of his favorite distinctions between mere speculative knowledge of religion and a true spiritual knowledge, Edwards points out that practice is no necessary part of the former but is always a consequence of the latter. Those who pretend to know Christ but do not keep his commandments are hypocrites and liars, for "It is the definition of grace that it is a principle of holy action." Principles and actions are interdependent; they are "correlates which necessarily have respect one to the other," like a root and a plant. "It is absurd to say of a root that it is a root of nothing. So it is absurd to talk of a principle that it does not tend to practice."[36]

Equally impatient, equally incredulous, Franklin would accept no pretension to virtue not evident in behavior. Nor would he tolerate doctrine that produced no visible effects. His involvement in the famous Hemphill affair in 1735 arose from his despair over Presbyterian preachers who seemed interested only in making more Presbyterians rather than good citizens. Samuel Hemphill, in sharp contrast to the majority of his fellow clerics, preached sermons notably devoid of dogma, but notably rich in their encouragement to virtue, "or what in the religious Stile are called Good Works." When Hemphill was accused of heresy and ordered to stand trial before an ecclesiastical court, Franklin sprang to his defense. Indignant that a preacher and promoter of morality should be treated in this fashion, Franklin demanded to know whether virtue has become heresy and universal benevolence a false doctrine. Everyone worries about opinion, and everyone believes his own to be infallible. The only point of faith that is completely clear and agreed to by all, Franklin wrote, is that "Morality is our Duty." Furthermore, "A virtuous Heretick shall be saved before a wicked Christian." Morality is the great end, and faith is only a means thereto—and not a necessary means at that. For virtue can come in different ways, "and if the End be obtained, it is no matter by what Means."[37] The Apostle Paul had spoken of the fruits of the Spirit; both Edwards and Franklin were vitally interested in those fruits, even if differing on what causal force made the fruit possible. True virtue could turn out to be useful, by Franklin's measure, even if useful virtue did not, by Edwards's measure, thereby become true.

Third, both men respected the place of even a prudential virtue, an ordinary morality, one not yet arising from or leading to a "second nature." In Paul Ramsey's phrase, for Edwards "ordinary morality was a rather splendid thing." There is a moral instinct to be found in all persons; there are laws of nature that are built into God's creation. Since God is responsible for these (just as he is for the superior gifts of grace), one cannot dismiss ordinary morality as though it had no value. In fact, ordinary morality and true virtue do resemble each other, can even be confused; adherents to true virtue and to ordinary morality, moreover, may often call a particular kind of behavior by the very same name. But these are not and never will be identical, since the latter arises chiefly from self-love however greatly extended, and the former from benevolence toward and union with Being in general. The golden rule, to take a single example, is an aspect of ordinary morality, since it merely would treat others in a way consistent with the way in which one would himself want to be treated. "To do that to another which we should be angry with him for doing to us, and to hate a person for doing that to us which we should incline to and insist on doing to him, if we were exactly in the same case, is to disagree with ourselves, and contradict ourselves."[38] Thus our behavior is based on self-love, even if on a more reflective form of it.

Behavior based on "consent, propensity and union of heart to Being in general" is, on the other hand, of a quite different order. In this instance, we love or hate particular actions "from a sense of the primary beauty of true virtue, and odiousness of sin." It is a natural principle to act in agreement with ourselves, so that we do not contradict and are not at war with ourselves. It is, however, a divine principle that enables us to act in "agreement or union of heart to the great system, and to God, the Head of it."[39] Nonetheless, civilization may be more often held together by ordinary morality than by true virtue, for the former (pertaining to the great masses) does include the instinctive affections for the family, the sense of proportion or harmony between an injury on the one hand and the punishment meted out on the other (a sense of fair play, or of justice), pity to others in distress, and the like. Ordinary morality, therefore, is part of God's structure in the universe; it is useful, it can even be noble.

This "ordinary morality" was, of course, Franklin's major concern. He names the virtues that he regards as important, extending the ancient cardinal virtues of justice, prudence, fortitude, and temperance to a list that included silence, order, resolution, frugality, industry, sincerity, moderation, cleanliness, tranquility, chastity, and humility. (Justice and temperance are the only two of the classical four to be specifically named, though prudence and fortitude are clearly implied in most of the items on the list.) If this list appeared to emphasize private virtue, Franklin had no doubt that public virtue rested on this prior foundation. So also did sound religion rest upon the art of being "a good Parent, a good Child, a good Husband, or Wife, a good Neighbour or Friend, a good Subject or citizen."[40] This is what Christianity was all about; this is what life was all about: virtue as the end, the goal, the *summum bonum*. Anyone who did not recognize that the "science of virtue" was worth more than all other learning put together was, said Franklin's Socrates, "a Fool, a Dunce, a Blockhead."[41]

Like Edwards, Franklin found virtue to be in the interest of all mankind. It was certainly not synonymous with self-denial, for so much depended upon the character, the nature, of the person in question. If one was not tempted to do injustice, his doing the just deed was no denial of himself: was it, then, not virtuous? Franklin found absurdity in defining virtue only in terms of sacrifice and self-abnegation. "The Truth is," he wrote, "that Temperance, Justice, Charity, &c. are Virtues, whether practis'd with or against our inclinations." Self-denial, like self-love, was neither good nor bad of itself; we simply need to know more, Franklin observed, about a person's interests or nature before we can decide. People can do vicious things that go against their inclinations ("like some mad Enthusiasts I have read of, who ran about naked"), but the act remains vicious just the same.[42] One is free, Edwards wrote in another connection, to do as he pleases—even on Calvinist terms; the question, however, is what pleases him. So for Franklin, the issue of temptation or denial is superficial; the question is, What sort of activity does one find consistent with his or her own character, consistent with those carefully cultivated habits of the heart?

And so Edwards and Franklin could agree on some of the same names for virtues that might, in Edwards's case, be unmistakably true and, in Franklin's case, preeminently useful. Sincerity, for example, was acclaimed by both men. Edwards declared that if "there be no love in what men do, then there is no respect to God or men in what they do; and if so, certainly no sincerity."[43] The whole of the third "Charity Sermon" expounds the idea that "nothing can make up for want of sincerity in the heart." Edwards observed that "God abominates great things without sincerity; but he accepts and delights in little things when there is sincerity. A cup of cold water given to a disciple in sincerity is worth more in God's sight than all one's goods to feed the poor."[44] Franklin was more interested in man's sight than in God's, but was likewise opposed to deceit: deceit of others that then brought harm, deceit of oneself that was perhaps the most treacherous vice of all.

Justice as well found favor with both men. Indeed, Edwards granted that the notion of justice was "founded in reason and the nature of things," that it was part of "a general moral sense, common to all mankind." Of course, different individuals and different nations may pursue justice in contrary ways, but this did not invalidate the universal allegiance to right over wrong, good over evil, justice over injustice.[45]

Humanity in general can understand, even on the level of "natural conscience," that justice requires that we yield all to God since we have received all from God. This is not quite true virtue, of course, but in such an instance of enlightened understanding natural conscience "concurs with the law of God, and is of equal extent with it, and joins its voice with it in every article."[46] High praise indeed for this cardinal virtue, a praise echoed by Franklin, as by the Whigs, the Commonwealth men, Enlightenment thinkers, and others. Franklin credited his allegiance to justice for having earned him the confidence of his country "and the honorable Employs it conferr'd upon him."[47] Most of that generality of "all mankind" preferred, of course, to speak of justice not in the abstract but in terms of particular grievances, inequities, and injuries.

Finally, humility, which, all things considered, came more easily for Edwards than for Franklin. Having a proper sense (even a sense of the heart) of God's excellency and perfection did much to encourage humility. Created intelligent beings, Edwards declared, "are all infinitely mean and little before God." All right, one can accept that without too much humiliation, but Edwards immediately added: "and most of them mean in comparison with some of their fellow creatures." At that point the sermon could be regarded as downright unfriendly. Man's "natural meanness is his filthiness."[48] As one would expect, this is not Franklin's mode of discourse when advocating humility. In fact, he admits that humility was something of an afterthought to his list of twelve virtues.

A Quaker friend, he wrote, "kindly inform'd me that I was generally thought proud," even "overbearing and rather insolent." Sobered by this confidence, Franklin promptly made humility the thirteenth on his list, "giving an extensive Meaning to the Word." He confessed, however, that he had little success achieving the reality behind the word, more success "with regard to the Appearance of it." As Franklin then proceeded to explain, even the appearance of virtue can be quite useful. He excused his failure to reach the level of true humility by noting that no natural passion is so difficult to conquer as pride. "Disguise it, struggle with it, beat it down, stifle it, mortify it as much as one pleases, it is still alive, and will every now and then peep out and show itself." Edwards and Franklin also agreed, however, that one problem with humility was that it could ironically itself become an occasion for pride.[49]

Since Franklin lived more than a generation beyond Edwards's life span, one might assume that in this matter of virtue he had the last word. And to some extent, he did. Edwards continued, however, especially in New England, to exercise a powerful sway. The New England theology, though not without competitors, maintained a coherence and intensity of thought that gave it unusual force. It did not decline into mere moralism, as William Breitenbach has convincingly shown, nor did it evaporate into an utterly irrelevant hyper-Calvinism, as the same author has demonstrated.[50] Samuel Hopkins translated true virtue into radical disinterested benevolence, this having powerfully explicit implications for slavery and the slave trade.[51] Joseph Bellamy took that "moral law embedded in the will of God" and thrust it into a republican and revolutionary ideology. The legacy of Edwards through his students was such as to give a vital moral and theological spin to the broad assumptions concerning republican virtue.[52] And in nearby North Haven, Benjamin Trumbull saw true virtue as impelling men and women to conspicuous social involvement, notably in the realm of missionary activity.[53]

But, to be sure, Franklin did not stand alone either. One sees in the 1760s and 1770s enormous attention by "natural men" to the matter of virtue. Not so much in theological terms as in political and historical ones did writers and speakers reflect on the necessity of virtue, or bewail its tragic passing. The history of ancient Greece and Rome was read and interpreted in terms of the respective virtue of each people. The right of a modern nation to rule was determined by that nation's adherence to the path of virtue. A successful outcome of the American Revolution rested upon the virtue of the people. Good government would survive, would deserve to survive, only if tendencies to vice were checked, opportunities for virtue magnified. "The only foundation of a free constitution," John Adams declared in 1776, "is pure virtue."[54] Religion was judged not by its doctrinal merit, but by its effectiveness as moral teacher and enforcer. Jesus, according to Jefferson, deserved to be honored not for his divinity (which was questionable), but for his contribution to morality (which was not). He greatly improved on the moral teachers of antiquity, said Jefferson, by emphasizing charity and philanthropy, by calling attention to our duties to "our neighbors, our countrymen, and the whole family of mankind."[55] At Franklin's death in 1790, the sides—New Divinity versus New Order of the Ages—remained divided, but both sides found the discussion of virtue very much to the point: increasingly relevant, if not passionately urgent.

It was noted at the beginning that both men, seeing order in the universe, sought order in the "images and shadows" on earth. Those images and shadows included personal life, social organization, political structures, economic regulations, and certainly prescribed paths to virtue. Both men, moreover, found order in an avoidance of extremes. Edwards charted a course between Arminianism on the one hand and Antinomianism on the other. The former encouraged humankind to take its moral ability too seriously, the latter not seriously enough. Franklin charted a course between sterile orthodoxies on the one hand and moral anarchy on the other. The former ("the spinning, splitting, nerveless refinements of theology," in the words of Horace Bushnell) turned men's attention and energies away from the momentous moral issues, while the latter found neither meaning nor moral purpose anywhere in the universe at all. Cosmic splendor was then, in the words of John Adams, only "a boyish Fire Work." Edwards and the New Divinity men became political in order that society might be moral. Franklin and the Enlightenment men became theological (the belief in immortality, for example) in order that society might be moral. True virtue in the Age of Revolution became useful; useful virtue in the world of politics became true.

## Notes

1. *WJE, 8:* 6, n. 5.
2. *Ibid.*, p. 132.
3. *Ibid.*, p. 133.
4. *Ibid.*, p. 136.
5. *Ibid.*, pp. 327–30.
6. *Ibid.*, pp. 332–33.
7. *Ibid.*, p. 377.
8. *Ibid.*, p. 392.
9. *Ibid.*, pp. 428, 433.
10. *Ibid.*, p. 446.
11. *Ibid.*, p. 447.
12. *Ibid.*, p. 448.
13. *Ibid.*, pp. 450–52.
14. *Ibid.*, pp. 454–55.
15. *Ibid.*, p. 467.
16. *Ibid.*, p. 540.
17. *Ibid.*, p. 541.
18. *Ibid.*, pp. 556–57.
19. *Ibid.*, pp. 559–60.

20. *PBF*, 2: 114. See also Norman Fiering, "Benjamin Franklin and the Way to Virtue," *American Quarterly*, 30 (1978): 199–223.

21. *PBF*, 8: 155.

22. *Ibid.*, 4: 505.

23. *Ibid.*, 2: 385.

24. *Ibid.*, 1: 118–20.

25. *Ibid.*, pp. 255–57.

26. *Ibid.*, 9: 104–5; 1: 121. Emphasis in original.

27. *Ibid.*, 2: 18.

28. *Ibid.*, p. 204.

29. Norman Fiering, *Jonathan Edwards's Moral Thought and Its British Context* (Chapel Hill, N.C., 1981), pp. 6, 8.

30. Paul Ramsey, "Infused Virtues in Edwardsean and Calvinistic Context," in *WJE*, 8: 740.

31. *PBF*, 1: 119–20.

32. *Ibid.*, 7: 294.

33. Ramsey, "Infused Virtues," p. 742. For an excellent discussion of the vital place of "habit" in the thought of JE, see Sang Hyun Lee, *The Philosophical Theology of Jonathan Edwards* (Princeton, N.J., 1988).

34. Ramsey, "Infused Virtue," p. 740.

35. See Fiering's *American Quarterly* article (cited above, n. 20) for pertinent discussion by Thomas Aquinas, John Locke, and others.

36. *WJE*, 8: 295–98. Also see *WJE*, 2, where JE locates the last and greatest sign of true religious affections in the consistency of one's holy practice.

37. *PBF*, 2: 27–31.

38. *WJE*, 8: pp. 589–90.

39. *Ibid.*

40. *PBF*, 9: 121.

41. *Ibid.*, 2: 19.

42. *Ibid.*, pp. 20–21.

43. *WJE*, 8: 137.

44. *Ibid.*, p. 181.

45. *Ibid.*, pp. 624–26.

46. *Ibid.*, pp. 594–95.

47. *The Autobiography of Benjamin Franklin*, ed. J. A. Leo Lemay and P. M. Zall (New York, 1986), p. 74. See also Caroline Robbins, *The Eighteenth Century Commonwealthman* (New York, 1968); Gordon S. Wood, *The Creation of the American Republic, 1776–1787* (Chapel Hill, N.C., 1969); and Forrest McDonald, *Novus Ordo Seclorum* (Lawrence, Kans., 1985).

48. *WJE*, 8: 234, 236.

49. *Autobiography*, ed. Lemay and Zall, pp. 75–76, and n. 5.

50. See William K. Breitenbach, "Piety and Moralism: Edwards and the New Divinity," in *Jonathan Edwards and the American Experience*, ed. Nathan O. Hatch and Harry S. Stout (New York, 1988), pp. 177–204.

51. See Joseph A. Conforti, *Samuel Hopkins and the New Divinity Movement* (Grand Rapids, Mich., 1981).

52. See Mark Valeri, "The New Divinity and the American Revolution," *William and Mary Quarterly 46* (1989): 740–69, especially pp. 746, 756, 769.

53. See James D. German, "The Preacher and the New Light Revolution in Connecticut: The Pulpit Theology of Benjamin Trumbull, 1760–1800," Ph.D. dissertation, University of California, Riverside, 1989.

54. *The Works of John Adams*, 10 vols., ed. Charles F. Adams (Boston, 1850–1856), *10*: 401.

55. *Jefferson's Extracts from the Gospels*, ed. Dickinson W. Adams (Princeton, N.J., 1983), p. 330.

# 5

# "A Wall Between Them Up to Heaven": Jonathan Edwards and Benjamin Franklin

ELIZABETH E. DUNN

During the first half of the eighteenth century, Anglo-Americans struggled to resolve a number of unsettling issues. The use of paper money as a circulating medium, growing power in the assemblies, and the popularity of evangelical revivalism were among the items that initiated heated public debates. Such conflicts provide evidence of the sort of turmoil often used as proof of the process of "modernization" at work.[1] But those and other disputes also prompted colonists to articulate assumptions about value and to reveal the depth of differences among themselves as they attempted to evaluate social, economic, and political change. By comparing the writings of two complex personalities, Jonathan Edwards and Benjamin Franklin, clues emerge that illustrate how values contributed to divisions in the colonies and shaped the attitudes of individuals caught in the vortex of cultural disruption.

Defined as clusters of beliefs used to order actions and thoughts, values emerge most clearly during intense arguments. They provide the basis for an individual's perception of reality and guide decisions concerning behavioral and intellectual choices.[2] Focusing on values provides

58

an alternative view of the stresses of change—one that avoids the pitfalls of directional analysis and the accompanying search for a transition period often associated with theories of modernization.

The "modernity" ascribed to Jonathan Edwards by his most famous biographer, Perry Miller, continues to influence how historians evaluate America's first great religious philosopher. This view contrasts with assessments labeling Edwards the last true Puritan, a theologian who reclaimed Calvinism while his contemporaries moved on to optimistic liberalism. Few scholars, however, question that Franklin symbolized the Enlightenment and the future of America. With his archetypal genius for applied science, his business sense, and his tolerant attitude, he seems to many observers today to have been worlds apart from the Reverend Mr. Edwards, who preached "Sinners in the Hands of an Angry God."[3]

Despite their differences, both Franklin and Edwards engaged in a lifelong debate with the society in which they lived, and their writings reveal how each defended his ideals in the face of threatening intellectual developments and social experiences. Comparing Franklin's and Edwards's approaches to science and religion, how they viewed the relationship between natural and religious philosophy, their uses of rationalism, and their attitudes toward particular aspects of reality clarifies their priorities and the strategies they employed to manipulate and protect their values.

When writing about the Great Awakening, Edwards emphasized the discord that revivalism had raised among his fellow colonists. "The people," he observed,

> are divided into two parties, those that favor the work and those that are against it, and the distinction has long been growing more and more visible, and the distance greater, till there is at length raised a wall between them up to heaven; so that one party is very much out of the reach of all influence of the other.[4]

Franklin and Edwards personified extreme possibilities evident in such a division, possibilities that went beyond differences over revivalism. Among the principles that separated them like "a wall" were Edwards's theocentrism and Franklin's humanism. Both men made assumptions about God that provided the basis for their notions of worth and affected their reception of cultural change.

At the most basic level, essentialist values colored Edwards's outlook. Essentialism is a value orientation that assumes worth to be a quality inherent to an object or idea. Superior authorities, ultimately God, serve as the initial font of value. Tendencies to view worth as an intrinsic quality translate into efforts to make language correspond to some preconceived notion of reality. Though Descartes had little direct influence in America, these theories harmonize with Cartesian assertions that the laws of physics derive from the essence of matter. In addition, like Malebranche's occasionalism, such reasoning assumes that two kinds of causation exist, natural (or occasional) and supernatural.[5]

By contrast, functionalism most often influenced Franklin's thinking. A utilitarian approach not only defines a thing by its intended purpose but evaluates it by how well it fulfills that purpose. This approach, therefore, relies on people to determine worth, and value itself becomes a variable concept rather than a given one. Functionalism finds its scientific counterpart in materialism, an interpretive framework that assumes a completed and mechanical universe subject only to the rules of natural law. Lacking a theocentric core, functionalism frequently bypasses tradition or any particular authority, such as the Bible, in favor of experience as the best guide in decision-making.[6]

Though they gravitated toward mutually exclusive sources of value, neither man was isolated from the effects of alternative approaches. What Franklin and Edwards shared was a need to make sense of the world while preserving basic beliefs. To accomplish that goal, both cultivated mediating strategies that protected their values from hostile cultural elements. Both used Enlightenment methods to solve intellectual problems, but each remained committed to a specific view of value. As a result, Franklin, the heretic, thrived, though he lived in a culture that blurred most distinctions between religion and science, and Edwards, the Puritan, absorbed into his theology the new science that threatened to force a separation of religious and natural philosophy.

The source of Edwards's essentialism lay in his consuming passion to understand God, and his dedication to that study colored his specific brand of essentialism. Because Edwards envisioned a theocentric universe and because theology was his metier, Edwards necessarily accepted the inherent worth of ideas, actions, or even people that harmonized with theories he gradually developed regarding God's role in the universe. Revelation provided Edwards with a fixed standard of interpretation. Though he sometimes appeared frustrated with the limitations of language, Edwards did believe that properly interpreted messages and imagery encoded in the Bible revealed God's preconceived plans for humanity. Physical nature, ideas, behaviors, and belief were all understood in terms of absolute truth of the Bible. Why did God forbid eating certain parts of animals? Edwards speculated it must be for "some mystical or typical consideration," not for mere "elegancy of speech."[7] Such laws ought not to be questioned but rather examined for an understanding of the verities they contained concerning God's mysteries. Human comprehension of the Bible changed, but its intended messages remained the same.

Revelation provided no assistance for Franklin when he speculated about religious issues, and he remained especially dissatisfied with his excursions into proofs of First Cause. Theology also played no important role in Franklin's thinking or writing, and he demonstrated little regard for the usual techniques and results of that discipline. In an earnest letter written to his parents in 1738, Franklin emphasized that religious musings in general held few charms for him. Accused of unorthodox beliefs ranging from Arianism to Arminianism, the young printer refused to deny or confirm rumors his mother and father had heard. Instead, he noted, "I make such Distinctions very little my Study," preferring to be judged by actions rather than by speculations.[8] By the mid-1740s, Franklin had settled for a bland public expression of deism, remarkable only for its consistency.

Though Franklin refused to ruminate on the existence of God, Edwards constructed at least two separate though related arguments to prove God's reality. In no. 199 of Edwards's private notebooks, known as the "Miscellanies," he wrote a proof of God's existence. The fact that we have souls, asserted Edwards, and that they are intricate "pieces of workmanship so curious and of such amazing contrivance," provides "exceeding glaring evidence" of God.[9] Who created souls, who assigned them to particular bodies, and who gave them immortality? he queried. If we have souls, Edwards deduced, then God must exist.

In an essay called "Of Being," Edwards took a different tack. He proposed that nothingness was impossible to imagine and therefore could not exist. Whenever one tries to form a picture of nothing, he asserted, something comes to mind. "The mind," Edwards wrote, "let it stretch its conceptions ever so far, can never so much as bring itself to conceive of a state of perfect Nothing."[10] Instead of nothing, all space was filled with something. That something, Edwards concluded, existed through the power, will, and purpose of an intelligent creator.

Edwards's feeling that nothingness was impossible echoed theories postulating that the distances between heavenly bodies must be filled with something, perhaps a fluid. Franklin's use of a reminiscent hypothesis illustrates how the assumptions of both men affected their religious beliefs. Asserting that something filled the void between humanity and God, Franklin turned to polytheism as a possibility. For his private worship service, he invented a group of intermediary gods. Proposing one god per solar system, Franklin described minor beings that would serve as objects of worship for humans. These gods, in turn, worshiped the supreme head who controlled all, thus creating a hierarchy of deities between humanity and its creator.[11] In keeping with his utilitarian character, Franklin offered a solution to his problem and made polytheism a part of his eclectic religious creed.

Disagreement over the shape of spiritual presence in the universe paralleled differences between Franklin and Edwards over doctrinal matters. Though Franklin, for example, willingly conceded the necessity of worship, creeds, and moral codes for successful socialization of most people, he had little sense of Edwards's aesthetic appreciation of the same things, and he especially found little use for conversion experiences.[12] Remaining suspicious of religious spiritualism throughout his life, Franklin preferred instead to concentrate on practical aspects of Christian morality and their role in the here and now. Ever the iconoclast, he explained his position in a letter rebuking an acquaintance who doubted Franklin's benevolent motives. I do not do good works to get into heaven, Franklin claimed, "I have not the Vanity to think I deserve it, the Folly to expect it, nor the Ambition to desire it." Although he trusted that the Father would "never make me miserable," Franklin focused on earthly deeds, rather than spiritual rewards.[13]

Edwards also rejected good behavior as a route to heaven, but he did have the ambition to desire salvation, and he trusted that grace gave it. For Edwards, conversion was the keystone of Christian life. Enjoined by scripture and valued as God's gift to humanity, the experience transformed individuals from natural persons into members of the elect. Despite moderation of his views during the Awakening, Edwards continued to favor identifiable conversion experiences as signs of true religious affections.[14]

Though he admitted that Christian belief had practical side effects, Edwards never lost sight of its ultimate goals. God created the universe out of goodness, Edwards believed, and Jehovah must enjoy seeing his creatures delight in his own existence. The universe, for him, was a giant funnel where existence narrowed down to one essential fact. "The end of the creation," Edwards concluded, "is that the creature might glorify Him."[15] He compressed religious purpose into one phrase, the glorification of God.

Franklin worked in exactly the opposite way. He used himself as a starting point and allowed his imagination to fan out across a broad range of ideas and potential explanations for reality. From this position he sympathized with functional explanations of phenomena, including religion. Franklin's penchant for avoiding explorations of first causes of the universe grew not only out of his desire to avoid public censure but also out of his inability to convince himself that there was a single first cause. Edwards, by contrast, never entertained any doubts about the reality of a creating, divine being, and his philosophy unfolded from there.

While Franklin, not unlike many conservative clergymen, found renewed interest in religious duties to be a useful tool for promoting morality, he harbored little sympathy for the emotionalism of revivalistic meetings. Edwards and other evangelicals could not have disagreed more. They searched for the core of religious experience in the very spiritualism that Franklin found disruptive and distasteful. Conversely, morality appeared to revivalists as an indicator of an individual's new awareness of God—not the ultimate goal. In their writings, Edwards and Franklin illustrate the diverse conclusions possible as colonials searched for the meaning and purpose of the Great Awakening.

Using the differences explored above as a basis, an investigation of Franklin's and Edwards's divergent interests in science and their view of the relationship between natural and religious philosophy clarifies both their values and the strategies they employed to manipulate those values. Because God served as his ultimate source of value, Edwards refused to interpret secular concerns as though they were unrelated to sacred ones. Science and theology existed as two categories in the same mental universe, and inevitably, Edwards's discoveries in each affected his conclusions in the other. Franklin, however, compartmentalized his thinking and separated categories that Edwards tied together.

Franklin's openness to novel explanations also led him to consider a variety of scientific hypotheses while leaving unanswered ultimate questions of causation. Though far more than a mere "gadgeteer," his orientation toward the practical led him to explore electricity, oceanography, heat transfer, and other areas with an eye to applying abstract principles to useful inventions. In Franklin's opinion, it was not important "to know the Manner in which Nature executes her Laws; 'tis enough, if we know the Laws themselves." It was useful to know that dishes, left unsupported, would fall to the ground and break. How and why this happened was interesting, "but we can preserve our China," he asserted, without knowing the answers.[16]

Edwards too saw purpose in studying science, but his goals were far removed from those of Franklin. Edwards pursued theoretical physics precisely because he wanted to achieve a clearer understanding of God and to give Calvinist religious philosophy a sound scientific basis. Though Edwards assumed that God was responsible for all creation, his faith served not to limit his imagination but to spur further research into the works of nature. Edwards's conclusions about matter, space, and existence, like his religious views, rested on the foundation of his essential belief in God's power.[17]

Three basic tenets shaped Edwards's scientific speculations. First, he assumed that creation was an arbitrary act of God. Drawing on the occasionalism of Malebranche, Edwards proposed that all existence depended continually on divine will. "The universe," he wrote, "is created out of nothing every moment."[18] Secondly, Edwards asserted that matter is not material, but a force that resists division. That force emanates from the divine being, and the existence of matter directly depends on God's power. It is obvious to all, Edwards asserted, that space exists everywhere and infinitely. "But I had as good speak plain," he clarified, "I have already said as much as, that Space is God."[19] Finally, Edwards honed his theory of matter by defining all existence in terms of relationships. In "Miscellanies" entry pages, Edwards asserted that existence required cognition. A thing cannot be in isolation. It must have a relationship to another entity—matter must be perceived in order to be.[20]

These three elements, the defining power of God, matter as an immaterial force dependent on God's will, and the relationship between existence and perception, provided the basis for Edwards's evaluation of scientific and religious ideas. All reality relied on the whim of a divine being, and Edwards's theories demanded absolute surrender to religious faith. At the same time, Edwards felt that his assumptions harmonized well with recent discoveries in natural philosophy. Our knowledge of the laws of nature might change with scientific discovery, but the reality of God's power did not.

Typically, Edwards drew religious corollaries based on these principles even in his simplest scientific essays. His earliest effort, "Of Insects," explained how spiders flew through the air on their webs. After detailing observations of webs and how they floated on the breeze to transport spiders from tree to tree, Edwards added an inference. "We hence see the exuberant goodness of the Creator," he declared, "who hath not only provided for all the necessities, but also for the pleasure and recreation of all sorts of creatures."[21] Physics explained the principles of a spider's flight, but God stood behind those principles.

Franklin, who rarely evoked the name of the creator in his scientific writings, usually avoided making parallels between natural law and the operations of God. Religion and science stood as two separate categories. The role of lightning as a symbol and subject for study illuminates the contrasting approaches Edwards and Franklin took when exploring the natural world. Thunderstorms terrified young Edwards until he accepted the sovereignty of God. Then he viewed storms as a source of inspiration and went out of his way to "see the lightnings play, and hear the majestic and awful voice of God's thunder." *In Images or Shadows of Divine Things*, Edwards chose lightning as the symbol of God's wrath and noted that it struck lofty places where pride dwells.[22] Representing an omnipotent deity, storms confirmed that God created the principles of natural science and arranged all physical phenomenon to deliver messages to humanity.

Franklin, by contrast, was popularly known as the man who snatched lightning from the heavens. Responding to criticisms of his work on electricity by the French scientist Jean-Antoine Nollet, Franklin complained that Nollet seemed to suppose "it Presumption in Man to propose guarding himself against the Thunders of Heaven! Surely the Thunder of Heaven is no more supernatural than the Rain, Hail or Sunshine," and we protect ourselves from those.[23] Pushing his argument further, Franklin denied that heaven produced cloud-to-ground lightning in the first place, for "it is not Lightning from the Clouds that strikes the Earth," he claimed, "but Lightning from the Earth that Strikes the Clouds."[24] The scientist-iconoclast seemed as proud to announce that lightning was not a production from heaven as he was to acknowledge that his lightning rod protected high places (where Edwards said pride dwells) from the supposed wrath of God! Franklin completely reversed Edwards's imagery.

While Edwards readily accepted scientific explanations for natural occurrences, even those he failed to comprehend fully, his use of lightning revealed a proclivity to harmonize natural descriptions with preconceived ideas about the universe as a text for understanding the supernatural. Edwards strove to reconcile nature with revelation, viewing the physical world as emblematic of a spiritual one. Franklin found such exercises superfluous to his purposes. Though recognizing his anomalous position in eighteenth-century society, Franklin steadfastly pursued his interests as a scientist and skeptic. As he wrote to Cadwallader Colden,

> 'Tis well we are not . . . subject to the Inquisition for Philosophical Heresy. My Whispers against the orthodox Doctrine in private Letters, would be dangerous. . . . As it is, you must expect some Censure, but one Heretic will surely excuse another.[25]

The commitments of Franklin and Edwards to particular ideas begin to emerge against the background of their orientation toward science and religion. Each constructed values according to suppositions about God and the role of scientific discovery. In addition they preserved the integrity of those beliefs despite a culture that was itself simultaneously changing and retaining certain conventions and traditions. Responding creatively to this tension, both men maintained their status as public figures (with varying success) while minimizing conflict and circumscribing the damage to their values. Among the mediating tools that both Franklin and Edwards used was rationalism. In science, for example, Edwards rarely used experiments to arrive at his conclusions. Instead he either observed nature, as in his essays on insects, or extrapolated from previously established scientific theories through the use of reason and logic. Franklin, by contrast, achieved much in the laboratory, yet he too manifested faith in the power of rational thinking.

As a young pastor, Edwards reminded himself to remain open to rational arguments. Recognizing that older men often became reluctant to accept new ideas, Edwards resolved, "if ever I live to years, that I will be impartial to hear the reasons of all pretended discoveries, and receive them if rational."[26] Thus he accepted Newtonian science without understanding the mathematics behind it and endeavored to apply reason to his own work, whether scientific or theological. We know by our own existence, Edwards postulated, and by our knowledge of it, that we are "intelligent and voluntary beings, [and] are the effects of this first cause; 'tis it that has made [us] and made us intelligent beings." Reason, he believed, was a gift from God.[27]

So thoroughly did Edwards embrace rationalism that he applied it to his most perplexing philosophical problems. In these efforts, Edwards's theoretical physics intersected with his religious concepts. There must be a reason for all things, he speculated; bare facts simply do not satisfy the human mind. If something is motionless, there must be a reason for it. If an object moves, then there must be a cause. "If it be said it is so because it was so from all eternity," he continued, ". . . how came it to be so from all eternity?"[28] Such reasoning underlay Edwards's habit of tracing long chains of cause and effect to arrive at the ultimate source.

Franklin, too, displayed extreme rationalism, especially in his early works. In his *Dissertation* he used logic to obscure distinctions between right and wrong and to present unorthodox religious opinions as truths. As expressions of Enlightenment sentiment, his writings often insisted on the primacy of reason over tradition and authority. Like Edwards, Franklin made a lifelong commitment to open-minded acceptance of well-constructed arguments and scientific evidence.

Both men also perceived the dangers of ratiocination, but their doubts sprang from different sources. Franklin began to question the utility of reason early in life. In an essay signed "The Casuist," meaning a person who applies clever but misleading logic to moral issues, Franklin posed and answered a query about adultery. If A's wife has an affair with B, the problem went, can A then justifiably have relations with B's wife? The published essay concluded no, but an unprinted reply justified an affirmative answer. Through adroit deduction, Franklin arrived at a determination that promoted immorality and further disorder. He kept those conclusions out of the public eye, but Franklin had revealed the short-comings of reason in fulfilling his criterion of utility (the goal in this case being to foster public morality) and made light of its possible consequences.[29]

Franklin especially questioned the legitimacy of rationalizing answers to religious problems. Confessing doubts about the truth of any of his theological opinions, he confided in an unsent letter to his father, I am "a weak ignorant creature, full of natural Imperfections, subject to be frequently misled by my own Reasonings or the wrong Arguments of others."[30] Though he chose a personal creed from an array of ideas, Franklin made no claim for its absolute truth.

Edwards more happily pursued reason, along the exact lines that Franklin found most dangerous. Yet Edwards's absolutism also forced him to circumscribe its power. No one could comprehend the deepest truths if unaided by the Holy Spirit. Because of the "natural stupidity" of an unsaved person, Edwards claimed, "his own natural strength, can do nothing towards getting such a sense of divine things."[31] A person could not reason his or her way to faith in God, according to Edwards, and his assumption that humans remained incapable of full understanding in their natural state necessitated a conclusion that rationalism had limits.

Given their respective stances regarding reason, use of the design argument by Franklin and Edwards comes as no surprise. Built on an assumption that patterns and purposefulness in nature proved the existence of an intelligent creator, the argument from design was popular among eighteenth-century deists and orthodox Christian thinkers alike. Dating from antiquity, the idea enjoyed a revival spurred by Newtonian science, and until the time of Darwin, it reconciled new discoveries regarding physical attributes of the universe with Christian belief in God as the creator. The theory, with its characteristic rhetoric and imagery, appeared in both Franklin's and Edwards's works.[32]

But while Edwards found the design argument unimpeachably valuable, Franklin abandoned and even parodied the theory in his later works. In the "Speech of Miss Polly Baker," for example, Franklin used design in nature as evidence that having babies could hardly be immoral, regardless of circumstances. In a brief meditation on the construction of the human arm, he proposed that the elbow had been perfectly constructed to allow people to drink wine. Luckily, as if to increase our "piety and gratitude to divine Providence," Franklin cheerfully concluded, ". . . we are in a condition to drink at our ease, the glass coming exactly to the mouth."[33] Franklin recognized the futility of imputing purpose to nature, and he came to regard theories based on design as inadequate to explain the structure of the universe.

Their uses of rationalism indicate the delicate balancing act that Franklin and Edwards performed as they evaluated scientific and religious ideas. Franklin satirized the new faith in rationalism because he discerned a fallacy in creating new dogmas, whatever their basis. For him, the answer to survival in the enlightened *and* religious eighteenth century lay in distinguishing between the conventions of public life and the privileges of private belief. Thus Franklin emphasized the need for religious values to encourage a virtuous citizenry at the same time that he undercut orthodox Christian beliefs in his own life. Similarly Franklin displayed perhaps the most reasonable public countenance of his time, while privately entertaining doubts about the power of rationalism as a method of inquiry. Tension between public and private philosophy often found expression in his personal correspondence or biting satires. Yet his utilitarian values told him there was much of use in rationalism and Christian morality.

Edwards expressed his own sort of duality, one that bore little relationship to that of Franklin. His solution allowed him to negotiate between an absolutist value system based on biblical truth and his acceptance of modern science and philosophical idealism. He fell back on distinguishing between natural and divine phenomena, limiting the scope of science and reason and necessitating reliance on faith and the power of grace. New scientific methods and discoveries prompted Edwards to reexamine Christian dogma, yet the design argument provided a bridge across the gap that threatened to separate religion and science. Edwards and many eighteenth-century colonials used that bridge to strengthen their faith. Franklin, however, found structural weaknesses, which forced him to withdraw and implicitly conclude that scientific discovery had little to offer religious philosophy or vice versa. Franklin's rejection of Edwards's solution did not indicate that he worshiped at the altar of reason only. He quickly recognized the shortcomings of such a position. Rather, Franklin used his own method to navigate in an overwhelmingly Christian culture, while harboring doubts about the legitimacy of Christianity itself.

\* \* \*

Differences in values not only emerge from Franklin's and Edwards's use of rationalism but also appear in their expression of specific concepts that play a role in evaluation. When discussing means and ends, for example, Franklin often disregarded ordinary assumptions. While God's revelation served Edwards as a universal standard, Franklin saw the Bible primarily as a means to inculcate virtuous behavior. Since he insisted on a functional purpose for religion, all aspects of Christianity became means rather than ends in themselves. "Morality or Virtue is the End," Franklin maintained, "Faith only a Means to obtain that End." Otherwise Christianity was not that valuable in and of itself. Indeed, Franklin concluded, "if the End be obtained, it is no matter by what Means."[34]

For Edwards means and ends exactly harmonized in God's scheme for ordering the universe. It all amounted to such perfect "correspondence, between means and the end as there is between the stamp and the picture that is designed to be stamped with it."[35] Speaking of the bodily effects of revivalism as a means, Edwards justified tolerance of disorder that sometimes resulted during the Great Awakening. Though others claimed the deity would not create chaos, Edwards pointed out that breaking the usual order might be God's way of working salvation. What appeared as "confusion" to people may be perfectly harmonious to God. "The end of the influence of God's Spirit," he noted, "is to make men spiritually knowing . . . not to increase men's natural capacities" or to "increase Civil prudence."[36] Because he believed that God's methods ultimately suited his objectives, Edwards read backward from the result to judge both.

In addition to addressing the issue of disorder during the Great Awakening, Edwards outlined criteria to judge the resulting conversion experiences. Here the issue turned not on means and ends but on appearance versus reality. Critics of evangelical methods often condemned superficial shows of faith, especially as manifested in fainting, crying out, or bodily contortions, but also in what they considered excessive public singing, praying, and religious meetings. How could one judge what signified real faith? While he hoped to defend revivalism against attack from those who stressed the deceiving nature of appearances, Edwards remained circumspect. "'Tis to the honor of God that a people should be so much in outward acts of religion," he emphasized, but ministers must guard against any defect that "deforms the experience." Flaws did not rob the Awakening of "the essence of truly Christian experiences," but Edwards could not condone the functionalist faith displayed by ministers like Connecticut's Andrew Croswell.[37] Edwards remained more than willing to distinguish between the show and the reality of Christianity, yet he preferred to give outward signs the benefit of the doubt.[38]

Franklin, like Edwards, often claimed to see harmony between appearances and reality.[39] He also encouraged others to accept things as they seemed to be. This was true despite (or because of) the fact that

Franklin frequently manipulated appearances. As he counseled one youth, "The Sound of your Hammer at Five in the Morning or Nine at Night, heard by a Creditor, makes him easy Six Months longer. But," Franklin warned, "if he sees you at a Billiard Table . . . when you should be at Work, he sends for his Money the next Day."[40] His advice rested on the assumption that appearances counted for everything in eighteenth-century society. Worry over perceived virtue grew out of Franklin's private strategy to succeed by manipulating social conventions to his own advantage. In his self-conscious duplicity, which allowed one set of values in public action and another in private thought, Franklin distanced himself from Edwards.

When conceptualizing means and ends and the reality of appearances, Franklin and Edwards returned again and again to strategies that preserved their value orientations, and those that allowed them to construct a world harmonious with their assumptions. Each analyzed human behavior within a framework that confirmed their basic priorities. In the process, they created individual realities that in turn molded their attitudes and reactions to daily issues and problems.

For his part, Edwards hoped to sweep aside false assumptions about reality and rebuild Christian thought on the basis of divine truth. Christianity contained mysteries that humans failed to understand; the problem lay not in the message or its author, but in our faulty reception and its imperfect expression in human language. In Edwards's system, truth existed only in God's mind and was accessible through his word. It was a concept crucial to Edwards's structure of religious philosophy and the bedrock of his essential values.[41]

Franklin had no similar anchor for his beliefs. His *Autobiography* made it clear that "Revelation had indeed no weight" with him, and he often spoke about truth as though it were relative. On other occasions, Franklin spoke of truth as a less slippery concept, as something recognizable to reasonable beings.[42] But his doubts about religion, lack of a core definition for truth or reality, and recognition of his anomalous status as an enlightened American cast a shadow over the optimism ordinarily identified with Franklin's character. When he wrote the *Dissertation*, Franklin was only nineteen. In it he developed a theory of pleasure that asserted "Pleasure is wholly caus'd by Pain" and achieved only in the attempt to relieve that pain.[43] With its surprisingly morbid theory for one so young, Franklin's paper revealed dark tones not usually associated with his character. Though he spent the rest of his life distancing himself from the pamphlet's implications, he never broke entirely free of the pessimism it voiced, and Franklin's attempts to construct a functional religious creed seem to have been aimed at relieving pain caused by those youthful philosophical excursions. Later Franklin reflected that "some Error" might have "insinuated itself unperciev'd" into the essay; though never denying the truth of the conclusions, he found little use for them.[44]

Perhaps it was the turmoil caused by his *Dissertation* that drove Franklin to such great activity. "The highest Pleasure," he wrote, "is only Consciousness of Freedom from the deepest Pain." Franklin's life could be interpreted as an edifice designed to protect himself from probing metaphysical uncertainties. Despite his best efforts though, Franklin's brooding side flits out in foreboding statements condemning humanity.[45] He turned to utilitarian values to construct a philosophy operable in eighteenth-century America, yet unthreatening to his own beliefs. His method, as Franklin knew all too well, could not resolve metaphysical issues, but it did provide a basis for evaluating worldly phenomena on most occasions.

Edwards too experienced deep pathos, but he focused on self-doubt. After his youthful conversion, Edwards said he never again questioned God's sovereignty. Indeed, he took great comfort in it. What he suffered over was his own unworthiness in God's eyes. The young clergyman once noted that awareness of his sins affected him "to such a degree as to hold me in a kind of loud weeping . . . so that I have often been forced to shut myself up." Edwards even had difficulty with personal joy, asking "whether any delight, or satisfaction, ought not be allowed, because any other end is obtained beside a religious one." Eventually he reasoned that everyday pleasures aided religious feeling, and having properly evaluated himself against his usual rigorous standards, answered yes to his question.[46]

Edwards and Franklin agreed on such everyday matters as the need for worship services, beauty in nature, and the capacity of science to impart new understanding. But Edwards found other answers—ultimate answers about the purpose of humanity and existence of God—that Franklin simply could not accept. Some individuals believe that people were made to be useful to each other, mused Edwards, but "if the highest end of the world be to have its parts useful to each other, the world in general is good for nothing at all."[47]

Both men responded in a similar way to the new knowledge of the Enlightenment and disruption of religious beliefs that followed. Rather than reject novel ideas simply because they were innovative, Franklin and Edwards judged unfamiliar concepts according to preestablished priorities. By devising successful mediating strategies, they protected and retained their values in the face of more superficial alterations. Each one created a broad-based stability for himself in the process. As an essentialist, Edwards viewed revivalism, science, and reason as means to an inherently valuable end, the glorification of God. For Franklin, means had become ends in themselves, and he applied his usual standard of utility in every case. Ironically, Edwards's student and first biographer, Samuel Hopkins, characterized the reverend minister as "one of the greatest, best, and most useful men of this age"—an epithet Franklin would have appreciated for himself infinitely more.[48]

## Notes

1. The continued influence of theories of modernization may be seen in such studies as Ronald P. Dufour, *Modernization in Colonial Massachusetts, 1630–1763* (New York, 1987); Jack P. Greene, *Pursuits of Happiness: The Social Development of Early Modern British Colonies and the Formation of American Culture* (Chapel Hill, N.C., 1988); and Michael Lienesch, *New Order of the Ages* (Princeton, N.J., 1988).

2. Florence R. Kluckhohn and Fred L. Strodtbeck, *Variations in Value Orientations* (Evanston, Ill., 1961), pp. 4, 45. For another definition of values, see J. E. Crowley, *This Sheba Self: The Conceptualization of Economic Life in Eighteenth-Century America* (Baltimore, 1974), p. 2.

3. The historiography dealing with JE and BF is too large to list here. Examples of those who portray JE as essentially modern include Perry Miller, *Jonathan Edwards* (1949; rep. Cleveland, 1959), p. vi; Paul K. Conkin, *Puritans and Pragmatists: Eight Eminent American Thinkers* (1968; rep. Bloomington, Ind., 1976), pp. 39–41; and Sang H. Lee, *Philosophical Theology of Jonathan Edwards* (Princeton, N.J., 1988), pp. 3–4.

Those who count JE among premodern thinkers include A. Owen Aldridge, *Jonathan Edwards* (New York, 1964), p. 22; R. C. De Prospo, *Theism in the Discourse of Jonathan Edwards* (Newark, N.J., 1985), pp. 9–36; Wilson H. Kimnach, "Jonathan Edwards's Pursuit of Reality," in *Jonathan Edwards and the American Experience*, ed. Nathan O. Hatch and Harry S. Stout (New York, 1988), p. 104; and M. X. Lesser, *Jonathan Edwards* (Boston, 1988), p. 34.

Confusion over JE's modernity is evident in a number of works. See C. C. Goen, *WJE, 4*: 32; James Carse, *Jonathan Edwards and the Visibility of God* (New York, 1967), pp. 29–30; and Patricia J. Tracy, *Jonathan Edwards, Pastor: Religion and Society in Eighteenth-Century Northampton* (New York, 1980), p. 93.

Others point to a double quality in JE that remains both modern and traditional. See Clyde Holbrook, *The Ethics of Jonathan Edwards: Morality and Aesthetics* (Ann Arbor, Mich., 1973), p. vi; William G. McLoughlin, *Revivals, Awakenings, and Reform: An Essay on Religion and Social Change in America, 1607–1977* (Chicago, 1978), p. 71; and Norman Fiering, *Jonathan Edwards's Moral Thought and Its British Context* (Chapel Hill, N.C., 1981), pp. 9, 60.

It has even been suggested that understanding JE depends on the reader's own religious beliefs. See Iain H. Murray, *Jonathan Edwards: A New Biography* (Edinburgh, 1987), p. xxvii. Henry F. May speculated that a dissertation might be written on whether "a fruitful discussion" of religious thinkers can be had among "believers, rejecters, and agnostics." See "Jonathan Edwards and America" in *Edwards and American Experience*, ed. Hatch and Stout, p. 31.

De Prospo describes BF as a truncated version of JE—a theist who neglects to mention God. De Prospo, *Theism in Discourse of Edwards*, pp. 192–94. For the most part, however, BF's biographers place him squarely in the path leading to the future rather than to the past. For examples see Ralph L. Ketcham, *Benjamin Franklin* (New York, 1966), pp. 3, 198; Arthur B. Tourtellot, *Benjamin Franklin: The Shaping of a Genius, the Boston Years* (Garden City, N.Y., 1977), p. 436; Mitchell R. Breitwieser, *Cotton Mather and Benjamin Franklin: The Price of Representative Personality* (New York, 1985), pp. 171–201; and Esmond Wright, *Franklin of Philadelphia* (Cambridge, Mass., 1986), p. viii. William Pencak traces the historiography of BF's image as a modern figure but emphasizes the influence of Puritanism on the *Autobiography* in his article, "Benjamin Franklin's Autobiography, Cotton Mather, and a Puritan God," *Pennsylvania History, 53* (January 1986): 1–3.

One of the first modern historians to realize the similarities between BF and JE was Carl Van Doren in his "Introduction," in *Benjamin Franklin and Jonathan Edwards: Selections from Their Writings,* ed. Will D. Howe (New York, 1920), p. ix. Aldridge occasionally compares BF and JE in his biography of JE. For examples, see *Jonathan Edwards,* pp. 55–56, 58, 109. For recent examples, see David Levin, "Edwards, Franklin, and Cotton Mather: A Meditation on Character and Reputation," in *Edwards and American Experience,* ed. Hatch and Stout, pp. 34–35.

De Prospo recognizes that the coexistence of BF and JE has been problematic for historians and mentions the historiography of the problem. *Theism in Discourse of Edwards,* pp. 185–86.

4. *WJE, 4:* 536.

5. *Ibid., 6:* 61, 67. On God as JE's source of value, see Holbrook, *Ethics of Edwards,* p. 5.

6. *WJE, 6:* 53–68. Materialism seemed to many to be reasonable in light of recent discoveries in natural philosophy. For a definition of subjectivism that applies well to BF, see Holbrook, *Ethics of Edwards,* pp. 5, 7.

7. JE, *Images or Shadows of Divine Things,* ed. Perry Miller (1948; rep. Westport, Conn., 1977), p. 103. Holbrook, *Ethics of Edwards,* p. 27.

8. BF to Josiah and Abiah Franklin, April 13, 1738, *PBF, 2:* 204. For a more complete analysis of this important letter, see my essay, "From a Bold Youth to a Reflective Sage: A Reevaluation of Benjamin Franklin's Religion," *Pennsylvania Magazine of History and Biography, 111* (October 1987): 17–18. Even BF's *Dissertation on Liberty and Necessity, Pleasure and Pain,* which established his tendency to espouse heretical opinions, began with the existence of God as a given. *PBF, 1:* 59–60. BF made his views of the study of theology known in one of his "Silence Dogood" (no. 4) essays, *PBF, 1:* 17.

9. *The Philosophy of Jonathan Edwards from His Private Notebooks,* ed. Harvey G. Townsend (Eugene, Ore., 1955), p. 76.

10. *Franklin and Edwards: Selections,* ed. Howe, p. 222.

11. *PBF, 1:* 102–3; Phyllis Franklin, *Show Thyself a Man: A Comparison of Benjamin Franklin and Cotton Mather* (The Hague, 1969), pp. 76–77; and Edward Grant, *Much Ado About Nothing: Theories of Space and Vacuum from the Middle Ages to the Scientific Revolution* (Cambridge, U.K., 1981), p. 150. De Prospo maintains that BF was not truly a polytheist because the gods he created were subordinate to a controlling being. *Theism in Discourse of Edwards,* p. 198.

12. *PBF, 2:* 54.

13. *Ibid., 4:* 505.

14. Carse, *Visibility of God,* p. 131. For a different interpretation of JE's views on conversion, see Conrad Cherry, "Conversion: Nature and Grace," in *Critical Essays on Jonathan Edwards,* ed. William J. Scheick (Boston, 1980), pp. 76–80.

15. *Philosophy of Edwards,* ed. Townsend, p. 193.

16. *PBF, 4:* 17. I. Bernard Cohen emphasizes that BF has been underrated as a pure scientist, especially by American historians. *Benjamin Franklin: Scientist and Statesman* (New York, 1972), p. 11. BF himself stressed the applicability of his experiments. Science, like religion, served a tangible purpose. Phyllis Franklin

contends that BF used science to understand God. *Show Thyself a Man*, p. 51. Though BF advised others to seek God through the study of natural history (for example, in his plan to educate Pennsylvania youths), there is little evidence to support the conclusion that he did so himself.

17. The best source on JE as a scientist is Wallace Anderson's introduction to JE's scientific writings. He notes that JE was "nearly unique" in America in his interest in physics. The familiar spider and insect essays that JE wrote were not representative of his enduring interests. *WJE, 6:* 39–40. On the role of Calvinism, see *ibid.,* p. 50. For a brief discussion of JE's studies in physics see Conkin, *Puritans and Pragmatists,* pp. 51–52.

18. *Franklin and Edwards: Selections,* ed. Howe, p. 227; *WJE, 6:* 59, 65–68.

19. *Franklin and Edwards: Selections,* ed. Howe, p. 223; *WJE, 6:* 65.

20. *WJE, 6:* 76–77.

21. *Ibid.,* p. 161.

22. *Franklin and Edwards: Selections,* ed. Howe, 348; *idem, Images or Shadows,* pp. 50, 71, 91; Lesser, *Jonathan Edwards,* pp. 22–23. Of course, JE accepted scientific explanations for lightning, and he and BF appear to have read some of the same sources on the subject. A. Owen Aldridge, "Benjamin Franklin and Jonathan Edwards on Lightning and Earthquakes," *Isis 41* (July 1950): 162–64.

23. *PBF, 4:* 463.

24. *Ibid.*

25. *Ibid.,* p. 301.

26. *Franklin and Edwards: Selections,* ed. Howe, pp. 264–65; Fiering, *Edwards's Moral Thought,* p. 343.

27. *Philosophy of Edwards,* ed. Townsend, p. 86; *WJE, 6:* 41. BF also referred to reason as a gift from God in his "Proposals to the Junto," *PBF, 1:* 262.

28. *Philosophy of Edwards,* ed. Townsend, pp. 74–75, 225.

29. *PBF, 1:* 234–37. Pushing logic beyond its conventional bounds was characteristic of BF. See J. A. Leo Lemay's comments and list of pieces where BF did this in *The Canon of Benjamin Franklin, 1722–1776* (Newark, Del., 1986), pp. 23, 29.

In their psychological study of values, Fred Weinstein and Gerald M. Platt suggest that it may be impossible to give oneself totally over to rationalism. *The Wish to be Free: Society, Psyche, and Value Change* (Berkeley, 1969), p. 6. BF and JE both fell short of that. Conkin sees BF as one-dimensional and limited by an unfettered belief in rationalism. *Puritans and Pragmatists,* p. 85. Clearly, this was not the case.

30. *PBF, 2:* 202–3.

31. *Philosophy of Edwards,* ed. Townsend, p. 123. Aldridge points out that Scripture remained JE's ultimate authority, not reason. See *Jonathan Edwards,* p. 24; Fiering, "Edwards's Metaphysics," in *Edwards and American Experience,* ed. Hatch and Stout, p. 87; and Carse, *Visibility of God,* pp. 42, 82.

32. Frederick Ferre, "Design Argument," in Philip P. Wiener, ed., *Dictionary of the History of Ideas,* 4 vols. (New York, 1973), *1:* 670–77; James Turner, *Without God, Without Creed: The Origins of Unbelief in America* (Baltimore, 1985), pp. 54–58. For examples of the design argument in the writings of JE and BF, see *Philosophy of Edwards,* ed. Townsend, p. 79, and *PBF, 1:* 105.

33. Franklin to Abbé Morellet [1779], trans. in Richard E. Amacher, *Franklin's Wit and Folly: The Bagatelles* (New Brunswick, N.J., 1953), p. 135. For an analysis of "The Speech of Miss Polly Baker," see J. A. Leo Lemay, "The Text,

Rhetorical Strategies, and Themes of 'The Speech of Miss Polly Baker,'" in *The Oldest Revolutionary: Essays on Benjamin Franklin*, ed. J. A. Leo Lemay (Philadelphia, 1976), pp. 91–120.

34. *PBF*, 2: 30.

35. *Philosophy of Edwards*, ed. Townsend, p. 84.

36. *WJE*, 4: 323. On revivals, see JE, *Distinguishing Marks of a Work of the Spirit of God*, in 4: 241, 266–67. Holbrook accuses JE of stooping to the "crassest" kind of utilitarianism when he preached "hell fire" sermons as a means to produce conversion. *Ethics of Edwards*, p. 37. But JE gave this means a value only because he thought God chose it as a route to conversion.

37. *WJE*, 4: 395, 462.

38. See, for example, JE to Thomas Prince, December 12, 1747, in *ibid.*, p. 556; Goen, "Introduction," *ibid.*, p. 76; and Edwin S. Gaustad, *The Great Awakening in New England* (Gloucester, Mass., 1965), p. 91.

39. See, for example, *PBF*, 2: 92.

40. *Ibid.*, 3: 307.

41. *WJE*, 4: 227. On biblical truth, see *ibid.*, pp. 330–31; *Philosophy of Edwards*, ed. Townsend, pp. 211, 230–31. The best analyses of JE's perception of truth include Perry Miller, "Introduction," *Images or Shadows*, pp. 19–20; James Hoopes, "Calvinism and Consciousness from Edwards to Beecher," in *Edwards and American Experience*, ed. Hatch and Stout, p. 212; Murray, *Jonathan Edwards*, p. 72; and Anderson, "Introduction," *WJE*, 6: 97. On JE's doubts about the accuracy of language to express the truth, see Kimnach, "Edwards's Pursuit," in *Edwards and American Experience*, ed. Hatch and Stout, p. 108; Amy S. Lang, "'A Flood of Errors': Chauncy and Edwards in the Great Awakening," in *ibid.*, pp. 165–67.

42. *The Autobiography of Benjamin Franklin*, ed. Leonard Labaree *et al.* (New Haven, 1964), pp. 114–15. For an example of truth as a more concrete concept, see *PBF*, 2: 95.

43. *PBF*, 1: 65.

44. *Autobiography*, ed. Labaree, pp. 96, 114. Though BF counted his "printing this Pamphlet," that is, making it public, among his Errata, he never admitted that he regretted *writing* it.

45. *PBF*, 1: 66. Historians have long slighted this side of BF. See, however, Ronald A. Boscoe's insightful analysis in "'He that best understands the world least likes it': The Dark Side of Benjamin Franklin," *Pennsylvania Magazine of History and Biography*, 111 (October 1987): 525–54. When this side of BF's character is missed, it is easy to view him as smug. See, for example, Breitwieser, *Mather and Franklin*, pp. 18, 178–79, 227. BF's dark interiors also counter Conkin's notion that he refused to deal with contradictions. *Puritans and Pragmatists*, pp. 79–80.

46. *Franklin and Edwards: Selections*, ed. Howe, pp. 356, 245–46. JE had recurring difficulty with the concept of happiness and its relationship to true virtue. Holbrook, *Ethics of Edwards*, 149–50; Richard L. Bushman, "Jonathan Edwards and the Puritan Consciousness," *Journal for the Scientific Study of Religion*, 5 (1966): 385.

47. *Philosophy of Edwards*, ed. Townsend, p. 127.

48. Samuel Hopkins, "Preface," in *The Memoirs of the Rev. Jonathan Edwards, A.M.*, comp. Samuel Hopkins (London, 1815), p. vii.

# 6

# Franklin, Edwards, and the Problem of Human Nature

## DANIEL WALKER HOWE

"Reason should govern Passion, but instead of that, you see, it is often subservient to it." So ran the conventional wisdom of the eighteenth century, in this case stated by Sir Richard Steele in *The Spectator*. Throughout the eighteenth century, the Western world typically thought of human nature in terms of a model of faculties or powers. There were two kinds of powers, "intellectual" and "active," which made up the "understanding" and the "will," respectively. The understanding encompassed the powers of perception; the will, those of action. It is with the latter that we shall primarily concern ourselves. The most common version of eighteenth-century faculty psychology arranged the "active powers" in a hierarchical sequence. First in order of precedence came the rational faculties of the will: conscience (or the moral sense) and prudence (or self-interest). Below them were the emotional springs of action, called either by the approving term "affections" or the more derogatory word "passions," as the context might dictate. Still farther down were mechanical impulses like reflexes, not subject to conscious control at all. The hierarchical structure of human nature, a later number of *The Spectator* explained, corresponded to humanity's intermediate position in the great chain of being, partly divine, partly animal.[1]

The model just described provided the basis for much of the philosophy, psychology, and literature of the eighteenth century. It was treated as the "common sense" of the matter by an age that idealized common sense. Embodied early in the century in such authoritative literary works as *The Spectator* and Alexander Pope's poetic *Essay on Man*, it was codified late in the century by the Scottish moral philosopher Thomas Reid. John Locke had worked within it, for the most part, in his great writings on human understanding and education; Francis Hutcheson and David Hume challenged it by proposing to treat the conscience as an emotional, rather than a rational, faculty. In America, the paradigm was adapted by the authors of *The Federalist Papers* to their discussions of the Constitution. Benjamin Franklin and Jonathan Edwards, both of them avid readers of *The Spectator* in their youth, were thoroughly conversant with this model.[2]

Eighteenth-century faculty psychology was both descriptive and normative, that is, it was not only a psychology but also an ethics. By right, conscience should govern the commonwealth of the mind, but in practice the passions were often too strong for it. The psychological fact, countless writers warned, was that the motivating power of the faculties varied in inverse proportion to their rightful precedence. Passion was the strongest faculty of the will, conscience the weakest, with prudential reason somewhere in between. This discrepancy between psychological fact and ethical imperative may be termed "the problem of human nature." It is no exaggeration to call it the central problem of eighteenth-century moral philosophy.

Benjamin Franklin and Jonathan Edwards were both informed participants in the world of eighteenth-century moral philosophy—Franklin knew many of its leading figures personally. Franklin and Edwards were in agreement on the importance of what I am calling the problem of human nature; both addressed it. "All things in the soul of man should be under the government of reason, which is the highest faculty," Edwards instructed his congregation; but "men's passions sometimes rise so high that they are, as it were, drunk with passion. Their passion deprives them very much of the use of reason." *Poor Richard's Almanac* taught its readers the same lesson: "He is a governor that governs his passions, and is a servant that serves them." "If passion drives, let reason hold the reins."[3] While agreeing on the nature of the problem posed by their community of discourse, Franklin and Edwards display for us, in the solutions they offered to it, differences of fundamental importance.

## I

"Men I find a sort of beings very badly constructed," Benjamin Franklin wrote his friend and fellow scientist, moral philosopher, and reformer Joseph Priestley. "They are generally more easily provoked than recon-

ciled, more disposed to do mischief to each other than to make repara-
tion, and much more easily deceived than undeceived." Franklin found
human motivation a complex mixture, but he had no doubt that the baser
impulses were the more powerful. For this reason, he felt Hobbes's
depiction of the state of nature "somewhat nearer the truth than that
which makes the state of nature a state of love."[4] Some of Franklin's
satires on human motives have a bite worthy of Jonathan Swift,
commentators have noted.[5] Characteristically, however, his low estimate
of human nature did not lead Franklin to express any personal *Angst*.
In the "Will" he drew up in 1750, he thanked God for giving him
"a mind with moderate passions, or so much of his gracious assistance
in governing them, [as] to free it early from ambition, avarice, and
superstition."[6]

As a good eighteenth-century scientist, Franklin celebrated the
rational order of the physical universe.[7] He took this rational order as a
norm to apply to human affairs, both social and individual. In a properly ordered society, there would be no conflict between individual
and community; each existed to serve the other. The moral faculty, for
Franklin, was the rational power to perceive the appropriateness and
utility of actions in promoting both individual and collective happiness.
"Virtue and sense are one," declared Poor Richard.[8] We may be confident that Franklin would have approved the teaching of his Scottish
contemporary, Francis Hutcheson: "That action is best which procures
the greatest happiness for the greatest numbers."[9]

Just as external nature could be made to yield the secrets of its divine
order to scientific research, so, Franklin was convinced, there could be a
science of human nature, that is, of morality. Like all good science (in
Franklin's view), moral science would have practical application to human
affairs. This was by no means an eccentric opinion in the eighteenth
century. The moral philosophy of the age was the ancestor of all the
modern social sciences, as well as of what we call ethical theory. Individual and social morality were governed by analogous principles: "No
longer virtuous, no longer free, is a maxim as true with regard to a
private person as a commonwealth." The danger posed by a usurping
vice or passion to the individual was the same as that of a demagogue
or tyrant in the state.[10]

To Franklin's mind, the order of the external universe, though a
model to be imitated, in another sense did not provide much encouragement for human moral strivings. The philosophical system that com-
mended itself to Franklin's science and logic was deism. Yet deism, with
its remote artificer-god, provided no basis for such human needs as prayer,
special providence, or moral incentives. As he observed in his *Autobiography*, "I began to suspect that this doctrine, though it might be true,
was not very useful." Having reached this conclusion, Franklin abandoned
deist system-making and devoted himself instead to inquiries with practical application.[11] To his good friend George Whitefield he confided,

"I rather suspect, from certain circumstances, that though the general government of the universe is well administered, our particular little affairs are perhaps below notice, and left to take the chance of human prudence or imprudence, as either may happen to be uppermost. It is, however, an uncomfortable thought, and I leave it."[12] Franklin's preoccupation with temporal goals, with human happiness rather than metaphysical values, should not be attributed to mere crassness of temperament. It followed from his conviction that the universe was ultimately indifferent, and that it was up to human beings to shape themselves and their destiny as best they could.

The most obvious alternative to deism was Christianity, in which Franklin had been reared by his Calvinist parents. The Christian religion seemed well suited to the needs of humanity, Franklin thought, provided it could be purged of intolerance and obsession with unanswerable theological conundrums. Like many subsequent Americans, he found refuge in the Anglican communion from the preoccupation with theology characteristic of the Reformed tradition. Anglicanism was traditionally concerned with issues of comprehensiveness and liturgy, both of which interested Franklin. It is a common mistake to suppose that Franklin involved himself with religion *solely* as a matter of social ethics; he also regarded worship and prayer as natural human impulses requiring expression.[13] Like Locke, whom he followed in so many things, Franklin believed that the core of Christian belief consisted of a few short affirmations. Beyond that, religions justified themselves by their contribution to temporal human welfare and should be judged accordingly. In a paper prepared in 1732, Franklin undertook to formulate a religious position that would be "a powerful regulator of our actions, give us peace and tranquillity within our own minds, and render us benevolent, useful, and beneficial to others."[14]

In a vivid letter to an unknown deist, sometimes thought to be Thomas Paine, Franklin refused to discuss the truth of his correspondent's philosophy, but strongly urged him not to publish it. Undermining respect for religion would not be socially beneficial, he explained.

> You yourself may find it easy to live a virtuous life without the assistance afforded by religion, you having a clear perception of the advantages of virtue and the disadvantages of vice, and possessing a strength of resolution sufficient to enable you to resist common temptations. But think how great a proportion of mankind consists of weak and ignorant men and women, and of inexperienced and inconsiderate youth of both sexes, who have need of the motives of religion to restrain them from vice, to support their virtue, and retain them in the practice of it till it becomes *habitual*, which is the great point for its security.[15]

It is clear in this passage that Franklin did not consider the Christian religion to be based on reason; on the contrary, he thought of Christian faith as an alternative to reason. ("The way to see Faith is to shut the eye of Reason," ran one of his aphorisms.) Encouraging religion was a concession to the strength of the nonrational component in human nature, especially appropriate for people in whom the rational faculty was undeveloped.[16]

Franklin's insistence upon discussing the issue entirely in terms of practical consequences became more and more typical of his attitude toward religion with the passage of time. In youth he had satirized Cotton Mather; later, however, he paid respectful homage to that Puritan patriarch for promoting philanthropic enterprises. "Opinions should be judged of by their influences and effects," he wrote to his parents.[17] A variety of different religions might all be deserving of support, provided they all promoted socially beneficial virtues. Accordingly, Franklin contributed money to the Philadelphia congregations of several denominations (including the synogogue), while maintaining his family membership in the Episcopal Christ Church.[18]

Organized religion was not the only form of association on behalf of virtue that Franklin endorsed. He formed a club in Philadelphia called the Junto, hoping that it would become the nucleus of an international "United Party of Virtue." During the years when the Junto was active, its founder probably thought of it as a nonpartisan political force sustaining reason and public virtue above the factionalism of ethnic or interest groups. Franklin apparently got the idea for the Junto from Mather's benevolent societies and the fictional club described in *The Spectator*. However, the Masonic movement had already preempted the role Franklin envisioned for his order. When the Masons established a lodge in Philadelphia, Franklin joined it, and the Junto was gradually eclipsed.[19]

But Franklin's best-known and most characteristic device for strengthening the conscience in its struggle to maintain supremacy over the baser motives was his invocation of prudential self-interest on the side of virtue. The prudential aphorisms of Poor Richard constituted Franklin's famous application of a general principle of eighteenth-century moral philosophy. This was the principle that conscience could compensate for its weakness by enlisting the motivating power of stronger faculties to do its bidding. For example, the love of fame—the "ruling passion of the noblest minds," according to Alexander Hamilton—could lead political men to serve the public interest when altruism alone might fail.[20] Franklin too relied on the love of fame this way; indeed, he regarded it as an enlightened form of prudence, akin to our concern with material well-being, rather than as a passion. Together, virtue and prudential self-interest made an effective combination in Franklin's scheme.

Franklin's use of prudence was part of a widespread upward revaluation of the faculty during the eighteenth century. At the beginning of the period, self-interest had generally been considered one of the "passions," but by the end, moral philosophers had definitely promoted it to the rank of a "rational" faculty.[21] A key to this development lay in drawing a distinction between self-interest and pride. Pride, Franklin maintained, was very different from self-interest and could even blind a person to his true self-interest. While self-interest was rational, pride was a passion.[22]

Religion, of course, had its own form of prudential incentive: a heavenly reward. This incentive found a prominent advocate during the eighteenth century in Archdeacon William Paley (1743–1805), who made it central to his system of moral philosophy, called "theological utilitarianism." Franklin did not ignore this motive to virtue,[23] but he devoted much more attention to tangible temporal rewards. By doing so he included in his audience those for whom religion had lost its appeal. Virtue, he argued—in both his own voice and that of Poor Richard, his most famous persona—was a good bargain. A virtuous way of life—honest industry, rational foresight, restraint of the passions—was "the Way to Wealth."[24]

For a person who is usually associated with the work ethic, Franklin had surprisingly little to say about the intrinsic satisfactions of work. In fact, the joy of work for its own sake did not fit into his theoretical model of human motivation. He himself, after all, quit work at the age of forty-two, once he had acquired a sufficient fortune. The remainder of his life he devoted to science and public service—gentlemanly pursuits which, in the eighteenth century, did not count as "work."

In 1730 Franklin printed in the *Philadelphia Gazette* two "Dialogues between Philocles and Horatio," treating the proper role of prudential self-interest. For a long time it was assumed that Franklin had composed the dialogues himself; thanks to Alfred Owen Aldridge, we now know that he reprinted them from the *London Journal* of the year before. But we may take it that Franklin did so because they set forth so well the view to which he subscribed. That Franklin picked up on the dialogues illustrates his involvement with the central issues of eighteenth-century moral philosophy. In the first dialogue, Philocles explains to the naïve young Horatio that self-love has two versions: self-indulgence and enlightened self-interest. The former is short-term and passionate; the latter, long-term and rational. Horatio is persuaded to subordinate his passions to prudential reason for the sake of greater happiness. In the second dialogue, Philocles argues that the highest happiness lies in a life of benevolent virtue, the pleasure of which can never cloy. The conventional hierarchy of the faculties—moral sense, prudence, passion—has been legitimated. Nothing is said about the satisfactions of work.[25] Though Franklin devoted much of his energy to reinforcing the lesson of Philocles' first dialogue, he seldom recurred to the subject of the second, which would interest Jonathan Edwards.

Despite all the care with which he crafted his appeals, no one could be more aware than Franklin himself of the likelihood that they would fail. Human nature being what it was, exhortations to virtue, even when coupled with prudential incentives, were seldom efficacious. Poor Richard admitted that hardly anyone could really live by his precepts:

Who is wise? He that learns from everyone.
Who is powerful? He that governs his passions.
Who is rich? He that is content.
Who is that? Nobody.

At the conclusion of "The Way to Wealth," Franklin's valedictory summation of Poor Richard's precepts, he notes, "the people heard it, and approved the doctrine, and immediately practiced the contrary, just as if it had been a common sermon."[26]

The problem was one of human nature, not one of knowledge. "Men do not generally err in their conduct so much through ignorance of their duty, as through inattention to their own faults, or through strong passions or bad habits." More succinctly: "Inclination was sometimes too strong for Reason."[27] What was needed, Franklin recognized, was a practical regimen, an applied "science of virtue" or "art of virtue" (he used both terms). The importance of such a program he outlined in a dialogue he wrote for discussion at a meeting of the Junto. In it, Socrates persuades Crito that an applied science of virtue would be the most important of all branches of learning.[28] As Franklin explained years later to his friend, the Scottish moral philosopher Lord Kames,

> Most people have naturally some virtues, but none have naturally all the virtues. To acquire those that are wanting, and secure what we acquire as well as those we have naturally, is the subject of an art. It is as properly an art as painting, navigation, or architecture. If a man would become a painter . . . he must be taught the principles of the art, be shown all the methods of working, and how to acquire the habits of using properly all the instruments. . . . My art of virtue has also its instruments and teaches the manner of using them.

Faith in Christ works as the requisite instrument for some people, Franklin acknowledged, though not for all. His own program would benefit everyone, including those with weak faith or none. The program involved systematic practice in a rotating sequence of individual virtues, and Franklin followed it himself over a period of many years.[29]

A modern scholar has noticed similarities between Franklin's program and the Puritan process called "preparation for grace."[30] But Franklin's "art of virtue" was intended to operate naturally, not supernaturally, and to be suitable for all, not only for the elect. The virtue it produced was an end in itself, not a manifestation of divine grace—or even of good intentions. The goal, in fact, was for virtuous behavior to become automatic, a conditioned reflex.[31] Ideally, it should be like the "mechanical powers": those unthinking reactions, not subject to conscious will, humbler than the passions, but nevertheless the strongest of all springs of action, being irresistible. The perfect person was one whose "knee-jerk" reactions were morally correct. "The strongest of our natural passions are seldom perceived by us; a choleric man does not always discover when he is angry, nor an envious man when he is invidious." Unreflective habit, an even stronger force than passion, could master it where reflective reason might not.[32]

For Franklin, the passions were to be denied only to the extent that they sacrificed long-term or general welfare. Like work, self-denial was not an end in itself. The end was happiness, that is, individual and collective well-being.[33] Self-denial, like work, was justified only in terms of its results. Acting contrary to one's inclinations was not the essence of virtue, he argued; a person who automatically acted right was to be preferred to one who pondered over it. Worst of all, in Franklin's eyes, was asceticism practiced for its own sake.

> He who does a foolish, indecent, or wicked thing, merely because 'tis contrary to his inclination (like some mad enthusiasts I have read of, who ran about naked, under the notion of taking up the Cross) is not practicing the reasonable science of virtue, but is a lunatic.[34]

Clearly, Franklin was interested in virtuous behavior (i.e., behavior productive of human happiness) regardless of the motive or means from which it stemmed. Christian love, voluntary associations like the Junto, prudential calculation, or ingrained habit—whatever worked would do. He concentrated his efforts on the young, because it was during their time of life that habits, the most promising of the "instruments" of virtue, were most effectively formed.[35] In the last analysis, Franklin was more interested in "merit" than in "virtue." "True merit" he defined as "an inclination joined with an ability to serve mankind, one's country, friends, and family." Virtue might only be a matter of intention, but *merit* joined this with ability, a behavioral test that took account of acquired skills and habits.[36]

Franklin never wrote the definitive handbook he projected on "the art of virtue." Instead he left his (incomplete) *Autobiography*, in which his own life story is related as a sequence of parables, each with its moral lesson. The book shows how to shape one's personality through fostering some impulses and restraining others. The rhetorical posture of the detached, self-controlled observer, like the postulated model of human faculties, is quintessential eighteenth-century moral philosophy and can be traced back to *The Spectator*. Overall, the lesson is that by shaping and controlling one's self, one can shape and control one's destiny, even in an uncaring world. Self-discipline is the key to success. The author Franklin is necessarily detached from the character Franklin in the book, since the character Franklin is meant to stand for Everyman, to be a model for universal imitation.[37]

It is a cliché, though none less true for being such, that Franklin was more interested in practice than in theory. This does not mean he was unsophisticated; the choice was quite deliberate on his part. He accepted the prevailing model of the human faculties and addressed himself with great shrewdness to the practical problems that model posed. He assumed that the autonomous, rational self would be socially useful and that society would appropriately reward, with fame, those who served it. He devoted little thought to the nature of virtue in and of itself. Once, when Franklin was planning the agenda for coming Junto meetings, he considered discussing "whether men ought to be denominated good or ill men from their actions or their inclinations." But then he crossed it off the list.[38] Very likely the question seemed too abstract to be interesting. It seemed quite otherwise to Jonathan Edwards.

## II

Though he never traveled outside the American colonies, the great Calvinist theologian and preacher Jonathan Edwards worked in a transatlantic intellectual context every bit as much as Benjamin Franklin did. As Norman Fiering has demonstrated, "Edwards's treatises on the will, on the affections, and on virtue are not readily classifiable in twentieth-century categories, but they can be comfortably fitted into the context of eighteenth-century moral philosophy debates."[39] These debates were predicated on a common model of the human faculties. Perry Miller's assertion that Edwards and Locke both discarded the model of faculty psychology was a careless judgment that has misled many a subsequent inquirer.[40] In fact, Edwards argued within the terms of the prevailing dual system of faculties: the "understanding," which consisted of the powers of perception, and the "will," which consisted of the powers motivating action. "Knowledge of ourselves consists chiefly in right apprehensions concerning those two chief faculties of our nature, the understanding and the will. Both are very important: yet the science of the latter must be confessed to be of greatest moment; inasmuch as all virtue and religion have their seat more immediately in the will, consisting more especially in right acts and habits of this faculty."[41]

Edwards's use of the model and vocabulary of faculty psychology was encouraged by his admiration for the Platonic tradition, particularly as exemplified in the writings of Shaftesbury and the seventeenth-century Cambridge Platonists. "God has given . . . all the faculties and principles of the human soul," he wrote, "that they might be subservient to man's chief end, . . . that is, the business of religion."[42] It was an affirmation typical of Christian Platonism. Among the God-given faculties were the affections, both benevolent and malevolent, prudential reason, and even a natural conscience, which "doth naturally, or of itself, . . . give an apprehension of right and wrong."[43]

Most of early-modern moral philosophy was the creation of theological Arminians, Christian thinkers seeking to refute both Hobbes on the one hand and Calvin on the other by establishing a natural basis for human moral values. They believed human beings had a meaningful power to choose between right and wrong. In addition to Locke, writers answering this description included Francis Hutcheson, Thomas Reid, Joseph Butler, most of the literary circle around *The Spectator*, and even the Cambridge Platonists whom Edwards so admired. Edwards respected the achievement of these moralists and undertook to relate it to another great system of thought, Reformed theology. Unlike Franklin, who thought religion mostly nonrational, though potentially useful, Edwards believed the doctrines of religion eminently rational: "there is the most sweet harmony between Christianity and reason," he declared.[44]

Jonathan Edwards set out to show that the moral philosophy of his age did not really dictate an Arminian theology, that it could be comprehended within a Calvinist system as well. Furthermore, Edwards believed that the Calvinist system was not simply viable but preferable on logical, scriptural, and empirical grounds. In fact, Edwards looked to Reformed theology to solve the problem of human nature posed by eighteenth-century faculty psychology. Edwards produced in the end a dual system of morality, one natural and one divine. What Edwards called natural morality was essentially the conventional moral philosophy of the eighteenth century, based on man's own unaided faculties. As a consequence of original sin, however, these faculties were corrupted by pride, which alienated humanity from God and prevented one from following the dictates of reason. Since this fallen human nature was hopelessly self-centered and incapable of true virtue, Edwards called a divine system of ethics into existence to rescue it.[45]

The problem, for Edwards as for Franklin and so many others, began with the weakness of the rational faculty in the human will. In the conventional model, conscience was a faculty of both the understanding and the will. As far as the perceptions of the understanding went, there was little difficulty: people were capable of *knowing* the right by means of their natural conscience. The problem lay in the will, in the helplessness of the conscience to *motivate* right action. The natural conscience was a rational power, which perceived moral obligations as part of the proper fitness of things. But it did not control the will. In its fallen state, the human will was incapable of transcending self-interest to achieve the austere altruism Edwards insisted was the one true virtue. Only God's grace could supply this.[46]

Edwards's decision to define conscience as a rational power was important. It meant that he was defending the conventional view, going back to Plato, that moral judgments were real judgments and not (as Hutcheson and Hume claimed) emotional reactions. But it also meant that conscience partook of the weakness of reason. Whether reason could motivate to action at all was the subject of a long-standing philosophical disagreement. The dominant school (sometimes called "intellectualism"), looking back to Aristotle and Aquinas, held in the affirmative, even while deploring the weakness of rationality. A rival school of thought ("voluntarism"), led by Augustine, held that reason had no motivating power whatsoever.[47] Edwards associated himself with the latter position, which helped him in his theological argument against free will. (Our actions are prompted by our emotions; but we don't voluntarily choose our emotions; therefore we do not have free will.)[48]

It might seem that Edwards, in espousing voluntarism, was excluding the rational conscience altogether from the operation of the will and defining it as solely a faculty of the understanding. Such was not the case. In matters of practical morality Edwards still expected reason to regulate and legitimate the motives, though it could not itself be a motive. "All things in the soul of man should be under the government of reason, which is the highest faculty."[49] He accepted the conventional terminological distinction that a "passion" was a bad "affection," one that had usurped the governing role of reason. The degree of rational justification and order that natural emotions displayed provided Edwards with a basis for judging them.[50]

Edwards, then, agreed with Franklin that there was such a thing as a natural morality, discoverable by human reason. "There are many in this world, who are wholly destitute of saving grace," he wrote, "but neveretheless have something of that which is called moral virtue."[51] In accordance with standard eighteenth-century moral philosophy, the natural conscience could invoke the aid of other faculties in the performance of its task; thus, Edwards explained, reason can ally with love "to keep men's irascible passions down in subjection, so that reason and love may have the regulation of them." Among the principles in human nature that Edwards recognized as potentially helpful to the natural conscience were prudential self-interest, benevolent affections, and the force of good habits.[52]

Edwards would have found nothing actually wrong with most of Franklin's homely devices for self-improvement, based as they were on nature and the general providence of God that made provision for human welfare in this world. No more would he have objected to the Founders' constitutional provisions for checks and balances, which imaginatively used human wickedness to combat wickedness. ("Ambition must be made to counteract ambition," as Madison explained it, invoking the principle of countervailing passions.)[53] Such devices took human nature as they found it, and did the best that could be done with it. They tamed the effects of evil without actually eradicating it. But, of course, all that could be achieved in such a fashion was better behavior; the basic self-preoccupation that corrupted the human heart remained untouched. True virtue, Edwards insisted, was a matter of inward disposition, not outward behavior.

Both Edwards and Franklin carried on inward dialogues with themselves in the course of trying to master their own subordinate faculties. Like Franklin, Edwards addressed good resolutions to himself.[54] Some of these private resolutions are as candidly prudential as anything Franklin ever expressed. The cover-leaf memoranda Edwards wrote for his projected monumental work on natural philosophy, for example, include: "The world will expect more modesty because of my circumstances—in America, young, etc. Let there then be a superabundance of modesty [in the work], and though perhaps 'twill otherwise be needless, it will wonderfully make way for its reception in the world."[55] Franklin, as we have seen, expected that his practice of self-discipline would eventually lead to the formation of good habits that would render virtue automatic and unproblematic. He realized that pride could never really be overcome but treated this as a minor exception to the rule.[56] Edwards worked just as hard at self-discipline and industriousness. ("By a sparingness in diet," he wrote in his diary while a student at Yale, "I shall doubtless be able to think more clearly, and shall gain time.")[57] But he harbored no expectation that self-discipline would ever come easily; it would always be a struggle, requiring conscious effort. The residuum of pride was no small matter for Edwards. Besides, any good behavior that came reflexively, without manifesting an intention, might be useful but could not be truly virtuous in his eyes.[58]

At most, Edwards's self-imposed rules of discipline might manifest a grace already received or might in some vague way prepare one to receive it. Whatever practical payoff they had in this life must be set against the unremitting toil they cost him. Edwards's life, like his writings, was organized methodically, even painfully.[59] Expecting so little from his regimen, why did Edwards subject himself to it? One is driven to the conclusion that he found austerity and hard work satisfying in their own right. If so, Jonathan Edwards was a more thoroughgoing exemplar of the work ethic than Benjamin Franklin.

There is a striking contrast between Franklin and Edwards in their attitude toward the faculty of prudence, or self-interest. In theory, Edwards admitted that self-interest, if properly enlightened, could be a legitimate motive.[60] In practice, however, he very seldom urged prudential considerations upon his audiences except with regard to the hereafter.[61] The self-preoccupation of human nature, after all, was the essence of its sinful alienation from God.[62] To exploit this ultimate vice, even for limited ends, must have been too distasteful for the great Christian philosopher. Instead, over and over again, he inveighed against it. "A Christian spirit is contrary to a selfish spirit." "Men are not to act as their own or for themselves singly, for they are not their own." "If you are selfish, and make yourself and your own private interest your idol, God will leave you to yourself, and let you promote your own interest as well as you can."[63]

Social ethics was really too important to be left to the second-best devices of natural morality. Edwards insisted upon applying the standards of divine morality in his social thought, demanding the transcendence of self-interest and the attainment of altruism. Only a religious awakening, therefore, could redeem secular society. Once a person had been converted, he would be "greatly concerned for the good of the public community to which he belongs, and particularly of the town where he dwells."[64] The specification of the town is significant; practically all of

Edwards's own interest in what we would call politics was expressed at the town level.

Rejection of individualism was a prominent feature of Edwards's social thought and social ethics. In one of his rare references to an American identity, Edwards criticized the individualistic culture he and his people shared: "We in this land are trained up from generation to generation in a too niggardly, selfish spirit and practice."[65] When he persuaded his parishioners to subscribe to a town covenant in 1742, he made its central theme the renunciation of "private interest" (including its corollary, party spirit).[66] For Jonathan Edwards, society was ideally an organic whole, in which persons treated each other as fellow members of the body of Christ. The proper model for society set forth in his great sermon cycle, *Charity and Its Fruits*, was not a contractual one, but the human family, with the magistrates acting "as the fathers of the commonwealth." In a good society, Christians "will not desire that all should be upon a level; for they know it is best that some should be above others and should be honored and submitted to as such."[67] (When Tryon Edwards published the work in the nineteenth century, he inserted some extra sentences at this point to try to soften and explain away his ancestor's endorsement of social inequality.)[68]

Edwards clearly believed social morality was important. As a manifestation of grace, social morality was more important than acts of worship were. He declared that "moral duties, such as acts of righteousness, truth, meekness, forgiveness, and love toward our neighbors . . . are of much greater importance in the sight of God than all the externals of his worship."[69] Edwards practiced what he preached and stood up for his social vision regardless of its unpopularity with a majority of his congregation. However, the social morality that interested him was properly only a by-product of true virtue, secondary to "internal" religion, "the worship of the heart." This relationship is clearly evident in the biography Edwards prepared of a model Christian saint, David Brainerd.

Although the account is nominally Brainerd's own journal, we know from the evidence presented by Norman Pettit that Edwards extensively edited and rewrote it, making it conform with his own theories concerning the religious affections.[70] The didactic life story that Edwards presented could hardly contrast more sharply with that of Franklin's *Autobiography*. Where Franklin chose himself as the subject, Edwards selected another. Where Franklin's subject lived to achieve wealth and fame at a ripe old age, Edwards's subject endured unremitting physical and psychological affliction, worked hard for very modest results, and died young. Yet Edwards held David Brainerd up as an example to young Christians of what life was really all about.

Like Franklin and Edwards, Brainerd was constantly in dialogue with himself. The dialogue concerns his relationship with God, the purity of his own motives, and his struggle to attain mastery over his baser faculties. His emotional "highs" and "lows" are graphically recorded. For all Brainerd's obsessive concern with overcoming pride, the dialogue seems in its own way totally self-absorbed. A missionary to the Indians, Brainerd only rarely notices the Indians as individual personalities. Most of the time they are means to his ends, his service to them an act of deter- mined self-abnegation.[71] Franklin had thought personal religious practice could be useful in prompting one to a life of public service, but Brainerd leads his life of service as a means to his personal religious practice. Franklin imposed personal discipline on himself as a means to temporal success; Brainerd imposes discipline on himself as a means to evangelical humiliation. In the end, the meager results Brainerd achieved from his mission were irrelevant to him and his editor; Edwards was interested in Brainerd's state of mind, not in what Franklin would call his merit.[72]

In practice, Edwards showed scarcely any concern with working for a just society through the devices of natural morality, the ones Franklin and the other Framers of the Constitution employed. While there was nothing wrong with those devices in principle, neither did they seem very important. They did nothing to liberate humanity from its prison of self- centeredness. Edwards wanted to change hearts, to be an instrument of divine grace for individuals. When enough individuals were saved, the community would be saved by the manifestation of their grace. In the meantime, a person would be foolish to attach much importance to what Edwards called "this world of pride and malice and contention and perpetual jarring and strife, . . . where all are for themselves and self- interest governs." The world Edwards described was the same one Franklin knew, but their responses to it were different. "What man acting wisely and considerately would concern himself much about lay- ing up a store in such a world as this?" demanded Edwards.[73] Franklin could have cheerfully responded, 'I would.'

For Edwards, society was too individualistic because the people who composed it were too selfish; the problem of society was rooted in the problem of human nature, most specifically in the defective human will. To supply the motivating power toward virtue that fallen human nature lacked, Franklin and the Arminian moral philosophers invoked prudence, instinctive emotions, and unthinking habits. But Edwards pointed out that none of these was *truly* virtuous: they might shape outward behav- ior, but they did not alter one's egocentric state of mind. Preoccupa- tion with self was a kind of prison, from which only Christ offered hope of deliverance.[74]

"There is a distinction to be made between some things which are truly virtuous, and others which only seem to be virtuous," Edwards wrote in what is probably his most famous philosophical distinction. "True virtue," as distinguished from the various halfway measures and imitation surrogates that Franklin and the Arminians discussed, Edwards defined as "benevolence to Being in general."[75] This was not part of fallen humanity's natural makeup; it could be bestowed only through God's saving grace. In His "ordinary method," to be sure, God would "give grace to those that are much concerned about it," those who had worked to attain "a preparatory conviction of sin." Ordinarily, "God makes use of . . . a good understanding, a rational brain, moral prudence, etc."[76] But of course there were many exceptions and "surprising" conversions. There was no secret sure method, no gradual progression up the ladder of love (as Plato had supposed). Grace was a matter of all or nothing, a blessing from God, which one could neither earn nor resist. When it came, it shed "a divine and supernatural light" upon experience.[77] Of course, even a sanctified person would not be sinless. But he or she had been definitively liberated from the prison of self and would be weaned away from this world of selfishness.[78]

True virtue, "benevolence to Being in general," was an affection, that is, an emotion. Franklin had considered religious belief nonrational and morality rational. For Edwards, it was just the opposite: Christianity was rationally justifiable, but true virtue was an emotional quality. Being an emotion, the God-given power of true virtue conferred no additional knowledge about right and wrong; the natural conscience, if well informed, "will approve and condemn the same things that are approved and condemned by a spiritual sense."[79] The difference was in the beholder, not in the principles beheld. Being an emotion, true virtue was involuntary: one does not love or hate as a result of a deliberate decision. Most importantly, true virtue, being an affection or emotion, had what the merely speculative, natural conscience lacked: the power to motivate. True virtue "not only removes the hinderances of reason, but positively helps reason,"[80] empowering one to act rationally, that is, rightly. True virtue overcame the limitations of self and opened the door to the world of love. Divine grace solved the problem of human nature.[81]

Like Franklin, Edwards was much interested in natural science; he projected, though he never wrote, a comprehensive work on "natural philosophy," as the physical sciences were then called. The differences between Franklin and Edwards, however, are as apparent in their approach to science as in their moral philosophies. Where Franklin was primarily an experimentalist, Edwards was primarily a theoretician. Franklin was interested in applied science; Edwards, in pure science. Edwards's interest in science stemmed from his love of harmony, symmetry, and beauty. "Always a metaphysician and an artist," even in his scientific writings, "he wanted to fit all loose parts into a perfect whole," in Paul Conkin's words. Scientist as well as logical determinist, Edwards wanted "to live in a universe in which nothing was left to chance."[82] Eventually, Edwards's scientific activities were crowded out of his life by his theological and evangelical ones. From his point of view, the latter were more relevant to the needs of the human condition.

Edwards was always clear about his priorities. The work of Redemption was more important than either the study of the material universe or the promotion of social reform.

> The conversion of one soul, considered together with the source, founda-
> tion, and purchase of it, and also the benefit and eternal issue of it, is a more
> glorious work of God than the creation of the whole material universe. . . .
> More happiness and a greater benefit to man, is the fruit of each single drop
> of such a shower [of grace], than all the temporal good of the most happy
> revolution in a land or nation amounts to, or all that a people could gain by
> the conquest of the world.[83]

Edwards could not more eloquently have summed up his differences with
Benjamin Franklin.

While Franklin and Edwards both addressed the problem of human
nature as posed by eighteenth-century moral philosophy, in the end each
transcended the conventional model of the faculties. That model was
based on the assumption that rationality ought to govern human nature
and led to the conclusion that its failure to do so was deplorable. Far
from simply bemoaning the failure of rationality, however, Franklin
and Edwards both found substitutes for it in the course of their quests
for virtue. Franklin substituted habit; Edwards, a divinely disinterested
benevolence. One came through practice and the other through grace.
Each was, in its way, an answer to the problem of humanity's perverse
irrationality.

## Epilogue

Edwards's message urged people to let God take over their hearts, and
all else would follow. Franklin's message was that God helps those who
help themselves. There have always been many Christians in America who
can't help feeling that both are somehow true. In the light of the differences between Jonathan Edwards and Benjamin Franklin, it may seem
remarkable that there should be an American tradition drawing upon
both of their approaches to the problem of human nature. But such there
is, and it goes all the way back to their contemporary, George Whitefield,
the Christian evangelist from England who came to know and admire
them both. Edwards and Whitefield had in common the desire to save
souls; Franklin and Whitefield had in common a concern with social
morality and organized social reform. Franklin welcomed Whitefield's
energy, rhetorical power, and organizational skills in humanitarian
causes.[84] The next several generations of evangelicals developed along
the lines Whitefield pioneered and Franklin approved. In the nineteenth
century, American evangelical Protestants created an impressive synthesis of the Edwardsean and Franklinian approaches to religion that had
momentous historical consequences.

The great Evangelical Movement of the nineteenth century, international and ecumenical in scope, active in both political and private
sectors, innovative in its use of the media of communication, became a
major culture-shaping force for its age. Like latter-day Franklins, the
evangelical Christians of the century after Franklin's death were utilitar-

ian, humanitarian, well organized, and not afraid to make big plans. But in the spirit of Edwards, they centered their personal lives upon an experienced relationship with Christ. As compared with both Franklin and Edwards, the evangelicals of the nineteenth century strike us as optimistic. They combined Edwards's faith in God's grace with a more positive estimate of human nature than either of the eighteenth-century thinkers we have been examining. When Jonathan Edwards's descendent Tryon Edwards edited "Charity and Its Fruits" in 1851, he found the conclusion of the seventh sermon, against selfishness, in need of revising. Edwards had ended on a note of pessimism regarding the likelihood of overcoming selfishness; his nineteenth-century successor added a more positive peroration ending: "Let us strive to overcome it that we may grow in the grace of an unselfish spirit, and thus glorify God and do good to man."[85]

Edwards had thought Franklin's devices to improve natural morality valid but not very important. Franklin, however, felt the same way about Edwards's "solution" to the problem of human nature. 'So Dr. Edwards assures us that a few people experience (now and then) a beatific vision of the divine,' one can imagine Franklin complaining; "so what? The world needs solutions appropriate for everybody, not just for a few saints." The evangelicals of the nineteenth century shared Franklin's attitude on this matter. They preached *plenteous* grace, enough grace for all. And instead of relying on occasional "showers" of grace in periodic revivals, the nineteenth-century evangelicals so organized and institutionalized their revival as to make it a continuous downpour. By the same token, they organized the charitable fruits of grace on a scale Cotton Mather could never have imagined.

The nineteenth-century evangelicals, as it happened, continued to conceptualize human nature in terms of a faculty psychology, for they continued to use and adapt the intellectual constructs of eighteenth-century moral philosophy. By their time, these had been codified by the Scots Thomas Reid and Dugald Stewart and the Scottish-American John Witherspoon.[86] The Scottish form of moral philosophy that the American evangelicals mainly used was actually closer to Franklin's than to Edwards's model, for the sentimentalist side of Edwards's ethical theory did not win broad acceptance, even within the Reformed community.

Some of the credit for adapting Edwards's legacy to a new age of Christian humanitarianism belongs to Edwards's disciple Samuel Hopkins (1721–1803). Hopkins taught that in the millennial age to come, there would be a larger population and more virtue, so that God would in the end save many more people than were damned. He reconciled divine sovereignty with revival preaching and individual preparation by teaching that these were the "occasions" of grace, if not the "causes" of it. He completed the divorce of salvation from the fear of hell by teaching that after conversion a person should be so caught up by benevolence to being-in-general as to be willing to be damned, if that was for the good of the whole. And through his courageous opposition to the New England slave trade, Hopkins pioneered the humanitarianism that would become such an admirable fruit of nineteenth-century evangelical piety.[87]

As mediated by Hopkins, Edwards became a heroic precursor and legitimator to the nineteenth-century evangelical humanitarian tradition. Joseph Tracy's magnificent centennial history of the revival of the 1740s (still indispensable for its lucid expositions of the context of events) typifies the respect that the Second Great Awakening felt toward the First.[88] Many a laborer in the vineyards of the Second Awakening drew inspiration and reassurance from *The Life of David Brainerd*.[89] (Franklin's *Autobiography* was popular too in Victorian America, though not assembled and published in its present form until 1868.) The mantle of Edwards became a prize for which rival evangelical schools of thought grappled through prolonged theological debates. Meanwhile liberal writers like Oliver Wendell Holmes the elder struggled to rid American culture of Edwards's towering presence.[90]

What happened in the nineteenth century was that evangelical Christians came to accept the importance of many of Franklin's concerns for temporal human welfare and incorporated them into their own version of the Edwardsean model of faith. Not only did Christian Sunday Schools and Temperance organizations inculcate the habits of industriousness and sobriety that Franklin wanted encouraged. Edwards's concerns with church discipline and the social morality of the town were grandly generalized by his nineteenth-century admirers into a commitment to making the United States as a whole a Christian nation. His postmillennial speculations were likewise grandly elaborated by Lyman Beecher and others as justification for social reform. This process reached a climax in the work of Charles Grandison Finney, the central figure of the antebellum revival. Finney has been called a man with a "divided conscience": a utilitarian like Franklin, yet still committed to benevolent and religious motives like Edwards.[91]

Thus evangelical piety energized humanitarianism as deism never could —just as Franklin had expected. Franklin, who encouraged Whitefield's social enterprises, would have approved of the Evangelical United Front, perhaps viewing it as a Christian version of his United Party of Virtue. Since he looked upon all religions as means to temporal ends, we may surmise that Franklin would have thought the emancipation of the slaves alone sufficient justification for the religious faith of the Victorian era. Edwards, on the other hand, might well have worried about the strict doctrinal purity of many of those who so proudly claimed him. Philosophies that logic declares different, history may still reconcile.

## Notes

1. *The Spectator*, no. 6 (March 8, 1711) and no. 408 (June 18, 1712), ed. Donald F. Bond (Oxford, 1965), I: 29 and III: 524. On early modern faculty psychology, see Norman Fiering, "Will and Intellect in the New England Mind,"

*William and Mary Quarterly*, 29 (October 1972): 515–58; Daniel W. Howe, *The Unitarian Conscience*, rev. ed. (Middletown, Conn., 1989), pp. 56–64; Arthur O. Lovejoy, *The Great Chain of Being* (Cambridge, Mass., 1936), ch. 6; and *idem*, *Reflections on Human Nature* (Baltimore, 1961).

2. On BF, see Albert Furtwangler, *American Silhouettes: Rhetorical Identities of the Founders* (New Haven, 1987), pp. 20–34; and Jeanette S. Lewis, "'A Turn of Thinking': The Long Shadow of *The Spectator* in Franklin's *Autobiography*," *Early American Literature*, 13 (Winter 1978–79): 268–77. On JE, see Norman Fiering, "The Transatlantic Republic of Letters," *William and Mary Quarterly*, 33 (October 1976): 642–60. Daniel W. Howe, "The Political Psychology of *The Federalist*," *William and Mary Quarterly*, 44 (July 1987): 485–509. James Madison was also among those influenced by *The Spectator*.

3. *WJE, 8*: 277; *PBF, 3*: 340, 441. I have chosen to follow the example of the Edwards editors rather than the Franklin editors by modernizing spelling.

4. BF to Joseph Priestley, June 7, 1782, in *Works of Benjamin Franklin*, ed. Jared Sparks, 10 vols. (Chicago, 1882), *9*: 226. I use Sparks's edition for years that the Yale edition has not yet reached. *PBF, 2*: 185.

5. See David Larson, "Franklin on the Nature of Man and the Possibility of Virtue," *Early American Literature, 10* (Fall 1975): 111–20; and Ronald A. Bosco, "'He That Best Understands the World, Least Likes It': The Dark Side of Benjamin Franklin," *Pennsylvania Magazine of History and Biography, 111* (October 1987): 525–54.

6. *PBF, 3*: 481. BF repeated this passage verbatim when he revised his will in 1757. *PBF, 8*: 204.

7. In a religious service he composed in 1728, BF prescribed the reading of lessons not from Scripture, but from John Ray's *The Wisdom of God in Creation* (1691) and other authoritative works of Enlightenment natural theology. *PBF, 1*: 105.

8. *PBF, 3*: 6.

9. Francis Hutcheson, *An Inquiry into the Original of Our Ideas of Beauty and Virtue* (London, 1729), p. 180. On BF as a proto-utilitarian, see also Norman Fiering, "Benjamin Franklin and the Way to Virtue," *American Quarterly, 30* (Summer 1978): 199–332.

10. *PBF, 2*: 223. See also Gladys Bryson, *Man and Society: The Scottish Inquiry of the Eighteenth Century* (Princeton, N.J., 1945); and Paul Conkin, "Benjamin Franklin: Science and Morals," in his *Puritans and Pragmatists* (Bloomington, Ind., 1976), esp. pp. 87–89.

11. *The Autobiography of Benjamin Franklin*, ed. Leonard W. Labaree *et al.* (New Haven, 1964). An example of BF's early interest in deism, *A Dissertation on Liberty and Necessity* (1725), *PBF, 1*: 57–71, expounded a system which, although internally logical, was not in the slightest useful to mankind.

12. *PBF, 16*: 192. After receiving the letter, the great evangelist wrote across the margin: "Uncomfortable indeed! And, blessed be God, unscriptural." *Loc. cit.*, note.

13. *PBF, 15*: 299–303 and *20*: 343–52.

14. *Ibid.*, *1*: 264.

15. *Ibid.*, *7*: 294. Emphasis in original.

16. *Ibid.*, p. 353.

17. BF to Samuel Mather, May 12, 1784, *Writings of Benjamin Franklin*, ed. Albert Henry Smyth, 10 vols. (New York, 1905–7), *9*: 208, *PBF, 2*: 203, and *3*: 125.

18. On BF's religion, see Elizabeth Dunn, "From Bold Youth to Reflective Sage: A Re-evaluation of Benjamin Franklin's Religion," *Pennsylvania Magazine of History and Biography, 111* (October 1987): 501–24; D. H. Meyer, "Franklin's Religion," in *Critical Essays on Benjamin Franklin*, ed. Melvin Buxbaum (Boston, 1987), 147–67; and A. Owen Aldridge, *Benjamin Franklin and Nature's God* (Durham, N.C., 1967).

19. See A. Owen Aldridge, *Benjamin Franklin: Philospher and Man* (Philadelphia, 1965), pp. 39–46. BF's own account is given in his *Autobiography*, ed. Labaree, pp. 162 ff.

20. Alexander Hamilton, in *The Federalist*, no. 72, ed. Jacob Cooke (Middletown, Conn., 1961), p. 488.

21. On this process, see Albert O. Hirschman, *The Passions and the Interests* (Princeton, N.J., 1977).

22. See, e.g., *PBF, 2*: 397; *Autobiography*, ed. Labaree, p. 160.

23. See *PBF, 7*: 89.

24. "Wealth" was a relative term for Franklin: "Who is rich? He that rejoices in his portion." *PBF, 2*: 395.

25. Since Jared Sparks supposed BF the author of the dialogues, he printed them in his edition of the *Works, 2*: 46–57. A. Owen Aldridge, "Franklin's 'Shaftesburian' Dialogues Not Franklin's," *American Literature, 21* (May 1949): 151–59.

26. *PBF, 5*: 473 and *7*: 350. See also Cameron Nickels, "Franklin's Poor Richard's Almanacs," in *The Oldest Revolutionary: Essays on Benjamin Franklin*, ed. J. A. Leo Lemay (Philadelphia, 1976), pp. 77–89.

27. *PBF, 8*: 123f; BF, *Autobiography*, ed. Labaree, p. 148.

28. *PBF, 2*: 15–19.

29. *Ibid., 9*: 105. BF's famous description of the regimen and his practice of it is in *Autobiography*, ed. Labaree, pp. 148–60.

30. David L. Parker, "From Sound Believer to Practical Preparationist: Some Puritan Harmonics in Franklin's Autobiography," in *Oldest Revolutionary*, ed. Lemay, pp. 67–75.

31. See Fiering, "Benjamin Franklin and the Way to Virtue," cited in note 9 above.

32. *PBF, 8*: 127; *Autobiography*, ed. Labaree, p. 148.

33. "A sound mind and a healthy body, a sufficiency of the necessaries and conveniences of life, together with the favor of God and the love of mankind," was BF's definition of happiness. The first part of the definition follows Locke. *PBF, 1*: 262.

34. *PBF, 2*: 19–21, quotation from p. 21. BF was probably arguing against Bernard Mandeville, though the position that virtue implies self-denial is also associated with Kant.

35. "General virtue is more probably to be expected and obtained from the education of youth than from the exhortation of adult persons; bad habits and vices of the mind being, like diseases of the body, more easily prevented than cured." *PBF, 4*: 41.

36. *PBF, 3*: 419. The Scottish moral philosopher Francis Hutcheson defined the "moral importance of any agent" as $M = B \times A$, where $B$ = benevolence and $A$ = abilities. See his *Inquiry* (cited in note 9), p. 185.

37. The *Autobiography* is the subject of an enormous body of literary criticism. Two rewarding works are Mitchell R. Breitwieser, *Cotton Mather and Benjamin Franklin: The Price of Representative Personality* (Cambridge, Mass.,

1984); and Ormond Seavy, *Becoming Benjamin Franklin: The Autobiography and the Life* (University Park, Penn., 1988).

38. *PBF, 1*: 263.

39. Norman Fiering, *Jonathan Edwards's Moral Thought and Its British Context* (Chapel Hill, N.C., 1981), p. 7. For JE's participation in transatlantic religious dialogue, see Harold P. Simonson, "Jonathan Edwards and his Scottish Connections," (British) *Journal of American Studies, 21* (December 1987): 353–76.

40. Perry Miller, *Jonathan Edwards* (New York, 1949), pp. 180–84, 237, 252.

41. *WJE, 1*: 133. A sensible study containing information on JE's use of faculty psychology is William J. Scheick, *The Writings of Jonathan Edwards: Theme, Motif, and Style* (College Station, Tex., 1975).

42. *WJE, 2*: 122. On JE's Platonism, see Paul Conkin, "Jonathan Edwards: Theology," in *Puritans and Pragmatists* (cited in n. 10 above).

43. JE, "A Divine and Supernatural Light" (1734), in *Jonathan Edwards: Representative Selections*, ed. Clarence Faust and Thomas Johnson (New York, 1935), p. 103.

44. *WJE, 8*: 286f.

45. *Ibid.*, p. 252; "Divine and Supernatural Light," *Representative Selections*, ed. Faust and Johnson, p. 103. Though he shared JE's low estimate of human nature, BF despised the doctrine of original sin. *PBF, 2*: 114.

46. *WJE, 2*: 206–7. See also Clyde Holbrook, *The Ethics of Jonathan Edwards: Morality and Aesthetics* (Ann Arbor, Mich., 1973), esp. pp. 56–71.

47. See Fiering, "Will and Intellect," cited in n. 1 above; and Fiering, *Edwards's Moral Thought*, pp. 263–69.

48. "All acts of the will are acts of the affections." From *Some Thoughts Concerning the Revival of Religion in New England* (1742), in *WJE, 4*: 297. Cf. "The Mind," in *ibid., 6*: 388, which equates the affections with "lively exercises of the will."

49. *WJE, 8*: 277. Malebranche had held that reason could regulate the passions, and his views carried weight with JE.

50. See *Ibid., 2*: 98, 350, and *8*: 277.

51. JE, *True Grace, Distinguished from the Experience of Devils* (1753), quoted in Fiering, *Edwards's Moral Thought, p. 61*.

52. *WJE, 8*: 278; Fiering, *Edwards's Moral Thought*, p. 92.

53. James Madison, in *The Federalist*, no. 72, p. 349.

54. See "Resolutions," *Representative Selections*, ed. Faust and Johnson, p. 38.

55. *WJE, 6*: 193.

56. *Autobiography*, ed. Labaree, pp. 159–60.

57. "Diary," in *Representative Selections*, ed. Faust and Johnson, p. 51.

58. Fiering, "Benjamin Franklin and the Way to Virtue," cited in n. 9, presents JE's logical arguments against the efficacy of habit-formation as a means to acquire virtue. These arguments are perfectly convincing with regard to what JE called *true* virtue—which is not what concerned BF.

59. See Holbrook, *Ethics of Edwards*, p. 91.

60. *WJE, 8*: 254.

61. Imprecatory sermons like the famous *Sinners in the Hands of an Angry God* were addressed to the prudential self-interest of sinners, in order to awaken them to a proper sense of their danger. Perhaps this would be of some help in

preparing them for grace. However, JE pointed out elsewhere that fear of hell was only a "natural," loveless motive, not to be equated with true virtue. *WJE*, 8: 176.

62. "Selfishness is a principle natural to us, and indeed all the corruption of nature does radically consist in it." *Ibid.*, p. 271.

63. *Ibid.*, pp. 260, 276, and 269.

64. *Ibid.*, p. 260.

65. *Ibid.*, p. 271.

66. The covenant is conveniently reprinted in Richard Bushman, ed., *The Great Awakening: Documents on the Revival of Religion 1740–1745* (New York, 1970), pp. 166–68.

67. *WJE*, 8: 242–79; quotations from pp. 261 and 242.

68. See Paul Ramsey's commentary, *ibid.*, pp. 105–6 and 242n. One of the few modern historians to analyze JE's social thought is Patricia Tracy; see her *Jonathan Edwards, Pastor* (New York, 1980).

69. *WJE*, 4: 522. BF cited this passage approvingly. *PBF*, 2: 384f.

70. See "Introduction" to *WJE*, 7.

71. E.g., *ibid.*, p. 261. An interesting exception is Brainerd's encounter with an Indian medicine man who explained a little of the native religion to him. *Ibid.*, pp. 329–30.

72. Cf. p. 82 above.

73. The two quotations are from *WJE*, 8: 393–94.

74. *Ibid.*, pp. 252–53; *Representative Selections*, ed. Faust and Johnson, p. 103.

75. *WJE*, 8: 540.

76. JE, "Miscellanies" no. 116, in *The Philosophy of Jonathan Edwards from His Private Notebooks*, ed. Harvey G. Townsend (Eugene, Ore., 1955), pp. 109–10.

77. *Representative Selections*, ed. Faust and Johnson, pp. 102–11.

78. *WJE*, 8: 396.

79. *Ibid.*, p. 596.

80. *Representative Selections*, ed. Faust and Johnson, p. 108.

81. As Norman Fiering has demonstrated, JE's theory of *natural* morality was rationalistic, but his theory of *divine* morality was a form of ethical sentimentalism. Fiering, *Edwards's Moral Thought*, pp. 64–66, 87, 103–4, 119, 143.

82. Paul Conkin, "Jonathan Edwards," in *Puritans and Pragmatists* (cited in n. 10 above), p. 46. See also Wallace Anderson's superb introduction to *WJE*, 6: 1–143.

83. *WJE*, 4: 344–45.

84. See David T. Morgan, "A Most Unlikely Friendship: Benjamin Franklin and George Whitefield," *The Historian*, 47 (February 1985): 208–18.

85. *WJE*, 8: 271n.

86. Sydney E. Ahlstrom, "Scottish Philosophy and American Theology," *Church History*, 24 (1955): 257–72.

87. See Joseph Conforti, *Samuel Hopkins and the New Divinity Movement* (Grand Rapids, Mich., 1981). Still very useful is Alexander Allen, "The Transition in New England Theology," *Atlantic Monthly*, 68 (December 1891): 767–80.

88. Joseph Tracy, *The Great Awakening: A History of the Revival of Religion in the Time of Edwards and Whitefield* (1842; rep. Edinburgh, 1976). I am here using the term Second Great Awakening, as historians sometimes do, to refer to the entire era of evangelical activity from 1800 to the Civil War.

89. See Joseph Conforti, "Jonathan Edwards's Most Popular Work: *The Life of David Brainerd* and Nineteenth-Century Evangelical Culture," *Church History,* *54* (June 1985): 188–201.

90. The fascinating subject of JE's influence may be pursued in *Jonathan Edwards and the American Experience*, ed. Nathan Hatch and Harry Stout (New York, 1988); Mark Noll, "The Contested Legacy of Jonathan Edwards in Antebellum Calvinism," *Canadian Review of American Studies,* *19* (Summer 1988): 149–64; and Daniel B. Shea, "Jonathan Edwards: The First Two Hundred Years," (British) *Journal of American Studies,* *14* (August 1980): 181–98.

91. James Moorhead, "Social Reform and the Divided Conscience of Antebellum Protestantism," *Church History,* *48* (December 1979): 416–30.

# CULTURE

# 7

# The Two Cultures in Eighteenth-Century America

### BRUCE KUKLICK

The study of the cultural significance of Franklin and Edwards is a time-honored, not to say old-fashioned, academic enterprise. For generations scholars have explored the ways in which the two men contribute to our understanding of American national character.[1] In relentlessly juxtaposing the personalities and careers of the two—in what might be called The Compare and Contrast Model—students hope to illuminate not just the colonial world but topics as diverse as twentieth-century corporate mores and the evangelistic revivalism of Billy Graham and his successors. This essay treats those conventions with respect but ultimately moves away from them to make a historiographical point about our understanding of the eighteenth century.

It is possible to view suspiciously the whole project of comparing the two men. Any attempt to point up similarities between them can be practically countered by narrowing the area of comparison and displaying instead a contrast. Franklin and Edwards were both conversant with Newtonianism. Yet within the camp of knowledgeable adherents of the New Learning, Edwards was concerned with the a priori dimensions of the *Principia*. Franklin was exclusively (and more deeply) interested in the experimentalism—the raw empiricism—of natural philosophy.[2] If we want to contrast the two men, a broadening of the spectrum on which the contrast exists will demonstrate similarity. Suppose we argue that Franklin was interested in vernacular culture while Edwards was committed to classical learning. Witness the curriculum of the College of Philadelphia in opposition to the sort of study Edwards received and respected at Yale. Nonetheless, both men were committed to "higher" education in the colonies—Franklin founded the College; Edwards became President of Princeton.

We can, moreover, always shift categories so that dissimilarites become similarities, and vice versa. Is it appropriate to contrast Franklin and Edwards as exponents, respectively, of vernacular and classical culture? Why not note their common extremism? Both disliked Harvard. Franklin's ideal of education contrasted with Harvard's orthodoxy; but Princeton's New Light orientation also distinguished Edwards's radical preferences from the orthodoxy of Harvard (and Yale). Franklin and Edwards were similarly interested in Newton. But in Edwards this interest was subservient to his desire to glorify God. Newton gave Edwards a new way to read off the character of the Deity in nature. Franklin's interest in physics was equally subordinate to his concern to promote practical improvements. Newton was no more central to Franklin than the postal service. Each man took whatever was available to advance his distinct purpose, in one case homage to God, in the other utilitarian progress.

Our notion of the relevance of any given series of contrasts and similarities must proceed from a more fundamental assumption about the representative quality each man had. Most modern scholars have considered the differences profound, and they have given us a Calvinist Edwards and a Yankee Franklin. But this disjunction has proceeded with a bad conscience, because scholars have usually also granted irreducible significance to many ways in which the two men were alike. Students see that the presumption of disparity between two cultural strands in America—Puritanism and the Enlightenment, Christianity and Republicanism—presents its own problems. The deep and axiomatic disjunction between religion and politics in the characters of Franklin and Edwards has produced one of the most challenging, if unsuccessful, books on colonial American history—Alan Heimert's attempt in *Religion and the American Mind* to link the two realms.[3] If there were critical differences in colonial culture embodied by the two men, why was the American Revolution such a relatively tame affair? Why was it so different from the French Revolution, which pitted militant atheism, on the one side, against clericalism, on the other? These hard questions continue to plague historians of the early republic. How could the evangelicalism of the Second Great Awakening develop during the presidency of Thomas Jefferson, the most secular holder of that office? We would not have these questions if we rejected the idea that Franklin and Edwards were so basically at odds, or that they represented two divergent social models.

I would like to shift around some of the central concerns that have dominated the study of Franklin and Edwards and change, just a bit, the parameters of discussion. My own view is that the two were not "representative men." They were both members of a colonial elite culture, but neither was the norm; each was at its fringes. More typical members were people like John Adams, George Whitefield, and John Witherspoon. As members of this culture, however, Franklin and Edwards shared the same intellectual and moral world.

Each became acquainted at an early age with not only the writings of Newton and Locke but also the thought of moralists like Shaftesbury and Hutcheson, as well as Reformed Protestant authors. Edwards was surely the more driven metaphysician, but Franklin was no fool when it came to philosophy. What strikes me about the critical speculative writings of each[4]—Franklin's *Dissertation* and other brief writings and Edwards's "Of Being" and *Freedom of the Will*—is how much they are speaking in the same idiom. The two agree on a Spinozistic monism that has reminded commentators of Hobbes. Each man, however, maintained that the structure of the universe was spiritual and not material.

After long observation of the social order, Franklin and Edwards were suspicious of the working of reason in human affairs. Each was dubious about the benignity of human nature.[5] Franklin scholarship has come a long way from the inadequate portrait of him as a fatuous optimist. Like the other Founders, he was convinced of the dark side to human endeavor. If it is objected that Edwards was not just distrustful but "knew" man to be evil, this obvious truth must be balanced by the equal truth that Edwards also "knew" that some people at least had a glorious future. In some ways he was more optimistic than Franklin. Moreover, studies have shown that Franklin was something more than a deist. He thought that God governed in human affairs, that the deity was providential and, incidentally, acted without regard to human merit, just as Edwards's God did.[6] The difference between the two in respect to the purity of our moral commitments and to the power of our rational faculties seems to me that Franklin had a sense of humor about our limitations, whereas Edwards found little to laugh about.

Whatever we make of the sort of learning each preferred, both men valued the role of education in bringing about whatever good could be achieved in human affairs. Each at the same time disdained mere book learning, theorizing, or talk and dismissed views that confined wisdom to the erudite. Here we come to a topic on which there has been some misunderstanding, at least of Edwards. Franklin's practical emphasis is well known. Less widely considered has been his coordinate contempt for the profession of good intent—his sense that the external evidences of religiosity and morality were often hypocrisy—and his dislike for cant.[7] This distinction is central, too, for Edwards. He was not opposed to good works; he was instead worried that most good works were selfishness masquerading as something else. *The Religious Affections* tries to fathom the differences between what Franklin called "real" good works and the feigned. Some scholars assume that the two men ask: What is more important, theory or practice, reflection or action? and that the two come up with different answers. Instead, each man stressed that we knew people by their "fruits," their deeds. Edwards did agonize more over which deeds were genuinely worthy, but Franklin was also aware of the capacity of people to deceive. His lifelong hankering for masquerade matched Edwards's attempts at uncovering masquerade.

Edwards believed that only God provided the grace necessary to "real" good works. But Edwards's role as an instrument of the divine consumed him, just as Franklin's role in promoting public good absorbed him. Both men were also concerned with didactic arts. Franklin's love of persuasive writing has appeared to his critics to be so overweening that they have excoriated certain features of the *Autobiography*. But Edwards too was so committed. He was not above reshaping material for maximal effect. Witness *Some Thoughts on the Revival* and his *Life of Brainerd*, both of which recast events to give them the structured order that Edwards thought was the pattern for appropriate preparation for and reception of grace. Perhaps more important is the contrast between Edwards's Diary and his "Personal Narrative," where his own experience is distorted, as was Northampton's and Brainerd's, to make it conform to certain Calvinist theories.[8] Like Franklin, Edwards refashioned his life in literature to make it more a standard of emulation than perhaps it was.

Franklin's persuasive talents were not limited to the written word. He was verbally effective in face-to-face encounters, at least according to many contemporaries. Edwards had a far more successful career in public speaking. If we credit the complaint of Franklin's critics that he told people what they wanted to hear, without regard for what Franklin himself believed, we should also recognize that Edwards altered the public expression of his ideas to secure what he took to be the maximum positive effect. *Sinners in the Hands of an Angry God* bases conversion on the self-serving fear of punishment, an idea that Edwards considered a sign of the worst sort of self-love.

This willingness of each man to "trim" his views in order to be most effective was, I believe, connected to the interest both had in their later repute. Consider what I take to be the most angry display extant from the pen of each man. Franklin showed rage at what he perceived to be his son's attempt to deprive him of his reputation. Edwards was beyond rage at his congregation for publically humiliating him in 1750.[9]

These examples hint at another quality common to both men, pride. This is an attribute that Franklin knew in himself more clearly. Indeed, his crafty way of speaking of it disarms criticism in a manner that has not disarmed criticism of Edwards.

In emphasizing these shared concerns, we can alleviate some of the scholarly discomfort that has arisen from postulating separateness while sensing some meeting of minds. The meeting occurred because the two were part of a provincial intellectual life defined in part by the common holding of the sorts of ideas I have reviewed. At the same time, however, if we also acknowledge that each man in his own way was perhaps at the periphery of this culture, we can move fruitfully to analyze the important distinctions between the two.

Franklin and Edwards were at the margins of the eighteenth century. Nonetheless, the nineteenth century would bring the American Yankee fully fledged into existence. Franklin could *then* be perceived as his progenitor. At the same time, only *after* Puritan New England had vanished could Edwards be seen as its final representative. That is, once colonial life passed—once the colonies became the United States—only then could the two come to represent opposing tendencies that later investigators saw in that culture. In exploring the colonial past, we have presupposed that it was essentially linked to the (New England) seventeenth century and to the (American) nineteenth century. From 1730 (or 1763) to 1800 (or 1828), American life is going *from* one thing to *another*.

In the second part of this paper I accept this framework and examine a critical difference between Edwards and Franklin that allowed them, after the fact, to serve, respectively, a retrospective and a prospective function.

Let me start by recapitulating the view of Franklin's self that is, I think, correct and, not incidentally, universal in the literature. In writing about the *Autobiography*, Ralph Lerner analyzes this conception of the self nicely. He says that Franklin asks us for the moment to adopt his own perspective while he tells a story, to join him as he relates to us how he looks at others. Lerner says that we are "taken in" by this rhetorical stance. We do not realize, or do not care even if we do realize, that at some point Franklin has "gotten out of" the perspective that he has coaxed us to adopt, and watches us, with a friendly yet distanced smile, while he looks on.[10] Franklin is able to step outside of what we at any point think his self is and to stand back, observing and dispassionate. Some such image as this runs through the work of all the Franklin scholars. Esmond Wright says Franklin is a "cultivated" character with a carefully manufactured control over himself. Robert Sayre and Ormond Seavey urge that Franklin is ironically detached.[11] This self behind or apart from all the projected selves explains, commentators argue, Franklin's love of personae, pseudonyms, poses, disguises, and practical jokes. John William Ward identifies this property as the ground for Franklin's constant distinction between appearance and reality. Franklin's critics complain that it is the source of his hypocrisy. Pretense becomes a way of life for him, and one can always doubt his sincerity.[12]

Scholars who want to get at the "real" Franklin, the self who is always able to step outside the man of the moment, concede the difficulty of their task, because Franklin keeps his own counsel. Data about his authentic emotions are scant. Esmond Wright argues that Franklin carefully made the private man private: he had a strong sense of who he was but didn't want his true person publically known. John Griffith has surveyed the scholarly work that tries to penetrate to this true self in the absence of facts. Was Franklin inwardly tranquil? a man motivated by money, success, and distinction? a Puritan driven by guilt? or an angry, marginal figure, eager for social and intellectual acceptance and willing to repress feeling to achieve them? Other scholars have hypothesized that the real Franklin traded intimacy and passion for a remote and generalized amiability to all. Finally, some critics have asserted that the real self was "hollow." At the extreme, Mitchell Breitwieser has contended that Franklin's self was blank and negative, a "void." "Behind the masks is [only] the universal capacity to take on masks."[13]

All the critics have concurred that this sort of self—be it good, bad, or "void"—reflected Franklin's belief in the range of human freedom, our ability, at least in a modest way, to mold our affairs. The *Autobiography* has exemplarily depicted the rewards of personal autonomy and the perceived ability of the self to transcend circumstance.[14]

This notion of the self is in counterpoint to that of Edwards. For Edwards the self is not an entity, something that stands behind appearances as their cause. Rather, the self is a construct—the structure of the series of an individual's momentary engagements with the world. Human beings have various impulses to action—motives, interests, desires, feelings, inclinations. Actions are linked to these various "volitions" and are inseparable from them. The synthesis of volition and act is an atom of consciousness. The organization of certain groups of these atoms is called a human self. The problem of *The Religious Affections* is to determine whether or not, for any person, this structure is directed virtuously, is oriented or not oriented to God. It would be a serious error to assume that in that book Edwards is trying to "read off" from what is given the genuine self behind the appearance. Appearance *gives* the genuine self; the question is properly to interpret the appearances, a job that only God can, in the end, accomplish. *The Religious Affections* leaves us with a series of hints, of negative disclaimers—don't necessarily think that A means B or that the absence of C means D. This is not to say that Edwards's concentration on the genuine fruits of religious belief rules out the inner life. Rather, Edwards believes it is metaphysically incorrect to separate the inner and the outer. Ultimately, for Edwards, nothing is hidden in the universe, certainly not the self. For Franklin, on the contrary, the self is just that item that can be hidden in our public world. Franklin's God can perhaps "see" into our secret soul; Edwards's God is the incontrovertible interpreter of what is there for all to see.

In Edwards's *Freedom of the Will* the constructional nature of the self is the starting point for the elaboration of an idea of freedom that makes it compatible with determinism. In its engagedness with the world, the self of *The Religious Affections* is identified with the human will in *Freedom of the Will*.[15] Like everything else, the will is caused. A determinate succeeding moment of consciousness inevitably follows each present moment of consciousness. We can never will otherwise than we have done. At the same time we have free will if we do what we want. Roughly speaking, freedom for Edwards is contrasted to physical constraint. The bride at the altar who says "I do" is free because she is doing what she wants. The prisoner locked in his cell is not free. When a prior moment that is considered part of the self (and not part of what is outside the self) determines the succeeding moment, we have freedom. Freedom implies a certain sort of causality, not the absence of causality; and we know that the causal agent finally at work in all cases is God.[16]

It is not strange that Edwards defended a view of freedom that many recent scholars regard as narrow or even absurdly minimal. It is, first of all, a notion whose logical presentation is in many ways compelling. Acute thinkers after Edwards have regularly defended it, and its alternatives are not easily justified.[17] Perhaps more important, Edwards was the leading Calvinist theoretician of the eighteenth century. Critical aspects of human behavior were rightly attributed to the spirit of God (or of Satan). Although this behavior was—in the most painful instances—the responsibility of the sinner, it was recognized as being beyond the sinner's control. The Calvinists made us blameworthy yet also astutely acknowledged that we seemed burdened with a self that that was given to us, somehow not our own making. We are guilty of being selfish yet utterly dependent on God, our wills bound. As a Calvinist, Edwards *needed* a minimalist idea of freedom.

God transformed the sinner. The Edwardsean saint was humble and dependent on the divine. He relied on God for guidance and sought above all else to become an instrument of the Lord. His self, again, was constricted. Edwards's philosophical analysis of the will conforms to the experienced reality of the Christian universe.[18]

On the other hand, Edwards held that those against whom he argued in *Freedom of the Will* did not just have false views about the practice of religion. His "Arminian" opponents did not just fallaciously think that people could somehow save themselves, that people could somehow merit salvation. This bad practice had a wrong theoretical justification—the "*modern* prevailing Notions" of freedom, as Edwards called them in his title. These notions, which Edwards confronted in one of the most extended and penetrating critiques in the history of thought, were of a self-determining will, a will that somehow stood apart from its acts and caused them. Edwards lashes out against just the sort of entity that scholars have found depicted in Franklin's writing. That peculiar thing—what Breitwieser calls "the universal capacity to take on masks"—is the crucial target of *Freedom of the Will*. There is no need to rehearse Edwards's three hundred pages of arguments against Arminian theory. Suffice it to say that just such a spontaneous, self-determining entity, of the kind that so many scholars have attributed to Franklin, could not exist; it was contradictory, said Edwards. When examined carefully, it was conceptually incoherent. Action based on such a will would be the hellmark of the irrational.

The direction of my analysis at this point should be clear. But before I draw some conclusions, let me suggest a way in which many critics have gone wrong, and wrong in a telling way, in appraising something like this distinction between the two men.

Norman Fiering is a great partisan of Edwards but has written eruditely on both men. He rightly sees Edwards as devoted to a religion of the heart and thus to the inner nature of the self. On the other side, for Fiering, is the "operationalist" Franklin, whom—in perhaps an unguarded moment—Fiering says is an early behaviorist, a follower before his time of B. F. Skinner.[19] Breitwieser too seems to believe that because the self in Franklin is reduced to an ability to project appropriate appearances, there is no real self, nothing in Franklin except what he actually does. In the most extended analysis, Ormond Seavey picks up an idea from Georges Gusdorf's *La Decouverte de Soi*. Gusdorf distinguishes self-knowledge from self-awareness. Self-knowledge is applied to selves: we have knowledge of the accumulated experiences whose product is the self. Self-awareness applies to souls and is given in an insight or perception or illumination about an entity—my soul or "being," a "substantial self." For Seavey, Franklin had self-knowledge, the admirable virtue of an intelligent and calculating man of affairs who was full of guile. But without a soul—or with only a minimal one—Franklin cannot be self-aware.[20]

After getting just right the felt difference between Franklin and Edwards, these writers have got their explanatory account of this difference almost precisely backwards. Franklin is the man with the soul, though that is giving the sort of self he believes in a connotation that may be inappropriate. In any event, for Franklin there is some thing—a self-determining power—that acts in the world. This is anathema to Edwards. For him there is no such entity as the individual soul. Edwards is the behaviorist, although this gives too modern a ring to it. In any event, for Edwards there is only the series of conscious acts; there is nothing behind the masks. For Edwards, there can be no introspection of a self, and the idea of a privileged inner life is invalid.

For Edwards the theoretical notion of a self-determining will and the worldly evils of Arminianism went hand-in-hand. As he saw it, the fight between his Calvinism and the beliefs of his adversaries was not just philosophical; it was a battle over what kind of man was to rule New England and America. On the one side was the saint who walked with the Lord and vividly experienced his limited power, typified by his tormented struggles. On the other side was the individual who felt he was autonomous, self-directing, and self-controlling, free equally of the domination of impulse and of authority.

A compelling example of Edwards's sense of the saint and the saint's limited power is given in his *Life of David Brainerd*. Edwards put aside his *Freedom of the Will* to write the biography, which, he thought, might be a more effective practical antidote to Arminianism than his speculative arguments. The *Life* would exemplify in practice the triumph of the Calvinistic idea over Arminianism. Brainerd was in some ways, however, a poor subject. His manuscript autobiography, from which Edwards worked, is filled with imaginative expressions of self-regard and intimations of desperation. This is not what Edwards wanted the Calvinist saint to be about. In consequence, as I have already noted, he had to rewrite parts of Brainerd's text for presentation in the biography. What is crucial here is the way Edwards reorganized the text he worked on. Edwards's Brainerd became less imaginative and desperate, more genteel and evenly balanced. As Norman Pettit, who has studied the texts, wrote, Brainerd's "inner life" is "concealed," his feelings "disguised." Edwards wrote of Brainerd as someone who had in his saintliness moved away "from the passions that had led to excesses in his own behavior." Edwards transformed Brainerd's heightened personal qualities, even after the reception of grace, into impersonal and steady affections.[21]

The kind of self attributable to Franklin became one of the guiding positive ideals of the postcolonial culture in which historians participated, but it is a nearly exact description of the Edwardsean sinner. Conversely, the Calvinist ideal is an ordered and controlled personality type that many people have disdained as rigid, conventional, and "not in touch with himself." Yankee "virtues" were the characteristics that led Adam to eat the apple. It was in response to that betrayal that man thereafter came to possess what the Calvinists called a "fallen" will. To behave, after the fall, as Adam did before it was the outstanding sign of wickedness. This, of course, was the way Franklin behaved, but even most of Franklin's severest critics share this self-conception. What they admire in Edwards is not the saint; they rather find relevant his depiction of the trouble that someone like Franklin eventually gets into. For Edwards, the person who (falsely) believed in Arminianism might start off expressing his autonomous control of the world, "feeling free," but he eventually became broodingly morose and self-castigating. At his most wicked, the sinner was most self-lacerating, full of despair and loathing yet unwilling to relinquish his misguided selfishness. Franklin's critics refuse to recognize in him the twentieth-century autonomous self that they admire. So, by a sleight of hand, they make Edwards's ideal self this sinner; and the Franklinian self becomes "behavioral." But such a self is just what Franklin was not—a self uninterested in triumphing over its environment, a self without resources or desire to assert itself in relation to its community, a self contingent on forces far greater than it. This behavioral self is just the sort of self Edwards thought conformed to the world as its truly was, the self of the saint.[22]

* * *

Scholars have long since pointed out that although Protestantism promoted aspects of the modern, it still had a great deal of the medieval
about it. The versions of Calvinism dominant in New England struggled
with the individualism that was more and more part of the landscape
of the eighteenth century. The reason that Franklin and Edwards were
so much alike is that they participated in the same historical moment,
eighteenth-century British colonial culture in America. But Edwards
gravitated to aspects of that culture that by the nineteenth century had
passed, while dominant in Franklin were those aspects that prevailed and
typified more recent times—what, for lack of a better term, I have called
the modern. A good way of getting at these differences is to examine
the conflicting conceptions of the self that each man had. These conceptions are in tension, and the practical consequences they were thought
to have differed. So in one sense I have reinforced an ancient distinction: the Puritan Edwards and the Yankee Franklin.

Yet in another sense I want to question the validity of this distinction: the Puritan and the Yankee were not social types indigenous to the
eighteenth century. They were constructs of a later scholarly era, which
saw a movement *from* the seventeenth *to* the nineteenth century and
beyond. The notion of Calvinism versus the Enlightenment might make
sense, but only in hindsight; it could not describe the eighteenth century before the nineteenth century.

More important, it is a description that historians who were part of
Yankee culture came to find persuasive. As the period we have called
modern itself passes into history, it is less clear how serviceable the
Edwards–Franklin character study will be. A consensus of American social
historians at the end of the twentieth century has joined in diminishing
the role of New England culture for the American colonies.[23] Some
historians of American religion have concluded that the sacred beliefs
of most New Englanders were far different from the theological niceties
of high Calvinism.[24] That is, as historians live through or past or out of
what they perceive as the certainties of Enlightment modernity, the transition to it has become more problematic, and the relevance of Edwards
to Franklin, or of either of them to us, is more mysterious.

Much of my critique is not invidious. The imposition of interpretive apparatus is inevitable in history, and it is surely small criticism of a
conceptual framework that it may have become outworn after a century
of use. At the same time the historiography of modernity has not been
transparent. Modern scholars in general liked what they saw in Franklin
but did not want to give up everything in Edwards. The result of these
discordant desires has been a confusion of the underlying ideas of the
selves attributed to "Calvinism" and to "the Enlightenment." For
Edwards the unconverted do not have the capacity for insight into a self.
The sinner errs in depicting his plight as that involving an agonized soul.
In reality there is only the torment of selfish moments, and the converted

saint is self-less. Only the modern Franklin has—or thinks he has—a substantial will. He is will*ful*, and it is at least possible for him to believe he is reflecting *on* his soul. The wrong thing in Edwards has attracted his champions—the sinner. They have consequently attributed to Edwards the angst-ridden substantial self that has been very much a part of twentieth-century life. Commentators have not recognized that it was repellent to Edwards. The soul-searching that some people found attractive in the modern period is not the Edwardsean ideal but the end to which the self of a man like Franklin must be driven. The self of the Edwardsean saint, as B. F. Skinner wrote in another context, was beyond freedom and dignity.[25]

## *Notes*

1. An excellent example of this kind of work that looks back to the nineteenth century as well as heralding more recent scholarship is Carl Van Doren's "Intro-duction" to *Benjamin Franklin and Jonathan Edwards: Selections from their Writings* (New York, 1920), pp. ix–xxxiv.

2. *WJE, 6*, particularly the "Spider Papers" (pp. 145–67) and *Of Being* (pp. 202–7). On BF the standard account is in I. Bernard Cohen, *Franklin and Newton* (Philadelphia, 1956).

3. Alan Heimert, *Religion and the American Mind from the Great Awakening to the Revolution* (Cambridge, Mass., 1966). For a recent discussion of the issue, see Mark A. Noll, *Princeton and the Republic, 1768–1822* (Princeton, N.J., 1989), pp. 4–9.

4. *PBF, 1*: 57–71; see also A. Owen Aldridge, *Benjamin Franklin and Nature's God* (Durham, N.C., 1967), pp. 75–79. For JE, see *Of Being*, and *WJE, 1*.

5. See *WJE, 1*: 13–14, 374; Aldridge, *Franklin and Nature's God*, pp. 75–79; and Ronald A. Bosco, "'He that best understands the World, least likes it:' The Dark Side of Benjamin Franklin," *Pennsylvania Magazine of History and Biography, 111* (1987): 531.

6. The complexity of BF's view of human nature is now generally recognized. See Bosco, "'He that best understands the World'"; Aldridge, *Franklin and Nature's God*, pp. 66–67, 73–74; and David M. Larson, "Franklin on the Nature of Man and the Possibility of Virtue," *Early American Literature, 10* (1975): 111–120. On BF's *providential deism* see Donald H. Meyer, "Franklin's Religion," in *Critical Essays on Benjamin Franklin*, ed. Melvin H. Buxbaum (Boston, 1987), pp. 161–62.

7. Aldridge, *Franklin and Nature's God*, pp. 99–101, 126.

8. There are excellent discussions of these writings. On *Some Thoughts*, see *WJE, 4*: 19–89; on *The Life of David Brainerd* see Norman Pettit, "The Life of David Brainerd: Comments on the Manuscript and Text," *Yale University Library Gazette*, April 1986, pp. 137–44; on JE's "Diary" and the *Personal Narrative*, see Daniel B. Shea, Jr., *Spiritual Autobiography in Early America* (Princeton, N.J., 1968), pp. 183–93.

9. On BF and his son, see Esmond Wright, *Franklin of Philadelphia* (Cambridge, Mass., 1986), pp. 258–49, and Claude-Anne Lopez and Eugenia W. Herbert, *The Private Franklin: The Man and His Family* (New York, 1975), esp.

p. 305; on JE and his parishioners, see Patricia Tracy, *Jonathan Edwards, Pastor: Religion and Society in Eighteenth Century Northampton* (New York, 1980), pp. 171–94.

10. Ralph Lerner, *The Thinking Revolutionary: Principle and Practice in the New Republic* (Ithaca, N.Y., 1987), pp. 58–59.

11. Wright, *Franklin of Philadelphia*, pp. 3, 7; Robert Sayre, *The Examined Self: Benjamin Franklin, Henry Adams, Henry James* (Princeton, N.J., 1964), pp. 20–25; Ormond Seavey, *Becoming Benjamin Franklin: The Autobiography and the Life* (University Park, Penn., 1988), p. 58.

12. On poses and so on, see Wright, *Franklin of Philadelphia*, p. 10, and John Williams Ward, "Benjamin Franklin: The Making of An American Character," in *Benjamin Franklin: A Collection of Critical Views*, ed. Brian M. Barbour (Englewood Cliffs, N.J., 1979), p. 57. On BF's possible hypocrisy, see John Griffith, "Franklin's Sanity and the Man Behind the Masks," in *The Oldest Revolutionary: Essays on Benjamin Franklin*, ed. J. A. Leo Lemay (Philadelphia, 1976), p. 126.

13. Wright, *Franklin of Philadelphia*, pp. 10–11; Griffith, "Franklin's Sanity," surveys various possible selves on pp. 134–35, and talks about the hollow self on p. 130. Seavey, *Becoming Benjamin Franklin*, talks of generalized amiability, pp. 129, 134. Breitwieser is quoted from *Cotton Mather and Benjamin Franklin: The Price of Representative Personality* (Cambridge, U.K., 1984), p. 233.

14. See Sayre, *Examined Self*, p. 23; Breitwieser, *Mather and Franklin*, pp. 7–8, 28; and Seavey, *Becoming Benjamin Franklin*, pp. 94–95, 137.

15. Throughout my discussion I have assumed the metaphysical stance JE took most vigorously in *The Great Christian Doctrine of Original Sin Defended*, *WJE, 3*, where the human self is clearly an arbitrary construct. Even in the eighteenth and nineteenth centuries, critics of JE noted that this position was not fully consistent with that taken in *Freedom of the Will*, where the human will is a less arbitrary construct, *real* enough, at least, to merit praise or blame intrinsically. JE's collapse of the distinction between the *inner* act of the will and its *external* expression is most clearly stressed when he takes up metaphysical problems. When he discusses practical responsibility, the metaphysics is in the background, although it is a persistent theme from the time JE wrote *Of Being*. The idealism of this metaphysics attracted many Calvinist divines—then and later—cogitating on philosophical theology.

16. This discussion of *Religious Affections* and *Freedom of the Will* is taken from Bruce Kuklick, *Churchmen and Philosophers* (New Haven, 1985), pp. 29–40, 62–63, where further citations can be found.

17. Historians, with little time for metaphysical niceties, have not appreciated the full significance of *Freedom of the Will*. JE's was the first of many subtle attempts in the post-Newtonian world to reconcile freedom with determinism. Positions similar to his and at least critically sympathetic to his continue to attract wide support among professional philosophers. Some exemplary recent writers include Harry G. Frankfurt, *The Importance of What We Care About: Philosophical Essays* (Cambridge, U.K., 1988); Brian O'Shaughnessey, *The Will: A Dual Aspect Theory* (Cambridge, U.K., 1980); Derek Parfit, *Reasons and Persons* (Oxford, U.K., 1984); Charles Taylor, *Philosophical Papers*, 2 vols. (Cambridge, U.K., 1985); and Richard Wollheim, *The Thread of Life* (Cambridge, Mass., 1984).

18. On the relation between the Edwardsean notion of the will and Calvinist religious practice, see the powerful argument in Murray G. Murphey, "The

Psychodynamics of Puritan Conversion," *American Quarterly, 31* (1979): 144–45, to which I am indebted for both the idea and the language to express it.

19. Norman Fiering, "Benjamin Franklin and the Way to Virtue," *American Quarterly, 30* (1978): 217.

20. Breitwieser, *Mather and Franklin*, pp. 178–79; Seavey, *Becoming Benjamin Franklin*, p. 58.

21. See Pettit, "Life of David Brainerd," *passim*. I am indebted to David Hall for this illustration.

22. Because *behaviorism* is a twentieth-century term, I do not think it is a designation for the Edwardsean saint. It is nonetheless true that B. F. Skinner saw in JE's determinism a precursor to his own ideas—and not without good reason. See Skinner's autobiography in *A History of Psychology in Autobiography*, ed. E. G. Boring and Gardner Lindzey (New York, 1967), 5: 387–413; *idem, A Matter of Consequences: Part Three of an Autobiography* (New York, 1983), pp. 402–3; and Daniel B. Shea, Jr., "B. F. Skinner: The Puritan Within," *Virginia Quarterly Review, 50* (1974): 416–37.

23. See Bernard Bailyn, *The Peopling of British North America: An Introduction* (New York, 1986); David Hackett Fischer, *Albion's Seed: Four British Folkways in America* (New York, 1989); and Jack P. Greene, *Pursuits of Happiness: The Social Developments of Early Modern British Colonies and the Formation of American Culture* (Chapel Hill, N.C., 1988).

24. See Jon Butler, *Awash in a Sea of Faith: Christianizing the American People* (Cambridge, Mass., 1990); David D. Hall, *Worlds of Wonder, Days of Judgment: Popular Religious Belief in Early New England* (New York, 1989); Nathan O. Hatch, *The Democratization of American Christianity* (New Haven, 1989); Harry S. Stout, *The New England Soul: Preaching and Religious Culture in Colonial New England* (New York, 1986).

25. B. F. Skinner, *Beyond Freedom and Dignity* (New York, 1971).

# 8

## The Laughter of One: Sweetness and Light in Franklin and Edwards

LEONARD I. SWEET

Benjamin Franklin was known to enjoy writing, in the mornings, in his bedroom, in the nude. Jonathan Edwards, who was known to strip his opponents bare intellectually, did some of his best writing in the woods, even while on horseback, returning to town with pieces of white paper pinned to his jacket looking less the august, dignified figure of the Puritan pastor than a misbegotten mess caught in a snowstorm. The two masterminds and "archsymbols"[1] of the eighteenth century were very different carriers of the comic touch.

Inevitably one contrasts these New World prodigies, Edwards and Franklin. By the birth of the "exemplary" Puritan (Edwards) and the archetypal Yankee (Franklin),[2] Puritan communal culture had essentially given way to Yankee individualistic society. Born in the same decade, in the same province, this son of a clergyman never met this son dedicated to be a clergyman. The closest they came was in shared sources, subjects, even sites. The Shippen House in Philadelphia, the home where the beautiful wife of the man known for barbecuing sinners over the coal pits of hell died, is also the home where Franklin introduced his battery-operated spit, America's first rotisserie. The closest the house of Franklin ever came to merging with the house of Edwards was in 1822, when one of the greatest nineteenth-century theological defenders of

Jonathan Edwards, the Reformed theologian Charles Hodge, married the great-great-granddaughter of Benjamin Franklin.

Edwards preached and wrote from 1727 to 1758; Franklin published *Poor Richard* from 1732 to 1757. Both Franklin and Edwards wrote essays on lightning and earthquakes that were strikingly similar, even word for word.[3] Both wrote treatments on the freedom of the will and the nature of virtue. Moral philosophy consumed both their minds, and each was powerfully influenced by Scottish thought.[4] Both flirted briefly with the fantasy of spending the closing years of their life in Scotland.[5] Both were literary stylists and English prose artists who pioneered a uniquely American form of literature.[6] Both testified to the Enlightenment power of rationality and orderly experiment to shape daily life. In their lifelong love of proverbs and respective course outlines for systematically cultivating virtue, both symbolized the modern era's replacement of community formation by "good sense" principles and "rules-of-life" maxims in the building of individual character.[7] Edwards composed seventy such precepts between 1722 and 1723; typically Franklin listed only thirteen virtues. Those maxims governed their lives and goaded them in the everyday ethics of industry, thrift, prudence, "common sense," and duty.

Both had scientific minds and interests, although Edwards was more original, Franklin more derivative; Edwards more a discoverer, Franklin more a colonizer. Both possessed a sharp sense of the absurd. Both proved martyrs to the "new science": each knew the irony of making "scientific" decisions—Franklin when he lost his son to smallpox after deciding not to risk inoculating him against the disease, and Edwards when he decided to get inoculated, and died of the vaccine. Both produced what each called "inventions": Edwards of a spiritual, Franklin of a technological sort.[8] Both were important influences on the history of American hymnody: Franklin for bringing out the first American edition of Isaac Watts's psalms in 1724 (a book that sat unsold on his shelves until Whitefield's use of Watts during his trip through the colonies in 1740), and Edwards for getting his Northampton church to adopt the radical Watts in 1742. Both wrote about passion: Edwards when he struggled to say what he meant by love to God, ending up comparing it to the love of a woman (one's wife); and Franklin when he struggled with what a young man should do if he could not control his passion, ending up counseling lovemaking to an older woman (one's mistress). Both created classics in their genres: Edwards the best-known and least-read sermon in American history—*Sinners in the Hands of an Angry God*; Franklin one of the best-known and least-read characters in American history—*Poor Richard*.

Franklin and Edwards may "share the eighteenth century between them,"[9] but they have embodied for historians the contrary tendencies of their age: either the "two halves" of the split American or "back-to-back" figures, one looking into the past, the other standing with face to the future.[10] Carl Van Doren stated the first view succinctly: Franklin and Edwards were "protagonists and symbols of the hostile movements which strove for the mastery of their age."[11] Was it the piety of Puritan Boston or the moralism of Yankee Philadelphia that molded most the American character? Franklin vied with Edwards, in Perry Miller's mind, for the distinction of which one "comes more directly and revealingly from the heart of New England culture."[12] While "Franklin snatched from heaven its electric fire," Eugene Lawrence observed, "Edwards pierced the skies to an eternal realm."[13] Vernon Louis Parrington classified Edwards as an "anachronism in a world that bred Ben Franklin."[14] In short, Franklin has come out on top as the architect of the American spirit. It is through the Franklin screen that generations of Americans have come to see Edwards, just as it was through the Franklin press that many eighteenth-century Americans came to read Edwards.[15]

Nowhere has the contrast been so severe as in the picture of a sour-spirited, ill-tempered, socially-inept Edwards versus the loose-tongued, nattily debonair, wittily effervescent Franklin. The only place one expects to find humor in Puritan New England, it is popularly thought, is on the stony graves of its rockbound coast. Even then, as Don Marquis observed, that "stern and/rockbound coast felt like an amateur/when it saw how grim the puritans that/landed on it were."[16] Glib Franklin, on the other hand, is said to have been prevented by the Continental Congress from writing the Declaration of Independence for fear he might smuggle a joke into the middle of it.

No danger of that from hard-driving, morbid Edwards, the stories go, endlessly. Two must suffice. One evening on the way home from Hartford, Mark Twain nodded approvingly through two-thirds of *Freedom of the Will*, confessing that "up to that point he could have written chapters III and IV of my suppressed 'Gospel'." Suddenly Edwards' "resplendent intellect" went "mad," Twain exclaimed, as he "wallowed and reeked" with Edwards until midnight "in his insane debauch." Twain awoke the next morning "with a strange and haunting sensation of having been on a three days' tear with a drunken lunatic. . . . By God I was ashamed to be in such company."[17] The reaction of Lyman Beecher's new bride to his attempt to read to her Edwards's sermon *Sinners in the Hands of an Angry God*—she jumped up with flushed cheeks and exclaimed, "Dr. Beecher, I shall not listen to another word of that slander on my Heavenly Father" and bolted out of the room—has been all too common in the vast literature of the past two hundred years.[18]

Benjamin Peirce writes that when Edwards spoke of God, it seemed "as if the devil must have been at his ear."[19] In a tortuous set of images Allan Pitkanen likens Edwards to a "dark and gloomy star in humanity's crazy-quilt."[20] Charles Angoff calls him a "pathetic, befuddled, sickly, angry, Puritan" who was "the most bitter hater of man the American pulpit ever had."[21] Few have been as condemnatory as George Godwin, who essentially calls Edwards every name in the dictionary of behavioral disorders: a sadistic, self-tortured, "morbid introvert," "half-insane," emotionally defective "psychopath" and spiritual quack whose forced solitude prevented him from doing more harm than he did.[22] Modern scholars have other ways of getting even. One editor of *The Works of Jonathan Edwards* rightly removes from the Edwards canon "The Soul," but wrongly because it is "almost profane in intellectual fun" instead of "unremittingly sober."[23]

In recent years scholars have been chipping away at the marblized image of Edwards and the enameled image of Franklin. But not enough. Impenetrably humorless, Edwards is still too often portrayed as a clenched-teeth apostle of spitfire sermons, skewered sinners, a spine-chilling God, and a theocratic culture. Impenetrably glib, Franklin is still too often portrayed as an apostle of paper sacks, money bags, kite strings, and enterprise culture. The image of an Edwards incapable of writing a humorous sentence, and a Franklin incapable of writing a serious sentence, as Harry S. Stout aptly summarizes the prevailing historiography, renders it as difficult to locate and discuss humor in one as in the other. When everything one writes is overlaid in levity, nothing is. And vice versa. Rollicking good humor is the last thing one expects to find in Jonathan Edwards, and lockjawed solemnity is the last thing one expects to find in Benjamin Franklin. For us to imagine either an Edwards for whom ultimate reality was sweetness and light, or a Franklin for whom ultimate reality was disillusionment and darkness, requires mental effort of considerable proportions. Edwards's favorite topic is supposed to be divine sovereignty and human damnation. Franklin's favorite topic is supposed to be bourgeois morality and self-made men.

In the ranks of people and ideas that time has been unkind to, Edwards rates high.[24] Ever since the Latin inscription on his Princeton gravestone spoke of him as second to no mortal, Edwards has been written about in such a way that he seems either not to belong to a world of reality, or to be more in his element in hell's torment than in heaven's delights. That both are gross distortions is evident to anyone who has ever looked at the 1740 Joseph Badger portrait hanging at Jonathan Edwards College. The picture of a decidedly nongloomy, nonglowering, markedly bright-eyed Edwards, almost puckering a smile, seems to vindicate his own belief that the redeemed are "much happier" than the wicked.[25] Indeed, the publication of every new volume in Yale's critical edition of Edwards's works makes as imperative a transformed image of America's greatest theologian as it does a deeper insight into his mind and ministry. In the same way the most violent anti-Franklin attack on record reveals D. H. Lawrence's lack of a sense of humor more than Franklin's bad humor,[26] so our inability to see comic sensibilities in Edwards says more about us than it does about him.

## I

The first part of our problem is that Edwards is too smart, too subtle, and too demanding for us—"too large for ordinary measuring rods."[27]

This person, who makes us learn three handwritings to read him, could be almost as much of a mask-wearer as Franklin.[28] Edwards himself expressed frustration over the inability of people to read him correctly at the height of the controversy with his congregation. He unwound to his friend Joseph Bellamy: "let me do or say what I will, my words & actions are represented in dark colours."[29] Alas, they still are.

In one of the most sensitive comparisons of Franklin and Edwards ever to be published, John F. Lynen notes how "Edwards' gloom is created by the art of chiaroscuro. The whole purpose is to define the light."[30] To see Edwards in this way is to reframe our understanding of his bouts with depression and the severity of self-discipline imposed on his physical and emotional life. In his diary (1722–24) Edwards admitted that he sometimes became "overwhelmed with melancholy."[31] In the most famous thing Edwards wrote, a published letter (dated November 6, 1736) to his friend Benjamin Colman of Boston, Edwards reported that "there is nothing that the Devil seems to make so great a handle of, as a melancholy humor."[32] Sarah would sing to bring her slope-shouldered husband out of his "humors," as he called them.[33] Although he was under a personal mandate not to engage in needless bantering and "small talk," he struggled against being an awkward conversationalist since he knew he needed communication to combat his tendency toward depression. Edwards fought depression all his life, adjusting his diet and daily regimen to minimize its visitations. Significantly, in his *Thoughts* on the revival of 1740–42, Edwards exempted "one case, wherein the truth ought to be withheld from sinners in distress of conscience"—melancholy.[34] In his *Life of David Brainerd*, Edwards again lifted up "one thing" that was an imperfection in David Brainerd's spiritual life: his "natural temper was so prone to melancholy."[35]

Edwards used the harum-scarum parts of his life to bring faith into a new focus, an Enlightenment focus, that through light-and-sight imagery he sharpened and illuminated what was becoming religion's blurred impressions and edges. Norman Pettit has brilliantly demonstrated, for example, that by scissors-and-pasting Brainerd's *Journal* of "joyless determination," Edwards created a visual commentary of the joyful, loving journey of faith that lay between Arminianism and antinomianism.[36] Edwards twitted those "who think that all serious strict religion is a melancholy thing, and that what is called Christian experience, is little else besides melancholy vapors disturbing the brain, and exciting enthusiastical imaginations."[37] Far from someone without an emotional side of life, as he has sometimes been portrayed,[38] Edwards confessed to being a deeply emotional person himself, although he did resolve to suppress any emotional expression, whether pleasure or pain, "joy or sorrow, but what helps Religion."[39] He wanted his life to give off an air of "love, cheerfulness, and benignity.[40] In his last letter before his death, Edwards asked his daughter Lucy to "give my kindest love to my dear wife," and admonish her to "submit cheerfully to the will of GOD."[41] Even death's darkness was used to bathe beauty on the light that never fades, the flame that never dies.

The weeping laughter tradition of Melville and Twain had its obverse side in Edwards. Joy so flooded his soul under the influence of White-field's wonderful voice that he sat weeping through the entire sermon.[42] Edwards wept his way through "dear David's [Brainerd's] papers," touched by the depth of his faith and devotion to God. Indeed, Edwards wept with joy from the experience of knowing God throughout his life— for example, on a Saturday night in 1739 when he found himself "break-ing forth into a kind of loud weeping" from the joys of serving God.[43] The importance of the experience of joy to Edwards is a recurring theme throughout Edwards's writings. It was the first thing he found attrac-tive in Sarah: her joyful faith. "Her religion had nothing gloomy or forbidding in its character," Sereno Dwight wrote. "Unusual as it was in degree, it was eminently the religion of joy."[44] Green was God's favorite color, and the principal color of the rainbow, Edwards suggested, because green symbolizes joy and gladness.[45] Dullness and joylessness were some of Edwards's most despised emotions, for they signified "per-fect indifference" to God.

"The sweetest joys and delights I have experienced, have not been those that have arisen from a hope of my own good estate; but in a direct view of the glorious things of the gospel."[46] The weeping of laughter, the crying for joy, represented faith's oxymoronic new range of experi-ences available to the believer, a state that Edwards called a "sweet con-junction" of feelings: "It was a sweet, and gentle, and holy majesty; and also a majestic meekness; an awful sweetness; a high, and great, and holy gentleness."[47] That famous Edwards ride into the woods in 1737, which led to his being "swallowed up" in God and for "about an hour . . . kept me . . . in a flood of tears, and weeping aloud,"[48] is but the most famous of many incidents of Edwards's passionate, sensitive temperament refusing to let experiences of the cloud of witnesses become a cloud of words.

Not surprisingly for someone whose understanding of holiness saw "nothing in it but what is sweet and ravishingly lovely,"[49] Edwards could enjoy good food, good wine (his beer mug still exists), good company, and good conversation, especially when it was on his home turf. The King Street parsonage was filled with happy sounds and sights: children chasing and teasing one another, lots of flowers and sunshine, pets galore (e.g., a mocking bird, a cat, which Edwards liked to stroke in his lap after supper, etc.), lengthy discussions punctuated by laughs and inter-rupted by crying children. In fact, Edwards's emotional expressions to his wife and family stand in marked contrast to Franklin's stiffness even to the point of insensitivity, at home. There is no evidence to suggest that Edwards appeared to his lively daughters as merely a grim stuffed shirt or a wet blanket on their gaiety. The second daughter, Esther, called the Edwards household "a singing family . . . our home is more like an aviary than the dwelling of a Colonial parson."[50] A solicitous father, Edwards sometimes wrote the letters his wife owed their children. Most of the children in later years paid tribute in one form or another to his tender and loving parenting of them.[51] If anything, Edwards was criticized by his community for lavishing too much affection and money on his family (jewelry for his wife, playthings for his children) at the expense of his congregation.[52]

A constant stream of visitors inundated the manse, some staying overnight, some staying months at a time, turning it into more a spiritual retreat center than an private home. Sarah kept the latch string out; Edwards, a heavy smoker himself, kept pipes ready for his guests who smoked. In a letter to the precinct asking for a "clear salary understanding," one that would come to terms with the pastor's hidden income sources, Edwards spoke without complaining of "the increase of my families acquaintances, whereby my house will probably become still more a place of resort, as it has been more and more for many years past."[53] One such guest was the revivalist George Whitefield, who found such spiritual refreshment and inspiration in their home that he resolved to resume praying himself for a wife: "A sweeter couple I have not yet seen."[54] Edwards humorously expressed his deep love for his wife, Sarah, and his dependence on her, in a marvelously funny note he wrote to Sarah when she was away helping out a family in distress while her absence was putting her own family into even greater distress: "We have been without you almost as long as we know how to be; but yet we are willing you should obey the Calls of Providence . . ."[55]

## II

The second part of our problem is our cramped understanding of the comic mode. Humor need not always issue in riotous laughter. Sigmund Freud's treatise on "Laughter" is humorous, not because it is funny but because it is arguably the most dull and dismal of all his works. Indeed, much of the humor in life is not even amusing. To identify all humor with laughing matter—jokes, raillery, pranks, invective, puns, mockery, burlesque, and bawdiness—is to let Franklin's almanac art set the agenda for what is humorous and what is not.

The highly competitive almanac business in colonial America may provide one of the best sources of early American middle-class wit and humor, an emerging literate audience almost unique to the northern and middle colonies of America. Franklin may have been our first truly great American humorist, and surely America's greatest humorist before Mark Twain. But the budding of American humor in New England included more than a highly derivative folk humor carried in from the old country to a new mass culture, street pop and pub humor which manifested itself in colonial newspapers and almanacs. American humor also embodies a literary tradition involving work in a finer grain and of a higher hue.[56]

Edwards's sense of humor was averse to being measured in decibels. This is not to suggest that Edwards did not laugh. Edwards's Resolution 38 made it a matter of principal "never to speak any Thing that is Ridiculous, or Matter of laughter on the Lord's Day."[57] Given Resolution 38, it must have been embarrassingly ironic for Edwards to have his children keep being born on a Sunday, when eighteenth-century cultural lore perceived the day one was born as the day of the week one was conceived.[58] The "free and catholik" opponents of Edwards in particular were not known for levity or their sense of irony. Edwards contrasted the "holy motions" of the Spirit in their midst at Northampton with "another way of thinking of things of religion, looking chiefly at morality and a sober life."[59]

But Edwards's humor was more likely to pull at the heartstrings than strike the funnybone. Above all, Edwards believed humor must have moral stature, if not be a moral virtue itself. Edwards clearly distinguished between the vanity and worthlessness of mere "mirth and jollity" and the "ravishing" joy and useful pleasures of what he termed "spiritual mirth" and happiness. The former, whether in the base form of adult carousing or youthful cruising (Edwards called it "frolicking"), was nothing but "the laughter of fools."[60] The one kind of humor Edwards consistently resisted, whether in his literary or his personal life, was that form which turned some people into perpetrators and others into victims. Writing on April 1, 1723, he said "I think it best not to allow myself to laugh at the Faults, Follies and Infirmities of others."[61] Especially and including, he might have added, himself. Edwards associated some laughter with morally degraded attitudes such as scorn, contempt, derision, envy, and pusillanimity. He was temperamentally allergic to, and morally repulsed by, the self-promoting, stagily exorbitant, hate-ensnaring humor of his day.

Stephen J. Stein has demonstrated the degree to which "the organs of speech are central to Edwards's description of the godly person."[62] In his "Blank Bible," Edwards found in Proverbs 10 proof that the "words of a wise man's mouth are like waters that come from a deep fountain or well-spring, and his words flow from his heart like a flowing brook, from a deep fountain that yields a sufficient, constant supply."[63] There is no evidence that Franklin ever relinquished his early guiding principle gleaned from the Latin proverb *Quod est in cordi sobrii, est in ore ebrii* ("That which is in the heart of the inebriated is in the mouth of the drunkard").[64] There is likewise no evidence that during a lifetime of more than fifty sermons on the Book of Proverbs Edwards failed to extend this proverb to the mouths of the sober as well as the drunk. Few people Edwards deemed more repulsive than those who, whenever they opened their mouths, the gates of hell parted and out rushed all manner of vulgarity and banality, not to mention run-of-the-mill, run-at-the-mouth waggery. Laughter can be humorless, especially when it vents feelings of superiority or selects "targets." The most devilish thing in Faust is the laugh of Mephistopheles. In this regard, Edwards has received less credit for a certain "humor" of spirit or person. Knowing melancholy at first hand, Edwards refused to deepen melancholy in others by cruel jesting and mocking.

Edwards's sense of humor was further constrained by his commitment to scholarship and his unclubbable constitution. There is a social dimension to laughter that Ralph Waldo Emerson touched on when he asked himself, "Why has my motley diary no jokes?" and answered his own question: "Because it is a soliloquy, and every man is grave alone." It would be a mistake to see Edwards as grave either alone or with others. Serious, most always; solemn, only sometimes. But Edwards's comic sense is best described as the laughter of one, not the laughter of two. He did not have at his command an extensive social vocabulary of "ahs," "oos," sighs, gasps, ughs, and shrugs, which, along with love and scandal, make the best "sweeteners of tea" (to paraphrase Henry Fielding).

Never losing his professional poise, Edwards never did find a social poise. He never could capitalize on situations that were undeniably humorous. Once, upon his late arrival to a preaching engagement, Edwards stealthily slipped his slender 6-foot frame into the back of the pulpit during the opening prayer. Thinking their guest had not yet arrived, the worthy leader, a Reverend Moody, launched into a fustian, fulsome panegyric to Edwards's virtues and gifts, only to turn and come face to face with the non-publically sainted preacher when he closed his prayer. Chagrined that Edwards's actual presence now undercut the majesty of the moment, Moody quickly brought Edwards back down to mere mortal status by proclaiming from his pulpit, "I didn't intend to flatter you to your face; but there's one thing I'll tell you: They say your wife is going to heaven, by a shorter road than yourself." Overcome by social embarrassment, Edwards was utterly incapable in this awkward yet comic situation of responding to either Moody's overblown purple prose or his purple-eyed comeback. Bowing, to both Moody and his social ineptness, Edwards simply stepped into the pulpit, read the Psalm, and preached.[65] "He stood in the pulpit with a head unmoved and a still hand, and what he had written he had written," is one description of Edwards's preaching style.[66]

Edwards would have been the first to admit he was not a social lion. His letter to the Trustees of Nassau Hall is almost as burlesque in its self-parody as it is biting in its conclusion.[67] Benjamin Franklin was not the only one who could pen deadpan self-criticisms.

Exposure to folk humor was a prime casualty of Edwards's waywardness around crowds and his withdrawal into the worlds of history, poetry, fiction, and science, as well as philosophy and theology. This "vain world" with "all its bubbles and empty shadows, and vain amusements," would lure one away from seeking the "Divine grace and comfort," Edwards warned his daughter.[68] He aimed ever to be circumspect in speech and conscientious of time. Even with his closest friends, according to his first biographer and most devoted disciple, Samuel Hopkins, Edwards did not lounge "in Scandal, Evil-speaking and Back-biting, or in foolish Jesting, idle chat, and telling Stories."[69] By not loitering where men gathered and talked, Edwards missed the rich tradition of oral tales, both folklore and woodlore, which the menfolk exchanged while strolling around the graveyard after church, on trips to the market, across the country, or on riverboats and by firesides. When judged by the Franklin standards of folksy pose, naughty charm, and lowbrow humor, Edwards could seem the least humorous of men.[70]

If lowbrow humor most often makes one laugh, high humor makes one nod, and sometimes smile. High humor is an aesthetic sensibility characterized by irony, satire, sardonic tones, paradoxes, oxymorons, verbal word play, sportive sentence constructions, rhetorical devices like ironic inversions, parallelisms, exaggerations, epigrams, and parodies, all of which are used to convey deeper meanings, reinforce points, even introduce new thoughts. Humor is seeing the familiar—the tragic, the philosophical, the theological, the sublime—in new ways that bring delight, pleasure, and playfulness. It is this comic aesthetic with which Edwards recruited the reader's and hearer's passion. Surprisingly, there is no mention of humor or laughter in the thirteen virtues Franklin touted incessantly in his quest for moral perfection. It was Edwards, not Franklin, who included a resolution on the role of laughter and humor in his rules of life. Franklin's matchless style expanded the range of American humor and the range of things Americans found humorous. Unlike Edwards, he could move almost effortlessly from crackerbox humor to highbrow humor, one moment writing "Silence Dogood" sketches for newspaper readers, the next moment writing satires like "An Edict by the King of Prussia" and the "Ephemera" for the world's politicians and nobility.[71]

To be sure, this is not how Edwards has been portrayed, even by his contemporaries. The Yale rector Timothy Cutler, who twenty years earlier had written to Jonathan's father congratulating him on such an outstanding son, in a letter to the Bishop of London discrediting the revival at Northampton, described his former student as so absorbed in his studies that "he is very much emaciated, and impair'd in his Health, and it is doubtful to me whether He will attain to the Age of 40. He was Critical, subtle and peculiar, but I think not very solid in Disputation. Always a sober Person, but withal pretty recluse, austere and rigid."[72]

With satirical touches worthy of Gargantua and Gil Blas, Edwards's oldest sister, Esther, refuted materialists who believed that the soul was corporeal.[73] A materialist (or what he termed "gross") definition of the spiritual drew forth Edwards's own astonishingly similar sarcasm and satire. "How large is that thing in the Mind which they call Thought?" he asked in "The Mind."

> Is love square, or round? Is the surface of hatred rough or smooth? Is joy an inch, or a foot in diameter? These are spiritual things. And why should we then form such a ridiculous idea of spirits . . . ?[74]

Alan Heimert has called our attention to the "magnificent sarcasm with which Edwards disposes of 'modern divines' in the *Will* and the *Original Sin*."[75] Edwards could also stoke the Franklin stove of satire.[76]

It is in Franklin's writings that we are told to find "the first well-known and fully expressed American humor of the absurd."[77] Yet Edwards found in the daily drama of humanity plenty of comedy, tragedy, and farce. At the height of his congregation's finagling and fighting, Edwards wrote a tender letter to Joseph Bellamy, which he signed off with the delightful closing: "My Love to your spouse, I am your Brother & near Friend." He traced the times he was undergoing with detachment, speaking wittily of how "There have been abundance of meetings about our affairs since you were here, society meetings, & church meetings, & meetings—of Committees, of Committees of the Parish & Committees of the Church, Conferences, Debates, Reports, & Proposals drawn up, & Replies & Remonstrances." He then went on to state bluntly: "The People have a Resolution to get me out of Town speedily."

One example of Edwards's highly developed sense of the absurd can be found in his farewell sermon to the American Indians at Stockbridge, delivered on January 8, 1758. "We Have No Continuing City" concluded with some personal reflections on his stoning-of-the-prophets experiences at Northampton and his short six-and-a-half-year ministry at Stockbridge. Edwards's personal sense of comic reversal with David Brainerd is here made evident.

Skepticism about a humorless divine personality also reached its peak in Edwards's reflection on the wry comic twist whereby God had sent one of the world's most celebrated theologians to spend his last years ministering in a mountainous, frontier Indian outpost with twelve families of white settlers and 250 native American Housatonnuck families who neither spoke nor understood English.[78] Edwards's premonition of the failure of his Northampton ministry, which Julie Ellison has shown Edwards communicated through the story of Sarah Edwards in *Some Thoughts Concerning the Revival*,[79] did not stop him from intending to spend the remainder of his ministry here. Similarly, Edwards's premonition of the absurdity of dying before putting his ideas into practice at Princeton, much less "stamp his iron heel" on the school (as Oliver Wendell Holmes put it unconscionably),[80] did not stop him from taking the job as President of Princeton.

Edwards could be downright witty. He lambasted the "Appetite of scratching when it itches."[81] He spoke of the devil as being "educated in the best divinity school in the universe, viz., the heaven of heavens."[82] In his farewell sermon at Northampton, he likened those in his congregation who think of themselves as "eminent saints" to "a smoke in God's nose."[83] He lamented having to define the will, which would not have been necessary "had not philosophers, metaphysicians and polemic divines brought the matter into obscurity by the things they have said of it."[84] One gets a flavor of the zest he enjoyed in the exercise of his formidable powers, and his delight in the thoughts rising from the text when placed in the context of his experiences in the town in a wonderful passage from "Notes on the Bible" based on a typology of the Ark as Church.[85]

Throughout the sermons, one finds sharp, humorous expressions, often verging on understatements and exaggerations. Stephen J. Stein has pointed to Edwards's use of biblical texts for "a kind of theological play, for amusement and relaxation."[86] One favorite text was James 2:19: "Thou believest that there is one God; thou dost well: the devils also believe, and tremble." In a scarcely somber tone Edwards described the Devil: "Although the devil be exceedingly crafty and subtle, yet he is one of the greatest fools and blockheads in the world, as the subtlest of wicked men are."[87]

When a certain play of mind manifested itself, Edwards could be a match for Franklin's playfulness. Humor is a matter of proportion and perspective. Edwards often became playful when he found himself struggling to find harmony in the ironies of existence. A humorous irony can be found even in the fearful pronouncement that the "God that holds you over the pit of hell, much as one holds a spider, or some loathsome insect over the fire, abhors you, and is dreadfully provoked." It is the same humorous irony of shouting at one's children to make them quiet.

To image the cruelest irony of all, Edwards used the language of the comedic to question the very Awakening itself. Perhaps "all Northampton religion," he wrote his Scottish confidants, would prove to be "nothing but strange tides of a melancholy and whimsical humor."[88] The irony of the worldwide attention on the awakening in Northampton, Edwards told his congregation, was that "While their mouths have been filled with praises, our mouths have been filled with backbitings." Edwards believed that certain situations justify, even require, a language that would not ordinarily be used. Sermons are places and spaces where names break bones. Even Edwards's best bone-breaking skills, he confessed, failed to stop the people of Northampton from gnawing on bones of contention and then on each other. In an implicit recognition that satire and verbal humor can be more effective in gaining attention and swaying sympathy than more linear literature, Edwards contrasted himself, a person who does not always have to win, with certain people who would do anything not to lose, even stooping to the tactics of the Roman Emperor Nero, whom Edwards humorously describes as wishing "that all the people of Rome had one neck, that he might cut it off at one blow."[89] Edwards's treatise on "The Mind" outlined an approach to how we all function within the limits of our prejudices that seethes of sharpened wit:

> How some churches would laugh at their ceremonies if they were without them. How a man's being rich or in high place gives great weight to his words; how much more weighty a man's sayings are after he becomes a bishop than before.[90]

Franklin, who called the Quaker meetinghouse he entered that first Sunday morning "the first House I was in or slept in, in Philadelphia," was not the only bright-eyed observer of churchly comedy.[91]

If one understands these two words, "sweet" and "sense"—the former incontestably Edwards's favorite word, the latter arguably Edwards's most original idea—one comes close to understanding the essence of Jonathan Edwards. The aesthetic component is close to the heart of Edwards's works. The dual concepts of beauty and sensibility, Roland A. Delattre has demonstrated, unify what is unique about this theologian, who shifted the axial center of faith from divine truth to divine beauty.[92] Much of humor, especially Yankee humor, is based on dissonance. That jack-of-all-genres, Franklin, had an aesthetic that was based on compartmentalization and dissimilarity. Edwards had an aesthetic that was based on harmony and agreement. Faith was a set of affective responses to a world that was fundamentally beautiful, issuing in a deep mystical joy. Not in good Enlightenment fashion, Edwards exhibited a rare holism and organicism that negated mind–body dualisms. For Edwards to accommodate low humor would have depreciated the "laws of union" and undercut his psychosomatic aesthetic.

Edwards's playful descriptions of nature testify to his love of life and his joy in "such a beautiful and lovely world."[93] In a phrase of exquisite poetic sensitivity, Edwards compares what it is like to think of spaceless nothingness as "think[ing] of the same that the sleeping rocks dream of."[94] Constantly Edwards extols the beauties of nature; he delights in the raptures of the gospel; he sees God's beauty and glory in the "blue skie," the "beauteous rainbow," or the buttercup. One of his most famous passages pictures the soul of a Christian as "a little white flower, as we see in the Spring of the Year; low and humble on the Ground, opening its bosom to receive the pleasant Beams of the Sun's Glory."[95] The "most charming of all Edwards's writings," his "Personal Narrative" (c. 1739), a piece that H. Richard Niebuhr called the most moving confession of faith in all religious literature,[96] is filled with raptures of delight in God's sovereignty and poetic ecstasies of nature.

For Edwards the gospel proclaimed the ultimate end of creation: the "happiness of creatures" and "the declarative glory of the Creator." Edwards devoted an entire sermon on God's promise of "positive happiness" to the believer. Another sermon summarized Jesus' chief end in dying: "to make those that should believe in him everlastingly happy in God's love."[97] "Praise," Edwards believed, "is the most joyful work in the world." His sermons are filled with incantations of exultations and rhythms of rejoicings, in much the same way Northampton was described in *A Faithful Narrative* as a town "full of joy" and "gladness," "alive in God's service," and resplendent in "remarkable tokens of God's presence."[98] Jonathan Edwards, Jr., claimed that his father was the first to show that our happiness and God's glory are "only one end, and that they are really one and the same thing."[99] Edwards could even find "happiness" and "delight" in the Fall, for here God displayed God's glory. "When I enjoy this Sweetness, it seems to carry me above the Thoughts of my own safe Estate. It seems, at such Times, a Loss that I cannot bear, to take off my Eye from the glorious, pleasant Object I behold without me, to turn my Eye in upon myself, and my own good Estate."[100] Frustrated by the inadequacy of language to convey what he felt, Edwards found more authentic expression in the medium of music: "it always seem'd natural to me, to sing or chant forth my Meditations; to speak my Thoughts in Soliloquies, and speak a singing voice."[101] Edwards's love of singing was transposed and transported into the key of eternity, where he looked forward to joining in "the glorious melody of heaven."

A life of faith and love, Edwards declared in a 1729 sermon on 1 Peter 1:8, is a "sweet and joyful life." He then went on to predict that many would misjudge the happiness of holiness. "Because you don't see the marks of that kind of mirth that others indulge, you are ready to look upon them as a melancholy and sorrowful kind of persons. But their happiness is such as a stranger intermeddles not with."[102]

For Edwards, humor was less something that brought laughter to others than an aesthetic that brought a faith-filled life to oneself. It was this "sense" of "humor"—Edwards's internal "sense" of "sweetness" and "light"—that enabled him to examine himself as a specimen when he wrote to the Princeton trustees; that enabled him to write so astutely and amusingly about the social and religious ironies of his last eighteen months at Northampton; that enabled him to experience a transcendent joy in the presence of Beauty and Being.

It is time to put to rest the Oliver Wendell Holmes portrait of Edwards's work, which he likened to "the unleavened bread of the Israelite: holy it may be, but heavy it certainly is."[103]

## Notes

1. For "archsymbols," see Perry Miller, *The New England Mind: From Colony to Province* (Cambridge, Mass., 1953), p. 344.

2. JE has sometimes been called "the greatest mind of New England," other times cited with Berkeley and Hume as "the greatest English philosophers of their century," and called by Peter Gay "the last medieval American." BF has sometimes been called "America's Newton" or "America's Voltaire," sometimes "the father of American philosophy" or "the first American," other times "the typical American" of "the venerable impersonation of democracy." David Levin, in his "Introduction" to *Jonathan Edwards: A Profile* (New York, 1969), pp. 257–59, calls JE the "exemplary Puritan." Gay's analysis of JE is found in *A Loss of Mastery: Puritan Historians in Colonial America* (Berkeley, Calif., 1966), p. 117. Thomas Jefferson is the one who called BF "the father of American philosophy." See *The American Enlightenment: The Shaping of the American Experiment and a Free Society*, ed. Adrienne Koch (New York, 1965), p. 51. Cf. Robert F. Sayre, *The Examined Self: Benjamin Franklin, Henry Adams, Henry James* (Princeton, N.J., 1964), p. 12.

3. This is primarily because both of JE's and BF's essays were derived from the same source: Ephraim Chambers's *Cyclopaedia: or, an Universal Dictionary of Arts and Sciences* . . . (London, 1728); see A. Owen Aldridge, "Benjamin Franklin and Jonathan Edwards on Lightning and Earthquakes," *Isis, 41* (July 1950): 162–64.

4. The Scottish philosophical lawyer Henry Home, Lord Kames, became a friend and correspondent of BF. For the JE and Kames connection, see G. D. Henderson, "Jonathan Edwards and Scotland," *Evangelical Quarterly, 16* (January 1944): 45. For the BF and Kames connection, see Alexander F. T. Woodhouselee, *Memoirs of the Life and Writings of the Honourable Henry Homes of Kames* . . . 3 vols. (Edinburgh, 1807), *1*: 262–71; *2*: 9–11, 16–26, 74–87.

5. See the January 3, 1760, letter BF wrote to Lord Kames in Wood-houselee, *Memoirs of . . . Henry Home of Kames, 1*: 268. For the efforts of JE's Scottish correspondents to bring JE to Scotland when his relationship soured with the Northampton church, see Henderson, "Jonathan Edwards and Scotland," p. 43. Of John Erskine's suggestion that he move to Scotland, see JE's letter to John Erskine, July 5, 1750, in Sereno E. Dwight, *The Life of President Edwards* (New York, 1830), p. 412.

6. See Sayre, *Examined Self*, p. 36.

7. BF advertised the almanacs with promises of "pleasant and witty Verses, Jests and Sayings," and filled the empty and odd spaces of his almanacs with what Richard Saunders called in 1747 "*moral* Sentences, *prudent* Maxims, and *wise* Sayings, many of them *much good Sense* in very *few* Words." See Bruce Ingham Granger, *Benjamin Franklin: An American Man of Letters* (Ithaca, N.Y., 1964), pp. 64, 65.

8. JE referred to his "Diary" as a handbook of "invention." See Dwight, *Life of President Edwards*, p. 77.

9. Van Wyck Brooks, *America's Coming-of-Age* (New York, 1915), p. 10. See also Howard Mumford Jones's contention that "the ethos of Jonathan Edwards and the ethos of Benjamin Franklin are complementary, not opposed," in Jones, *O Strange New World: American Culture—The Formative Years* (New York, 1964), pp. 64, 65.

10. Quentin Anderson, "Practical and Visionary Americans," *The American Scholar, 45* (1975–76): 405; Claire McGlinchee, "Jonathan Edwards and Benjamin Franklin, Antithetical Figures," *Studies on Voltaire and the Eighteenth Century*, ed. Theodore Besterman (Geneva, 1987), p. 814. In *The American Heritage History of the Writers' America* (New York, 1973), p. 50, Marshall B. Davidson contends that "two more disparate personalities could hardly be named."

11. *Benjamin Franklin and Jonathan Edwards: Selections from Their Writings*, ed. Carl Van Doren (New York, 1920), p. ix.

12. Miller, *New England Mind*, p. 344.

13. Eugene Lawrence, *A Primer of American Literature* (New York, 1980), p. 33.

14. Vernon Louis Parrington, *Main Currents in American Thought: An Interpretation of American Literature from the Beginnings to 1920*, 2 vols. (New York, 1927), *1*: 162.

15. A profit-minded BF obliged a public hungry for sermons. Second only to public documents, sermons and religious works (including some JE sermons) were the principal output of BF's press. See Edwin Wolf, *Franklin's Way to Wealth as a Printer* (Philadelphia, 1951), p. 12.

16. Don Marquis, *Archy and Mehitabel* (Garden City, N.Y., 1930), p. 45.

17. Twain to the Reverend J. H. Twichell, February 2, 1902, *Mark Twain's Letters,* ed. Albert Bigelow Paine (New York, 1917), 2: 719–20.

18. Lyman Beecher Stowe, *Saints, Sinners and Beechers* (London, 1935), pp. 44–45.

19. *Sketches and Reminiscences of the Radical Club of Chestnut Street, Boston,* ed. Mrs. John T. Sargent (Boston, 1880), p. 370.

20. Alan Pitkanen, "Jonathan Edwards—Scourger of the Wicked," *Social Studies, 37* (October 1946): 269–71.

21. Charles Angoff, *A Literary History of the American People* (New York, 1931), *1*: 290, 299. In Jonathan Bennett's "The Conscience of Huckleberry Finn," Edwards's moral philosophy is called "worse than Himmler's," *Philosophy, 49* (1974): 188.

22. See George Goodwin, *The Great Revivalists* (Boston, 1950), pp. 113–23.

23. *WJE, 6*: 401.

24. To see how wrong and nasty something as basic as an encyclopedia entry on JE can be, see *The Encyclopaedia Britannica,* 14th ed., *8*: 19–21 (e.g. JE's "12 children"; his "little feeling for poetry or for the beauties of the natural world").

25. As quoted in Stephen J. Stein, "'Little Apples of Gold in Pictures of Silver': The Portrait of Wisdom in Jonathan Edwards's Commentary on the Book of Proverbs," *Church History, 54* (1985): 332.

26. D. H. Lawrence, "Benjamin Franklin," *Studies in Classic American Literature* (New York, 1964), pp. 9–21.

27. These are the words of Egbert Coffin Smyth as he opened his 200th anniversary address ("The Theology of Edwards") on the birth of JE in *Exercises Commemorating the Two Hundredth Anniversary of the Birth of Jonathan Edwards* (Andover, Mass., 1904), p. 75.

28. Often it is enormously difficult to tell whether BF is serious or jesting. See his March 14, 1764, letter to the physician John Fothergill as an example. *PBF, 11*: 101.

29. JE to Joseph Bellamy. See also JE's comments to a colleague, Peter Clark, May 7, 1750, as quoted in Loren Baritz, *City on a Hill: A History of Ideas and Myths in America* (New York, 1964), p. 173.

30. John F. Lynen, *The Design of the Present: Essays on Time and Form in American Literature* (New Haven, 1969), p. 104.

31. The best treatment of this is Gail Thain Parker, "Jonathan Edwards and Melancholy," *New England Quarterly, 41* (June 1968): 193–212.

32. *WJE, 4*: 162.

33. *The Journal of Esther Edwards Burr, 1754–1757,* ed. Carol F. Karlsen and Laurie Crumpacker (New Haven, 1984), February 13, 1741, entry.

34. *WJE, 4*: 392.

35. *WJE, 7*: 91.

36. See "Introduction" to *WJE, 7*: 1–10.

37. *WJE, 7*: 91.

38. See Kate M. Cone, "Jonathan Edwards," *Outlook , 75* (October 30, 1903): 255–66.

39. Quoted in Dwight, *Life of President Edwards,* p. 80. This is JE's Resolution 45, written in January 1723; see *ibid.,* p. 71.

40. JE's Resolution 58, written on May 27 and July 13, 1723, as quoted in Dwight, *Life of President Edwards,* p. 72.

41. As quoted in Samuel Hopkins, *The Life and Character of the Late Reverend Mr. Jonathan Edwards* (Boston, 1765), p. 81.

42. See entries for October 17 and 19, 1740, *George Whitefield's Journals*, ed. Iain Murray (London, 1960).

43. Hopkins, *Life and Character of Edwards*, pp. 36–38.

44. Dwight, *Life of President Edwards*, p. 131.

45. The color green, JE wrote in his "Notes on Scripture," "fitly denotes Life, flourishing prosperity and happiness." See Stephen J. Stein, "Jonathan Edwards and the Rainbow," *New England Quarterly, 47* (September 1974): 444.

46. With none of the self-deprecating quality of BF's humor, JE's could be deeply humble and often harder on himself than anyone else. See, for example, his June 9, 1741, letter to Eleazar Wheelock, later founder and first president of Dartmouth College, in Dwight, *Life of President Edwards*, p. 148.

47. Hopkins, *Life and Character of Edwards*, p. 26; also quoted in Dwight, *Life of President Edwards*, p. 61.

48. Hopkins, *Life and Character of Edwards*, pp. 36–37.

49. JE's initial entry in the "Miscellanies" is as follows: "We bring in strange notions of holiness from our childhood as if it were a melancholy . . . and unpleasant thing, but there is nothing in it but what is sweet and ravishingly lovely." See "Miscellanies" no. a. In his "Personal Narrative," JE defined holiness as "Purity, Brightness, Peacefulness, and Ravishment to the Soul." See Hopkins, *Life and Character of Edwards*, p. 29.

50. *Journal of Esther Edwards Burr*, ed. Carlsen and Crumpacker, February 13, 1741, entry. See also Esther's October 1754 letter to Sarah Prince, whom Edwards and Burr were visiting in Boston: "I Imagine now this Eve Mr. Burr is at your house. *Father* is there and some others. You are set in the Middleroom, *Father* has the *talk*, and Mr. Burr has the *laugh*, Mr. Prince gets room to stick in a word once in a while." For Ola Winslow's answer to the question "did Jonathan Edwards ever unbend from his rigidities?" see Ola Winslow, *Jonathan Edwards, 1703–1758: A Biography* (New York, 1940), p. 128.

51. See the letter from JE to his eldest daughter, Sarah, June 25, 1741, which begins "Your mother has received two letters from you, since you went away." Throughout the letter JE conveys messages to Sarah from her namesake: "Your mother would have you . ."; "She would have you . . ." See Dwight, *Life of President Edwards*, pp. 148–49.

52. See Patricia Tracy, *Jonathan Edwards, Pastor: Religion and Society in Eighteenth-Century Northampton* (New York, 1979), pp. 157–59. An excellent treatment of Edwards's home life and family relations is Kenneth P. Minkema's "Hannah and Her Sisters: Sisterhood, Courtship, and Marriage in the Edwards Family," *The New England Historical and Genealogical Register*, January 1992.

53. JE, "To the inhabitants of the first Precenct in Northampton at their meeting Novem. 8, 1744," The Edwards MSS, Yale University Library.

54. *George Whitefield's Journals*, ed. Murray, October 19, 1740, entry.

55. JE to Sarah Edwards, July 22, 1748, as quoted in Winslow, *Jonathan Edwards*, p. 291.

56. See Daniel Royot, *L'Humour Americain, des Puritains aux Yankees* (Lyon, 1980).

57. JE's Resolution 38, as quoted in Hopkins, *Life and Character of Edwards*, p. 7. The writing of the resolution was recorded matter-of-factly in his "Diary" for December 23, 1722: "Made the 38th Resolution." Hopkins, *Life and Character of Edwards*, p. 10.

58. Six of the Edwards children—Sarah (1728), Jerusha (1730), Esther (1732), Mary (1734), Jonathan (1745), and Pierpont (1750)—were born on the Puritan Sabbath. A seventh child, Eunice (1743), missed being born on Sunday by a half-hour. See Dwight, *Life of President Edwards*, Appendix K, p. 762.

59. JE, Sermon on Matthew 5:14, July 1736, p. 28, transcribed by E. Edwin Burtner, p. 24, Edwards MSS.

60. *WJE, 4*: 146, 147, 152, 183, 585–600, and *7*: 131–58.

61. For JE's diary entry of April 1, 1723, see Hopkins, *Life and Character of Edwards*, p. 14.

62. Stein, "'Like Apples of Gold,'" p. 334.

63. JE quoted in *ibid.*

64. This was the frontispiece to BF's essay on drinking in *The New-England Courant*, no. 58, September 3–10, 1722.

65. Dwight, *Life of President Edwards*, p. 284.

66. Park goes on to say, "But his hearers looked up, and the tears stole down their cheeks, and they shook like aspen-leaves, and on some occasions screamed aloud." See Edwards Amasa Park, "Duties of a Theologian," *American Biblical Repository, 2* (October 1839): 373.

67. Quoted in *ibid.*, p. 372.

68. JE to his daughter Mary Edwards, quoted in Dwight, *Life of President Edwards*, p. 286.

69. Hopkins, *Life and Character of Edwards*, p. 45.

70. I am making a somewhat different point here than Van Wyck Brooks's attempt to portray BF and JE as the "two grand progenitors" of the rift in the American character between highbrow and lowbrow culture that developed in the eighteenth century. See Brooks, *America's Coming-of-Age*, pp. 8–14, 21.

71. James C. Austin, "The Cycle of American Humor," *Papers on English Language and Literature, 1* (Winter 1965): 86.

72. Timothy Cutler to Edmund Gibson, May 28, 1739, as reprinted in Douglas C. Stenerson, "An Anglican Critique of the Early Rise of the Great Awakening in New England: A Letter by Timothy Cutler," *William and Mary Quarterly, 30* (July 1973): 482.

73. *WJE, 6*: 405. For Esther's authorship of "The Soul," see Kenneth P. Minkema, "The Authorship of 'The Soul,'" *Yale University Library Gazette, 65* (October 1990): 27–32.

74. *WJE, 6*: 338.

75. Alan Heimert, "The Yale Edwards: Review Essay," *Early American Literature Newsletter, 20* (Winter 1985–86): 262.

76. E. B. White and Katherine S. White, in *A Subtreasury of American Humor* (New York, 1941), place BF under the heading of "Satire," reprinting portions of his "Three Love Letters" to Madame Helvetius, attractive widow of the famous French philosopher, written while BF was United States Minister to France. See pp. 362–64.

77. See Richard Boyd Hauck's study of American absurd humor entitled *A Cheerful Nihilism: Confidence and "The Absurd" in American Humorous Fiction*

(Bloomington, Ind., 1971), p. 21. Hauck is exactly on target in his contention that "in the Puritan struggle to posit faith can be seen the seeds of the perplexities that delight the American absurdist." Hauck is exactly backward in his contention that "Jonathan Edwards was painfully aware that faith could appear to be absurd, and any moment in which he could escape that awareness was a moment of spiritual joy." Also p. 21.

78. Portions of this sermon were published for the first time by J. E. Rankin, "The Jonathan Edwards Letters: A Supplementary Article," *Independent*, November 28, 1895, p. 1603.

79. Julie Ellison, "The Sociology of 'Holy Indifference': Sarah Edwards's Narrative," *American Literature, 56* (December 1984): 493.

80. See Oliver Wendell Holmes, "Poem for the Two Hundred and Fiftieth Anniversary of the Founding of Harvard College," *The Poetical Works of Oliver Wendell Holmes* (Boston, 1975), p. 283, which includes the lines: "O'er Princeton's sands the far reflections steal,/Where mighty Edwards stamped his iron heel."

81. *WJE, 6*: 372.

82. *The Works of President Edwards*, 4 vols. (New York, 1869), 4: 454–57.

83. *Ibid., 1*: 67.

84. *WJE, 1*: 137.

85. I owe this example to E. Edwin Burtner, an Edwards scholar who helped me see more in Edwards than I ever would have on my own. See *Works of President Edwards* (New York, 1968; reprint of Edinburgh 1847 ed.), *9*: 58.

86. Stein, "Edwards and Rainbow," p. 456.

87. Quoted in Clement Elton Holmes, "Edwards and Northampton," *Zion's Herald*, September 30, 1903, p. 1240.

88. *WJE, 4*: 566.

89. Quoted from JE's manuscript sermon on 2 Sam. 20:19, as published by Perry Miller, "Jonathan Edwards' Sociology of the Great Awakening," *New England Quarterly, 21* (March 1948): 59, 61.

90. *WJE, 6*: 387.

91. See *The Autobiography of Benjamin Franklin* (New York, 1909), p. 27.

92. Roland Andre Delattre, *Beauty and Sensibility in the Thought of Jonathan Edwards* (New Haven, 1968). Unfortunately, Delattre gives short shrift to the "new sense," which JE posited as the basis of regenerate affections.

93. *Images and Shadows of Divine Things*, ed. Perry Miller (New Haven, 1948), p. 137.

94. *WJE, 6*: 206.

95. Hopkins, *Life and Character of Edwards*, pp. 29–30.

96. *Jonathan Edwards: Representative Selections*, ed Clarence H. Faust and Thomas H. Johnson (1935; rev. ed. New York, 1962).

97. See JE's "Sermon on Genesis 28:12," March 1736; "Sermon on Jeremiah 31:3," March 1730, p. 20, as transcribed by E. E. Burtner, Edwards MSS, p. 14.

98. *WJE, 4*: 151. See also Helen Petter Westra's study of the ordination sermons in "Jonathan Edwards on 'Faithful and Successful Ministers,'" *Early American Literature, 23* (1988): 281–90.

99. *The Works of Jonathan Edwards, D.D.*, 2 vols. (Andover, Mass., 1842), *1*: 481.

100. For JE's "delight" in "God's Absolute Sovereignty, and Justice, with respect of Salvation and Damnation," see Hopkins, *Life and Character of Edwards*, p. 35.

101. *Ibid.*, p. 27.

102. From JE, Sermon on 1 Peter 1:8 (1729), Edwards MSS, Yale University Library. I am indebted to Kenneth P. Minkema for pointing out this sermon to me.

103. Oliver Wendell Holmes, "Jonathan Edwards," originally published in *International Review, 9* (July 1880): 1–28; reprinted in *Oliver Wendell Holmes: Representative Selections*, ed. S. I. Hayakawa and Howard Mumford Jones (New York, 1939), p. 401.

# 9

# Women, Love, and Virtue in the Thought of Edwards and Franklin

## RUTH H. BLOCH

As major American intellectuals in the midst of the transition from Puritanism to the new Protestant middle-class morality of the late eighteenth and early nineteenth centuries, Jonathan Edwards and Benjamin Franklin stood at an important juncture in the development of ideas about women and marital love. Although neither of them wrote extensively about relationships between men and women, their often implicit ideas reveal difficulties they had reconciling traditional Puritan with newer points of view. Their shared preoccupation with human morality, as well as their personal relationships with women, unavoidably raised basic questions about the role of human attachment in the generation of virtue. Their often internally contradictory answers to these questions at once resisted and encouraged broader changes in the American cultural understanding of women and love.

The Puritans before them, as many historians have shown, accorded marriage fundamental social value as the core of the "little commonwealth" of the family. Regarded as the basic unit of society, familial relationships served as the primary locus of religious education and the enforcement of the moral code. Love between men and women, defined largely in terms of duty, was conceived as a consequence rather than a precondition of marriage. Wives were deemed valuable as both economic and spiritual "helpmates," and traditional criticism of women as danger-ously sexual and prone to sinful temptation was gradually giving way to a positive image of female piety and domestic devotion. Love of God, which was always, of course, to supersede conjugal love, was in the late seventeenth century increasingly symbolized in terms of marital bonds.[1]

During the eighteenth century, this earlier positive conception of women and marriage was transformed into a newly sentimental under-standing of marital love. No longer stressing the tension between divine and human love, moral commentators increasingly viewed virtue as based in sympathetic connections between human beings. Influential British moral philosophers such as the Earl of Shaftesbury, Francis Hutcheson, and their popularizers rooted virtue in the emotions and posited the existence of an innate moral sense. A growing emphasis on the redemp-tive qualities of human love, including romantic love between men and women, as something distinct from sexual attraction, pervaded both religious and secular literature. Writings on courtship and marriage com-monly attributed especially keen moral sensibilities to women, who as wives and mothers promised to cultivate benevolent emotions in men. According to this increasingly gendered ideal of virtue, feminine intui-tion and empathy balanced masculine industriousness and self-reliance. Whereas the earlier Puritans had typically characterized good wives as dependable assistants to men, late-eighteenth-century domestic moral-ists highlighted gender differences and the psychological interdependence of husbands and wives.[2]

On first impression, neither Edwards nor Franklin seems to have contributed to the development of this sentimental conception of women and human love. Neither was particularly concerned with the family as a social institution. Neither regarded virtue as either produced or real-ized in human relationships. Whatever their differences, the fundamen-tal perspectives of both on the sources of human morality remained essen-tially individualistic. Virtue was never for either of them the result of emotional involvement with other people. It was instead a quality inter-nal to the individual—for Edwards the product of the gracious awaken-ing of one's spiritual sense, and for Franklin the disciplined quest for worldly happiness. Each in his own way assumed benevolent social rela-tionships to be a necessary outcome of virtue, but neither regarded marriage or the family as distinctive or especially valuable arenas for the expression of virtue.

Both Edwards and Franklin found relations between men and women more problematic, however, than the ostensible clarity of these positions suggests. While biographers have, of course, paid attention to each of their relationships with women, they have made little effort to relate their personal attitudes and experiences to the general framework of their thought.[3] The dominant tendency of both men was to disregard or to trivialize the issues of gender difference and domestic attachments. Yet they each employed gender imagery and periodically sought to define the moral status of marriage. Inasmuch as their thinking did touch on these issues, they both played unwitting but significant parts in constructing the sentimental outlook toward women and marriage that was emerging in the middle of the eighteenth century. Their sporadic and often inconsistent comments about these matters also reveal underlying tensions in their moral theories. These tensions point to the intrusion of their complex personal relationships and deep-seated cultural assumptions about women into the seemingly gender-neutral structure of their thought.

To my knowledge, Edwards left no sustained discussion of his views on women or on love between the sexes. What documentation exists consists of several pieces of indirect evidence: his philosophical speculations about the relationship of the so-called natural affections and instincts to true virtue; his use of examples of women and sexual transgressions in his evangelical writings and ministry; and a few moving expressions of his love for his wife, Sarah. Taken together and set against the backdrop of major events in his life and the general development of his thought, these scattered bits and pieces fall into a discernable pattern.

Edwards was essentially of two minds about the moral status of love between women and men. He held, on the one hand, that love between human beings could be spiritual and, on the other, that such love was fundmentally selfish and instinctual. At times he elevated love above sex and self-interest, at other times he reduced it to them. Similarly torn between an idealization of female spirituality and an abhorrence of female seductiveness, he vacillated in his religious use of feminine symbolism. His overt position was always, of course, to maintain the genderless and transcendent quality of grace. Toward the end of his life, partly in response to pivotal experiences in his own marriage and ministry, this insistence finally drove him to assume a more absolute position equating love between the sexes with sinful self-love. This position was never, however, entirely consistent, and, despite all his efforts to differentiate love of God from human love, an ambiguous and suggestive connection remained between them.

No concept was as fundamental to Edwards's thought as love. The "first and chief" affection propelling the will, love caused desire, hope, joy, and gratitude; the negative affections of hatred, fear, and anger resulted from the absence of love.[4] Love was, he wrote in his "Notes on the Bible," "the sum of all saving virtue."[5] The most holy affection, love of God, was for him the essence of religious experience, the source of beauty, and the basis of virtue. The all-inclusive object of this spiritual love, which Edwards termed "being in general," of course rendered it different in kind from the mundane and unregenerate love of fellow human beings. Indeed, as Norman Fiering has argued, one of Edwards's major intellectual projects was to distinguish himself from the Scottish sentimentalists by denying the moral sufficiency of mere natural affections.

Yet, despite these clear intentions, problems of definition remained. On the one hand, Edwards consistently maintained that love of other human beings—whether of the opposite sex, one's children, neighbors, or humanity generally—arose from self-love rather than from true benevolence. Only love of God, which he variously called spiritual love or Christian love, was essentially selfless. On the other hand, he wavered considerably in his assessment of the morality of self-love, especially when it involved love of other people.[6] Until the early 1740s he often wrote eloquently in defense of the value of love between human beings, even allowing for an intermixture of divine and human love. Around the time of his engagement to Sarah he maintained that love between the sexes was the same "inclination" as Christ felt toward his spouse, the church. Far from hindering one's attraction to the opposite sex, "love of God only refines and purifies it."[7] Although love between human beings remained for him fundamentally an expression of self-love, it was not, he reasoned in 1732, the "simple" self-love that delights only in one's own exclusive good. Instead, the "compounded" self-love that delights in the good of another "is not entirely distinct from love of God, but enters into its nature."[8] In a 1738 sermon entitled *The Spirit of Charity the Opposite of a Selfish Spirit*, he similarly argued that the personal happiness derived from seeking the good of others "is not selfishness, because it is not a confined self-love."[9] "The self which he loves is, as it were, enlarged and multiplied, so that in those same acts wherein he loves himself he loves others. And this is the Christian spirit . . . divine love or Christian charity."[10] Condemning the wickedness of the heathen, who lacked natural affection, he strenuously objected to the "notion that no other love ought to be allowed but spiritual love, and that all other love is to be abolished as carnal, . . . and that therefore love should go out to one another only in that proportion in which the image of God is seen in them."[11] To the contrary, he advocated love on the natural basis of family ties, even at one point claiming "the nearer the relation, the greater is the obligation to love."[12]

Edwards's dual perspective on human love as distinct from, and yet infused by, the love of God, shifted significantly sometime prior to 1755, when he published *True Virtue*. Earlier he had simply insisted that love of other people be "well-regulated" or kept "under the government of the love of God."[13] In *True Virtue*, however, he emphasized a direct antagonism between natural and religious affections. Love of other people, as he now put it, "is contrary to the tendency of true virtue" and "will set a person against general existence, and make him an enemy to it."[14] The only virtuous love was directly dependent on love of God.[15] For the regenerate, love of other human beings varied in proportion not to the nearness of their familial relationship but to the degree of their holiness. "When anyone under the influence of general benevolence sees another being possessed of the like general benevolence, this attaches his heart to him, and draws forth greater love to him."[16] Mere natural, particular love for one's children or for one's husband or wife Edwards classified as narrow and instinctual self-love, in opposition to "a principle of general benevolence."[17]

This shift in focus within his theory of human love can, as Norman Fiering has suggested, be partly explained by Edwards's increased intellectual efforts to refute the naturalistic premises of sentimental philosophy.[18] Whereas his earlier discussion of human love assumed the presence of grace, he now turned to refute the benevolists' argument for a natural, universal principal of love independent of grace. The difference between his earlier and later perspectives reflects these different intellectual premises. Yet there was a personal dimension to Edwards's intellectual development as well, involving two critical experiences of his middle age: the growing disaffection of his parish and the spiritual crisis of his wife Sarah. Patricia Tracy's study of his pastoral life shows Edwards to have been singularly preoccupied with the danger of youthful sexual transgressions, a concern that may well have reflected a painful history of adultery and divorce in his own family.[19] His sermons during the revival of 1734–35 passionately denounced both parental negligence and the "sensual filthiness" and "abominable lasciviousness" of the town's young.[20] The practices of premarital "bundling" and late-night "frolicking" received his particularly strenuous criticism.[21] Indeed, one of his chief objectives as a minister was to purify souls by divesting religious affections of dangerous sexual tendencies: ". . . certainly the mutual embraces and kisses of persons of different sexes, under the notion of Christian love and holy kisses, are utterly to be disallowed and abominated, as having the most direct tendency quickly to turn Christian love into unclean and brutish lust."[22] For this reason, he made it his policy during the revivals that informal religious meetings be sexually segregated. In his account of the 1735 Northampton revivals he focused on the conversion of a young woman, "one of the greatest company-keepers of the town," whose change of heart "seemed to be almost like a flash of lightning, upon the hearts of young people all over the town and upon many others."[23]

Successful in the short run, Edwards's efforts to arouse the consciences of the wayward young men and women of Northampton almost immediately resulted in a wave of youthful conversions. Later on, however, his tenacious efforts to enforce strict moral discipline apparently cost him the support of much of his original youthful constituency. In the "bad books" incident, he infuriated many parishioners by publicly humiliating a group of young men who had surreptitiously examined anatomical drawings of women in a midwife's manual and then knowingly jeered at a female companion.[24] In another case, Edwards tried hard to force the marriage of parents of an illegitimate child, despite the fact that their sexual affair was over and their families had already agreed on a financial settlement.[25] In these episodes Edwards acted in part to defend the reputation of women victimized by irresponsible young men, as well as to serve, as he put it, "the well being of society."[26] But instead of awakening religious consciences, these disciplinary efforts only contributed to the growing resentment of his ministry. Edwards's later categorization of love between men and women as unregenerate instinct can be understood in part as a response to his failed pastoral exertions.

The second development in his personal life that throws light on Edwards's shifting theories about human love was his wife Sarah's religious experience of 1742. In sharp contrast to his response to the sexual impulses of parish youth, his relationship with Sarah Pierrepont had from the beginning an otherworldly quality. His well-known, lyrical description of her, written shortly after they met, sets her in blissful solitary communion with nature and God: "She loves to be alone, walking in the fields and groves, and seems to have someone invisible always conversing with her."[27] However much sexual passion may have permeated their marriage, Edwards left no written record of his attraction to her. His few recorded words about their relationship stress only their attachment through faith. As he poignantly assured her on his deathbed, "the uncommon union that has so long subsisted between us has been of such a nature as I trust is spiritual and therefore will continue for ever."[28] Unlike earlier Puritans who worried lest marital love become obsessive desire and thereby displace the love of God, Edwards seems to have distinguished sharply between examples of illicit sexuality and the spiritual love of his marriage.

His idealization of Sarah's spirituality took extensive written expression only once, in *Some Thoughts Concerning the Present Revival* of 1743. Borrowing from her account of her recent religious crisis, he described it as a model spiritual experience. To a degree, his use of her as an ideal of religious piety was continuous with the promotion of female examples of faith in his previous evangelical writing. In *A Faithful Narrative* of 1736, the most salient illustrations of the glorious work of the spirit were women: the notorious loose young woman whose reformation catalyzed a round of conversions, an "aged woman" who suddenly saw scripture in a new light, the invalid Abigail Hutchinson, and the four-year-old Phoebe Bartlett. In this earlier choice of female examplars, Edwards conformed to a growing tendency among New England ministers to associate women with religious faith.[29] But what distinguished Edwards's depiction of Sarah in 1743 was precisely his refusal to identify her as a woman. His description meticulously omitted all mention of gender. The exemplary character modeled after Sarah became in print simply "the person," rupturing Edwards's earlier pattern of associating piety with femininity.

Heavily editing Sarah's own written account of her experience, Edwards expunged all references to the intimate interpersonal context of her crisis. Her version poignantly reveals her dependency on his approval of her, confessing her special sensitivity to "the esteem and love and kind treatment of my husband."[30] As she tells her story, the sources of her spiritual anxieties of 1742 were twofold, both resulting from her deep attachment to Edwards: she became upset because he reprimanded her for being tactless in a conversation with a relative, and she felt acutely jealous of the visiting minister Samuel Buell, who proved to be a more popular preacher than he.[31] After her conversion experience, she described herself as having reached a greater spiritual distance from Edwards. "If the feelings and conduct of my husband were to be changed from tenderness and affection, to extreme hatred and cruelty, and that every day, I could so rest in God that it would not touch my heart, or diminish my happiness."[32] Edwards's published rendition, to the contrary, omits this entire emotional context, only reporting briefly that the joys of grace removed the "person's" former melancholy and censoriousness.[33]

These deletions go far beyond an understandable effort to maintain anonymity. They reveal Edwards's refusal to accord the experience of human love a role in spiritual regeneration, evidence from his own marriage notwithstanding. Whereas he might well have used the occasion to expound upon the way that mortal attachments are superseded by the love of God, he eliminated the marital drama altogether. Sarah's account commendably affirmed the transcendent quality of divine love, but it also more ambiguously pointed to the religious repercussions of mundane human attachments. Edwards left out the entire interpersonal emotional process and chose to endorse only the spiritual conclusion.

Indeed, Sarah's successful disengagement from Edwards may well have pushed him still further towards disparaging the moral value of natural human love, the position he articulated most clearly in his later treatise on *True Virtue*. The scarce evidence permits only the most tentative interpretation of their emotional relationship, but Sarah's experience of religious transcendence seems to be linked to an unusual degree of tension between them. As Patricia Bonomi has suggested, perhaps 1742 marked a period of crisis in their marriage, which led to their assuming a greater emotional distance. Without expressing overt hostility, Sarah's account, written exclusively for Jonathan, dwells repeatedly on his rival's superior preaching, and in it she claims to have finally "rejoiced" over Buell's success. The spacing of the births of their children also suggests the possibility of increased estrangement. Only in 1742 did they not conceive a child within two years of the previous birth—a pattern Bonomi has found otherwise unbroken during more than twenty years of childbearing.[34] On a personal level, Sarah's religious experience and the possibly related change in their marriage can be placed alongside Edwards's disappointment in the revivals and his increased antagonism to the optimistic philosophical arguments of the British sentimentalists.[35] What he most disliked in the moral philosophers—their confidence in the benign quality of human relationships—his wife's inspiring (and perhaps also painful) emotional detachment from him had already powerfully and intimately challenged.

Corresponding to Edwards's growing pessimism about the value of human love was a revealing shift in his use of gender imagery. His earlier description of subjective religious experience had used the passive, often implicitly feminine and sexual metaphors of taste, sight, physical incorporation, and infantile dependency: "an inward sweetness," "the light of the sun," the soul "swallowed up," "intercourse . . . as a child with a father."[36] While this passively sensual language continued to be used in his later accounts, in the 1746 *Religious Affections* he employed far more aggressive and explicitly male symbolism to convey the intensity of religious affections. "The business of religion is . . . compared to those exercises, wherein men are wont to have their hearts, and strength greatly exercised and engaged; such as running, wrestling or agonizing for a great prize or crown, and fighting with strong enemies that seek our lives, and warring as those that by violence take a city or kingdom."[37] And, whereas his earlier evangelical writings had highlighted female conversion experiences, his *Life of David Brainerd* of 1749 exalted a singularly male model of piety. Bravely forsaking the comforts of family and community to venture into heathen lands, pushing himself to the point of death in the service of God, Brainerd's life of continuous "striving and violence in religion," as Edwards put it, could hardly contrast more with the childishness of Phoebe Bartlett or the sickbed confinement of Abigail Hutchinson.[38]

Despite these notable changes in both his perspective on natural affection and his use of gender symbolism, Edwards never fully resolved the thorny moral and spiritual questions posed by human love. Insisting upon the centrality of love in religious life, he equivocated in his judgments about the value of love between people, particularly in relationships between men and women. For a time he assumed an ambiguous compromise position in which human love occupied a kind of middle ground between love of God and base self-love. During the same period he publicly elevated examples of female piety, while consistently expressing abhorrence of female physical seductiveness and sexual desire. In these ways, Edwards can even be seen as indirectly contributing to the more positive evaluation of romantic love and female morality that was gradually developing in the eighteenth century. Yet, in his insistence on the absolute superiority of divine love, he powerfully resisted these sentimental implications. In the 1740s, in response to a combination of intellectual and personal experiences, he began moving toward the more extreme position taken in *True Virtue* of 1755. Uncompromising in his moral castigation of all forms of human attachment, he finally relegated love between men and women simply to the category of instinct. By instinct he first and primarily meant sexual drive. But even in this passage he equivocated, agreeing with Hutcheson and Hume that the "kind affections between the sexes" arose not only from "sensitive pleasure" but

from "a disposition both to mutual benevolence and mutual compla-
cence." He acknowledged that God implanted such affections not just
to reproduce the race but to provide, more diffusely, for "the comfort
of mankind."[39] The notion that human beings instinctively promote the
comfort of mankind through their love of the opposite sex is not a view
ordinarily associated with Edwards. For all his efforts to deflate the moral
and spiritual status of human love, Edwards still left a small opening for
the sentimental naturalist arguments about marriage that were gaining
currency by the middle of the eighteenth century.

Franklin's relationship to the wider development of middle-class domestic
morality is in many respects more straightforward. According to his
basic moral philosophy, the pursuit of private, this-worldly happiness promoted rather than undermined the larger moral good. As Poor Richard
once expanded on the image of a pebble thrown in a lake, he described
self-love as benignly radiating outward to encompass "Friend, Parent,
Neighbor, . . . all [the] human Race."[40] For Franklin there was no intrinsic conflict between promoting one's own happiness, benevolently promoting the happiness of others, and pleasing God. As he outlined strategies for achieving success, moreover, he frequently designated marriage
as a key to both personal happiness and a beneficial social life. "The good
or ill hap of a good or ill life," the almanac put it, "Is the good or ill
choice of a good or ill wife."[41] Repeatedly, he characterized single men
as "the odd halves of scissors" or as lone volumes "of a set of books."[42]
"A Man without a Wife, is but half a Man."[43]

For Franklin, of course, virtue inhered not in one's inner disposition but in one's outwards acts. Just as Edwards drew from a side of
Puritanism in his emphasis upon the emotional experience of grace,
Franklin enlarged upon the Puritan commitment to vocations. His writing on women and marriage stressed above all the practical affairs of the
domestic economy and the larger social benefits of reproducing the race.
As wives, frugal and hardworking women served as invaluable assistants
to upwardly mobile men. Franklin frequently drew the equation between
good wives and money. "A good Wife and Health," read one of Poor
Richard's typical aphorisms, "Is a Man's best Wealth."[44] Commenting
in a letter to his sister on his nephew Benny's bride, he wrote, "If she
does not *bring* a fortune she will help to *make* one. Industry, frugality,
and prudent economy in a wife, are . . . in their effects a fortune."[45]

As mothers, women possessed perhaps even greater value, for in
Franklin's view fertility was an index to social happiness. Linked to inex-
pensive tastes, a high birthrate such as that found in America, he argued,
stemmed from the affordability of early marriage made possible by frugal women.[46] Deploring the single life of many English acquaintances,
he reported, "The great Complaint is the excessive Expensiveness of
English Wives."[47] Franklin's spirited speech in the personna of the unwed

mother Polly Baker satirically underscores her "natural and useful Actions" in adding citizens to the commonwealth. Far from attacking marriage, she boasts all her Franklinesque qualifications to marry, "having all the Industry, Frugality, Fertility, and Skill in Oeconomy appertaining to a good Wife's Character."[48]

For all Franklin's appreciation of the economic and reproductive aspects of marriage, he made considerably less room for intimate relationships than Edwards. The ultimate goal of personal happiness inhered, in his view, in material success, sound health, and good reputation.[49] He used the term love in a highly diffuse manner. "*Love* and be *loved*," advised an aphorism he included twice in his almanac.[50] In letters home he sent love to his wife, family, and friends with no effort to discriminate among them, once jokingly acknowledging his wish to have "everybody" love him.[51] Benevolence and efforts to make others happy ranked high for him as human virtues, but he always described the recipients of these acts impersonally. His famous discussion of the "art of virtue" altogether dispenses with such traditional interactive virtues as charity, mercy, kindness, and fidelity. The thirteen virtues included on his list were instead all purely individual and instrumental, chosen for their usefulness in the attainment of happiness for the autonomous self.[52]

Franklin's quality of individual detachment permeated not only his moral theory but his attitude toward his own life. The *Autobiography*'s well-known accounts of his own singularly unromantic courtships perhaps best illustrate this point. He indignantly broke off one engagement when he suspected the family of cheating him out of a dowry. His eventual marriage to the penniless Deborah Read, whom he had several years earlier planned to marry but had forgotten about during his trip to England, as he tells it, came only after his painful discovery that he could command no better price on the marriage market.[53] A similarly utilitarian perspective on marriage led him much later to oppose as "a very rash and precipitate step" the engagement of his daughter Sarah to the debt-ridden Richard Bache.[54]

The repeated effort to secure financial position through marriage was consistent with his apparently affectionate but doggedly practical relationship with his wife. His praise of her centered on her helpfulness in his business, her frugal and efficient housekeeping, and her unwavering loyalty. The song he composed about her for a club of male friends, entitled *I Sing My Plain Country Joan*, expressed appreciation of her down-to-earth qualities in an implicit critique of more exalted ideas of romance.[55] However genuine his regard for her, the emotional content of their marriage clearly dwindled to next to nothing through the fifteen years of separation while he was negotiating for America abroad. Their correspondence was mainly about household matters. He professed homesickness, and doubtless meant it, but was at the same time able to lead a largely satisfying life without her. She claimed that the reason she stayed home was her fear of the sea, but one suspects that both he and she prefered that the "plain country Joan" not risk embarrassment by joining him in the polite social circles of England and France.

In the meantime, beginning already prior to his departure, Franklin developed a series of personal relationships with younger people, particularly young women, to whom he freely gave paternalistic advice. Late in life, during his years in France, he especially cultivated the role of fatherly flirt. Even in his most effusive and charming moments, however, "Cher Papa," as he was known among his female admirers, characteristically used humor to keep his emotional distance.[56] An ironic tone even permeates what we know of his ostensible efforts to proposition Madame Brillon and to propose marriage to Madame Helvetius. Madame Helvetius commented to a friend that Franklin "loved people only as long as he saw them."[57]

Yet beneath Franklin's evasive humor and cool utilitarianism vied deeply conflicting conceptions of women. His scattered comments on sexuality, courtship, and marriage presented dichotomous images of women as irrelevant and invaluable, undermining and uplifting. His focus remained, of course, on men, with himself as the primary model. In the fundamentally male quest of virtue and economic success, women played a profoundly ambiguous role. For Franklin, individual self-reliance was an essential value, the key to the attainment of happiness. Yet within the context of his culture women unavoidably represented the opposite qualities of dependency and attachment. Faced with this basic problem, Franklin wavered between praising women as productive assistants and criticizing them as wasteful spendthrifts. In neither capacity could they comfortably fit into a theory extolling the achievements of autonomous males.

Just as Edwards's ideas about human love played themselves out in his portrayal of Sarah Edwards, Franklin's ambivalence about women are perhaps best revealed in his conflicting assessments of Deborah Franklin. True to his public admonitions about the financial value of a well-chosen wife, the dominant image he conveyed of Deborah was that of "a good & faithful Helpmate," hard-working and economical.[58] Toward the end of his life he fondly recalled in a letter to one of his young female correspondents: "Frugality is an enriching virtue; a Virtue I never could acquire in myself; but I was once lucky enough to find it in a Wife, who thereby became a Fortune to me."[59] The main passage about Deborah in the *Autobiography*, illustrating the proverb, "He that would thrive/ Must ask his Wife," similarly counts his good fortune in having a wife "as much dispos'd to Industry & Frugality as myself."[60] Yet immediately following this proud depiction of their mutual parsimony, Franklin relates the famous anecdote about finding his breakfast one day "in a China Bowl with a Spoon of Silver." Presenting this episode as an example of the way "Luxury will enter Families, and make a Progress, in Spite of Principle," he describes his wife as having "no other Excuse or Apology to make but that she thought *her* Husband deserved a Silver Spoon & China Bowl as well as any of his Neighbors."[61] This contrary, critical view of his wife as a frivolous consumer appears most vividly in his private correspondence. His letters from England periodically remind her to be "careful of your Accounts," warning her of his declining income and even raising the specter of poverty.[62] "I know you were not very attentive to Money-matters in your best Days," he chastised her.[63] He gave her a memorandum book and pressed her, unsuccessfully, to keep a close record of her expenses.[64] In the last years of her life, while she suffered from partial paralysis and deteriorating memory, Franklin put her on an inadequate allowance and refused to acknowledge her financial difficulties, even though she was borrowing from friends.

Vacillating between his proud appreciation of Deborah's economic value and his harsh criticism of her excessive expenditures, Franklin seems to have been genuinely unsettled in his basic evaluation of her worth as his wife. This double image of her as both frugal and extravagant expressed Franklin's ambivalence about women generally. Especially in his relatively youthful writings of the 1720s and 1730s, women often appear as vain, lazy, irresponsible, and hopelessly addicted to the latest expensive fashions.[65] His essay on the industrious Anthony Afterwit, driven to despair by his wife's status-seeking and luxurious taste, seems modeled, in part, on his own experience with Deborah's purchase of the china bowl and silver spoon.[66] Repeatedly, in his public and private writings, he juxtaposed the symbols of tea tables and spinning wheels: "Many estates are spent in the getting/Since women for tea forsook spinning and knitting."[67] Often Franklin issued his warning against female acquisitiveness in the context of a comic battle of the sexes. In the opening issues of *Poor Richard's Almanack*, for example, Richard's wife Bridget, whom he regards as "excessive proud," carps at him about their poverty and the necessity of her "spinning in her shift of tow" while he uselessly gazes at stars.[68] In addition to impugning them for their vanity, Franklin frequently caricatured women as malicious gossips, overly talkative, and domineering.[69] He ridiculed the sexual pride of aging, unwanted spinsters who had found too many faults with suitors when young and poked fun at the unfulfilled needs of frustrated widows and old maids.[70]

Taken together, these numerous misogynist pieces depict women as sexually demanding, haughty, and contentious. In keeping with these images, Franklin himself occasionally used the comic mask of a female pseudonymn in order brazenly to publicize controversial opinions and attack adversaries.[71] At one point, following Defoe, the young Franklin even had the forceful widow Silence Dogood argue for better female education on the grounds that female failings were mostly due to ignorance, a position that, however, Franklin never espoused elsewhere.[72] Instead he insisted that the proper antidote to overbearing women was male domination. As Poor Richard put it, "Ill thrives that hapless Family that shows/ A Cock that's silent and a Hen that crows."[73] Objecting in the *Pennsylvania Gazette* to a recent critique of marriage as a form of slavery for women, Franklin responded, "Every Man that is really a Man is Master of his own Family; and it cannot be Bondage to have another submit to one's Government."[74]

Later on, beginning in the 1740s, Franklin increasingly developed a less hostile (if also less humorous) outlook on women and marriage. Whereas in the early issues of *Poor Richard*, only lawyers receive as much ridicule as wives, after 1738, and especially after 1748, the number of verses and aphorisms that comment on women or marriage dramatically declined.[75] The few that are printed were notably less misogynist as well, giving way to practical recommendations to marry and sensible bits of advice about the prudent choice of a spouse.[76] By 1746 even the acrimonious Richard and Bridget had settled into an idyllic, harmonious, and prosperous married life.[77]

Occasionally in this later period Franklin even espoused a more sentimental attitude. One verse extolled women's benign, civilizing influence; another claimed that men were drawn to women not by their bodies but by their "souls."[78] Deploring the destructive influence of sophisticated taste and high fashion, pieces that dispensed marital advice idealized uncorrupted wives for their "native Innocence," being "form'd in Person and in Mind to please."[79] In other writings as well, Franklin increasingly underscored the benign aspects of innate gender differences. "It is the Man and Wife united that make the compleat human Being," he wrote in his famous 1745 letter on the choice of a mistress; "Separate, she wants his Force of Body and Strength of Reason; he, her Softness, Sensibility, and acute Discernment."[80] Women, he variously observed in the later decades of his life, were less rivalrous and more impressionable than men.[81] In a letter to Madame Brillon of 1780 he went so far as to claim to trust feminine intuition more than male intellect, "for women, I believe, have a certain feel, which is more reliable than our reasonings."[82]

In the end, however, for all these lighthearted concessions to a sentimental ideal of women, Franklin remained as much opposed to idealized expressions of romantic love as Edwards. As he wrote characterically in a spoof on hot air balloons in the Parisian press, "an element ten times lighter than inflammable air" can be found "in the promises of lovers and of courtiers and in the sighs of our widowers."[83] The dominant tendency of his thought held that virtue was a quality of autonomous males, an attitude well illustrated by the membership restriction in his proposed United Party of Virtue to "young and single Men only."[84] According to his proverbial expression, "it is hard for an empty Sack to stand upright," virtue hinged on the achievement of economic independence.[85] As dependents, women were at best aides, at worst parasites, in this prototypically masculine quest. The fundamental lack of clarity in Franklin's view of women—the vacillation among images of vain and impulsive consumers, industrious helpmates, and intuitive innocents—suggests the underlying difficulty he had determining the relationship of women to his model of the self-reliant, upwardly mobile man. For Edwards, to the contrary, virtue was a quality of genderless saints in communion with God, extended diffusely to all people as part of "being in general." Both men stopped well short of a sentimental conception of women or of love between human beings. In this, though in sharply contrasting ways, both remained faithful to their common Puritan past.

Yet, in other respects, each of them unwittingly helped set the stage for the transformed gender ideology of the late eighteenth century. In his depiction of female exemplars of piety, Edwards took measured steps in the direction of upholding a female standard of virtue. Even the elderly Franklin did so briefly in his extravagant statements about female moral intuition and judgment. Still more importantly, however, Edwards's insistence upon the centrality of love in religious life, coupled with his ambiguous description of the spiritual and moral status of human attachments, point toward more positive interpretations of marital love. Franklin's most decisive contribution lay instead in the formulation of a new male utilitarian standard of virtue. Although he himself only vaguely and inconsistently endorsed an alternative feminine ideal, he defined the male standard against which the sentimental female one was quick to emerge.

Despite the fact that neither of these figures systematically addressed the issue of gender or romantic love, their sketchy and often contradictory depictions of women and marriage point to their troubled ambivalence as much as their intellectual indifference. To a degree, their difficulties with the subject can be understood biographically as the product of each of their very different relations to women. When considered from a wider historical perspective, however, both the omissions and the inconsistencies point to their transitional position as theorists of human psychology and morality. Edwards's towering achievement consisted in integrating modern moral philosophy with Calvinist pietism, an accommodation that problematized the relationship between religious and natural affections despite his own repeated efforts to draw a sharp distinction between them. Franklin, too, was poised between Puritanism and contemporary secular thought, in his case balancing a traditional commitment to hard work and frugality—norms he applied to men and women both—against a more resolutely masculine and utilitarian endorsement of the value of individual economic success. Romantic love between men and women, I would suggest, symbolized the ambiguous and even threatening element of human interdependence and emotional fusion. While these two intellectuals managed for the most part to avoid this increasingly troublesome issue, it would emerge with full force in the sentimental literature and religious moralizing of the following generation.

*Acknowledgments*: I should like to thank Joyce Appleby, Patricia Bonomi, Daniel Walker Howe, and Thomas Shafer for their helpful readings of an earlier draft of this paper.

## Notes

1. The many works on the Puritan family and women from which this paragraph is drawn include Edmund S. Morgan, *The Puritan Family: Religion and Domestic Relations in Seventeenth-Century New England*, rev. ed. (New York, 1966); Laurel Thatcher Ulrich, *Good Wives: Image and Reality in the Lives of Women in Northern New England, 1650–1750* (New York, 1980); Carol F. Karlsen, *The Devil in the Shape of a Woman: Witchcraft in New England* (New York, 1987); Margaret Masson, "The Typology of the Female as a Model for the Regenerate," *Signs: Journal of Women in Culture and Society, 2* (1976): 304–15; and Gerald F. Moran, "'Sisters' in Christ: Women and the Church in Seventeenth-Century New England," in *Women in American Religion*, ed. Janet Wilson James (Philadelphia, 1980), pp. 47–65.

2. The less extensive literature on this transitional period includes Nancy F. Cott, *The Bonds of Womanhood: Women's 'Sphere' in New England, 1780–1835* (New Haven, 1978); Linda Kerber, *Women of the Republic: Intellect and Ideology in Revolutionary America* (Chapel Hill, N.C., 1980); Mary Beth Norton, *Liberty's Daughters: The Revolutionary Experience of American Women, 1750–1800* (Boston, 1980); and Ruth H. Bloch, "The Gendered Meanings of Virtue in Revolutionary America," *Signs: Journal of Women in Culture and Society, 11* (Fall 1987): 37–58. On Scottish moral philosophy, see Norman Fiering, *Jonathan Edwards's Moral Thought and Its British Context* (Chapel Hill, N.C., 1981); Daniel Walker Howe, "Why the Scottish Enlightenment Was Useful to the Framers of the American Constitution," *Comparative Studies in Society and History, 31* (July 1989): 572–87; and John Dwyer, *Virtuous Discourse: Sensibility and Community in Late Eighteenth-Century Scotland* (Edinburgh, 1987).

3. See especially Elisabeth D. Dodds, *Marriage to a Difficult Man: The 'Uncommon Union' of Jonathan and Sarah Edwards* (Philadelphia, 1971); Claude-Anne Lopez, *Mon Cher Papa: Franklin and the Ladies of Paris* (New Haven, 1966); and Claude-Anne Lopez and Eugenia W. Herbert, *The Private Franklin: The Man and His Family* (New York, 1975).

4. *WJE*, 2: 107–8.

5. *The Works of President Edwards*, ed. Sereno Dwight, 10 vols. (New York, 1830), *9*: 511.

6. See also Fiering, *Edwards's Moral Thought*, pp. 150–199.

7. "Miscellanies," no. 189, as quoted in *WJE, 8*: 617–18, n. 3. Thomas Shafer allerted me to this passage and pointed out that JE probably wrote it in the spring or early summer of 1725, about the time of his engagement.

8. "Miscellanies," no. 530, in *The Philosophy of Jonathan Edwards from His Private Notebooks*, ed. Harvey G. Townsend (Eugene, Ore., 1955), pp. 203–4.

9. *WJE, 8*: 258.

10. *Ibid.*

11. *Ibid.*, 4: 469–70.

12. "Great Care Necessary, Lest We Live in Some Way of Sin" (1734), *Works of President Edwards*, 4 vols., (New York, 1843), *4*: 522.

13. *WJE, 4*: 470. Fiering notes that JE turned his full attention to exposing the deceptions of self-love only in *True Virtue* (though there are earlier foreshadowings in "Miscellanies" nos. 473 and 534 of the earlier 1730s). See Fiering, *Edwards's Moral Thought*, p. 174.

14. *WJE, 8*: 555.

15. *Ibid.*, pp. 558–59.

16. *Ibid.*, p. 546. See also pp. 545, 571. This argument is presaged in *WJE, 2*: 257.

17. *WJE, 8*: 605.

18. Fiering, *Edwards's Moral Thought*, pp. 174, 197.

19. Patricia J. Tracy, *Jonathan Edwards, Pastor: Religion and Society in Eighteenth-Century Northampton* (New York, 1979), pp. 56, 218–19, n. 38.

20. "The Justice of God in the Damnation of Sinners" (1735), *Works of President Edwards, 4*: 233–34. For a long quotation from this sermon, see Tracy, *Jonathan Edwards*, pp. 81–82. See also *WJE, 4*: 146.

21. "Joseph's Great Temptation and Gracious Deliverance," *Works of President Edwards, 4*: 595–96.

22. *WJE, 4*: 468.

23. *Ibid.*, p. 149.

24. Tracy, *Jonathan Edwards*, pp. 160–64; Thomas H. Johnson, "Jonathan Edwards and the 'Young Folks' Bible," *New England Quarterly, 5* (1932): 437–514.

25. Tracy, *Jonathan Edwards*, pp. 164–66; Kathryn Kish Sklar, "Culture Versus Economics: A Case of Fornication in Northampton in the 1740s," *University of Michigan Papers in Women's Studies*, Special Issue, May 1978, pp. 35–56.

26. Sklar, "Culture Versus Economics," p. 45, as quoted from Jonathan Edwards Papers, Folder n.d. 2, item 15, Andover Newton Theological School, Newton Centre, Mass.

27. Sereno E. Dwight, *The Life of President Edwards* (New York, 1830), pp. 114–15.

28. *Ibid.*, p. 578.

29. *WJE, 4*: 158. On earlier feminine religious imagery, see Moran, "'Sisters' in Christ," and Masson, "The Typology of the Female."

30. Dwight, *Life of President Edwards*, p. 172.

31. *Ibid.*, pp. 171–72. For a similar interpretation, see Julie Ellison, "The Sociology of 'Holy Indifference': Sarah Edwards' Narrative," *American Literature, 56* (1984): 479–95.

32. Dwight, *Life of President Edwards*, p. 183.

33. *WJE, 4*: 334–35.

34. Patricia Bonomi, "Comment," unpublished paper, National Conference on Jonathan Edwards and Benjamin Franklin, Yale University, February 24, 1990.

35. Fiering, *Edwards's Moral Thought*, p. 174.

36. Dwight, *Life of President Edwards*, pp. 60–61, 65, 132–33; *WJE, 4*: 194–95, 332.

37. *WJE, 2*: 100.

38. *Ibid., 7*: 500.

39. *Ibid., 8*: 603–5.

40. *PBF, 3*: 5.

41. *Ibid.*, p. 8; also *2*: 9.

42. *Ibid., 15*: 184; *The Works of Benjamin Franklin*, 10 vols. (New York, 1904), *10*: 81; *Autobiography and Other Writings*, ed. Kenneth Silverman (New York, 1986), p. 207.

43. *PBF*, 5: 471; see also 2: 396.

44. *Ibid.*, 3: 62; see also 2: 5, and *Autobiography*, ed. Silverman, p. 88.

45. *PBF*, 7: 216; see also 3: 479–80.

46. *Ibid.*, 4: 227–43.

47. *Ibid.*, 9: 175.

48. *Ibid.*, 3: 120–25.

49. On how BF's definition of happiness reduces to the instrumental satisfaction of natural, physical wants, see Herbert Schneider, *The Puritan Mind* (New York, 1930), p. 251; Flower and Murphey, *History of Philosophy*, 1: 110–11.

50. *PBF*, 6: 324; also 5: 471.

51. Benjamin Franklin, *Dr. Benj. Franklin and the Ladies* (Mt. Vernon, N.Y., 1939), pp. 17–18.

52. *The Autobiography of Benjamin Franklin*, ed. Leonard Labaree *et al.* (New Haven, 1964), pp. 91–92.

53. *Ibid.*, pp. 74–75.

54. *PBF*, 15: 185.

55. *Ibid.*, 2: 353–54.

56. These relationships are described vividly in Lopez, *Mon Cher Papa*.

57. *Ibid.*, pp. 261–62.

58. *Autobiography*, ed. Labaree, p. 76.

59. "To Miss Alexander," Passy, June 24, 1782, in *Dr. Benj. Franklin and the Ladies*, p. 32.

60. *Autobiography*, ed. Labaree, p. 88.

61. *Ibid.*, pp. 88–89.

62. *PBF*, 6: 425, and 14: 193–94.

63. *Ibid.*, 18: 91.

64. *PBF*, 7: 167–68, and 10: 100–01.

65. See, for example, *PBF*, 1: 21–23, 240–43.

66. *Ibid.*, pp. 237–40. Also see Gary E. Baker, "He That Would Thrive Must Ask His Wife: Franklin's Anthony Afterwit Letter," *Pennsylvania Magazine of History and Biography*, 109 (January 1985): 27–41.

67. *PBF*, 1: 315. See also pp. 100 and 239; and *The Private Correspondence of Benjamin Franklin*, 2 vols. (London, 1817), 1: 42.

68. *PBF*, 1: 311. See also 2: 137, 169, 191, 371.

69. For example, *ibid.*, 1: 39–40, 243–48, 316, and 2: 139, 223, 235, 369, 400.

70. *Ibid.*, 1: 37–38; 2: 166–67, 251, 399; 3: 65.

71. Examples are the pseudonyms Silence Dogood, *ibid.*, 1: 8–46; Cecilia Single, pp. 20–43; and Martha Careful and Caelia Shortface, pp. 112–13.

72. *PBF*, 1: 18–21.

73. *Ibid.*, p. 356.

74. *Ibid.*, 2: 22–23.

75. Whereas I counted twenty-two short pieces on women and marriage in the almanac from 1733 through 1738 (3.6 per issue), there were only ten in 1739–44 (1.6 per issue), twelve in 1745–50 (2 per issue), and two in 1751–58 (less than 0.5 per issue).

76. For example, *PBF*, 2: 294; 3: 62; 5: 471.

77. *Ibid.*, 3: 60.

78. *Ibid.*, pp. 65, 66.

79. *Ibid.*, pp. 103, 342.

80. *Ibid.*, pp. 30–31.

81. *Ibid.*, 8: 92.

82. Letter to Mme Brillon, November 29, 1780, as quoted in Lopez, *Mon Cher Papa*, p. 82.

83. Lopez, *Mon Cher Papa*, p. 222.

84. *Autobiography*, ed. Labaree, pp. 103–5.

85. *Ibid.*, p. 106.

# 10

# The Selling of the Self: From Franklin to Barnum

## MICHAEL ZUCKERMAN

Each of them straddled his century like a colossus. Each was born near its beginning—one in 1706, the other in 1810—and each lived almost to its end—one to 1790, the other to 1891. Each of them began in obscurity, each had half a century of celebrity, and each died acclaimed as the representative American of his age.

Benjamin Franklin was the embodiment of the Enlightenment. David Hume declared him "the first philosopher and indeed the first great man of letters for whom we are beholden to America." The Parisians lionized him while he lived among them and lamented him when he died far from them; his fame in France was so extraordinary that the National Assembly proclaimed a period of national mourning when word of his death reached the Continent. Even caustic John Adams conceded enviously that, in Europe, "his reputation was more universal than that of Leibniz or Newton, Frederick or Voltaire, and his character more beloved or esteemed than any or all of them."[1]

Phineas Taylor Barnum was the most celebrated American of the nineteenth century. His own posters modestly hailed him as the "hero about whose name clusters so much of romantic interest and whose brilliant deeds are themes of poetry and prose." Others praised him more effusively. American presidents anointed him the most admired American in the world. Europeans pronounced him the symbol of an era of unprecedented amusements for the masses. Upon his death the

*London Times* grieved his passing and called him "an almost classical figure." The French press proclaimed him "the character of our century": a "great benefactor of humanity," an "incomparable," whose "name is immortal."[2]

Thomas Carlyle called Franklin "the father of all the Yankees." Barnum implicitly acknowledged that paternity, not only patterning his own autobiography unmistakably upon Franklin's but also dedicating it to "the universal Yankee nation, of which I am proud to be one." American copywriters would one day salute Franklin as the "Patron Saint of Advertising." Memorialists marked Barnum's death by crowning him "king of advertising." Balzac celebrated Franklin as the inventor of the lightning rod, the republic, and the hoax. Barnum built his national notoriety on a succession of scams and flimflams long before he launched the circuses by which Americans still know his name.[3]

These convergences were more than merely casual. They were but a very few of the many commonalities, and indeed uncanny coincidences, in the careers and concerns of the two men. Since those commonalities and coincidences spanned almost two full centuries of American history, it would seem plausible to propose that they issued from deep continuities in our character and reveal persisting preoccupations and perplexities in our collective life.

Franklin wrote the most popular and influential American autobiography of our entire history. Barnum wrote the best-selling American autobiography of the nineteenth century. And they both told a tale of ascent from humble origins through discouragements and hardships to inspiring triumphs. Each account was damned by a fastidious few as the confession of a con artist—the preachment of "our wise prophet of chicanery," as William Carlos Williams derided Franklin's narrative, "a perfect pattern-book for would-be Yankees and 'cute' businessmen," as others assailed Barnum's—and each was discovered by the multitudes "as evidences of the American genius."[4]

Franklin and Barnum alike went forth to forge in the smithies of their operations if not of their souls the uncreated psyche of their country. And they both did so by empowering ordinary people as ordinary people had never been empowered before. Franklin calculated the increase of commoners with a demographic sophistication unsurpassed in his era. He rejoiced in them as a rising people and cherished their happy mediocrity. He offered them the story of his own advancement as a talisman of the future he had plotted for them all. Barnum too took his own tale emblematically, as at once an object lesson and a tribute to the middling masses of the Yankee nation. He was a populist in his artistry as in his politics. He insisted again and again that "what gave pleasure to democratic audiences was good" and that "standards were fixed by the entertained, not the entertainer." His hoaxes did not infuriate the groups he gulled, because, as Constance Rourke realized, "a hoax is an elaborate form of attention." Barnum's humbugs delighted the multitudes they deluded, because no one else "had ever taken the pains to delude them on so preposterous a scale before."[5]

On the conventional understanding of their careers and their writings, both Franklin and Barnum exemplified the opportunity America afforded ordinary people to get ahead on their own initiative, predicated this improving endeavor on distinctively American conditions of competitive enterprise, and thereby promoted the materialistic individualism at the core of American culture.

There is much to be said for this conventional understanding. Both Franklin and Barnum took for granted the salience of self-interest among men's motives. Both expected people to act on calculations of private advantage. Both moved in milieus of deceit and disappointment, and both became connoisseurs of conniving. Both presented their youth and early manhood as an insistent saga of sharp practice and chicane, in "a world where mutual hostility [was] the norm" and a wary attentiveness to one's own ends a necessity. As early as 1731, Franklin recorded his conclusion that "the great affairs of the world" were "carried on and effected by parties," that parties were actuated by "their present general interest," that each man within each party harbored simultaneously "his particular private interest," that "as soon as a party . . . gained its general point" each member became "intent upon his particular interest," and that few in public life sought the common good, "whatever they may pretend."[6]

But despite its undeniable force, there are difficulties with this conventional understanding as well. Even as Franklin came to a keen appreciation of American egoism and articulated the logic of its eventual ascendancy, for example, he remained convinced that "men are naturally benevolent as well as selfish." Indeed, his *Autobiography* is in many ways his account of the means by which he weaned himself from the gratifications of aggression and from his youthful delight in defeating others. As a boy in Boston, he proceeded by "abrupt contradiction and positive argumentation." In his maturity in Philadelphia, he saw that there was no point in "obtaining victories that neither my self nor my cause . . . deserved" and that "the chief ends of conversation" were information, pleasure, and persuasion, not the temporary titillation of triumph. He cultivated a "modest diffidence" that served him better than contentiousness or Socratic method ever had when he "had occasion to inculcate [his] opinions" and persuade men into "measures" that he was "engaged in promoting."[7]

Similarly, even as Barnum insisted that he was "always looking out for the main chance" and that others too were "very apt to think of self first" in cases of "conflicting interests," he remained essentially steadfast in his commitment to the common weal. Indeed, his commitment was the more striking because it was not nearly so necessary to him as a comparable commitment had been to Franklin.[8]

Franklin lived in a society still hedged about by the prerogatives of patronage. He made his way by ingratiating himself with his betters and securing their sponsorship. He had therefore to master or mask his aggressiveness in order to achieve advancement and influence. Barnum never had to suppress his ambition. Barnum never even had to muffle his avidity to vanquish all rivals. He lived in an era of unbridled competition among men who acknowledged no betters. He came of age amid the liberal scramble and the capitalist clamor that Franklin only forecast.

Contemporaries caught the irony in Barnum's recurring acclamations of self-interest and his pervasive presumption of the priority of the public good. As a reviewer of the autobiography observed, the great impresario frequently ascribed his actions to selfish motives when more charitable interpretations of his behavior were equally plausible. "He seems to fear," the reviewer wrote, "that he shall be suspected of having sometimes acted without an eye to the main chance."[9]

In a country without a titled elite, everyone was under suspicion, because, in a country of "confidence men and painted women," everyone had a hustle. One way to dispel such suspicion was to affect honesty by conceding cunning. Aware that he had to move in the maze of appearances and realities which Franklin had heralded, Barnum disarmed doubt by anticipating his doubters. Operating intuitively on a principle Charles Dickens enunciated explicitly—that Americans would "strain at a gnat in the way of truthfulness" but "swallow a whole caravan of camels if they be laden with unworthy doubts and mean suspicions"—he turned the very rhetoric of self-regard into another persuasive ploy, a humbug, as it were.[10]

In the dense thickets of semblance and substance of nineteenth-century America, Barnum concentrated first on the management of impressions. Indeed, he devoted "a large part of his daily existence" to an unabashed manipulation of public opinion. In the retrospect of his long career, he concluded that he was "indebted to the press of the United States" for "almost every dollar" he possessed and "every success as an amusement manager" he had "ever achieved." As he summed up his "universal plan" for his partner and successor, James Bailey, an essential item was "to advertise freely and without fear." Advertising was "the first, second, and third elements of 'success.'"[11]

Nonetheless, Barnum never mistook the necessity of advertising for its sufficiency. Despite his special sensitivity to promotion, he still made plain to Bailey that an integral aspect of his "methods" was "to get the best of everything and the most of it." Despite his occasional conviction that people had only to "put on the appearance of business, and generally the reality [would] follow," he still swore that his own exhibitions always gave his patrons "more than [their] admission was worth" to them. The humbugs—the "little 'clap-trap' . . . and puffing advertisements"—were merely "skyrockets" to "attract attention and give notoriety" to the "wonderful, instructive, and amusing" enticements that he offered. Beyond that, Barnum declared his disbelief "that any amount of advertising . . . would make a spurious article permanently success-ful." It was possible to make money from the public only by "giving a full equivalent therefore" in amusement and in edification.[12]

Franklin was, of course, entangled in similar brambles of images and actualities a century before. Recent revisionists of his legend have been quick to point out how "typically" he settled for "an indulgent appear-ance of virtue rather than the exacting reality," and in some regards they are surely right. Franklin himself admitted as much in his account of his efforts to attain humility (to "imitate Jesus and Socrates," as he put it in his initial plan, as if to capitulate before he began). But if Franklin conceded that he could "boast" of success only in acquiring the appear-ance of humility, that is not yet to say that his every virtue was only an apparent one. With virtues he accorded more consequence than humil-ity, he mastered himself as well as the arcane arts of self-promotion. He rose not only by "the conscious and calculated display of diligence" but also by diligence itself. As he said, he "took care . . . to be *in reality* industrious and frugal" as well as "to avoid all *appearances* to the contrary."[13]

When Franklin paraded his paper home in a wheelbarrow, clanking noisily over the cobblestone streets as he went, he did indeed demon-strate devotion to his business with a brilliant flourish, but he did not engage in an exercise in empty ostentation. Lest anyone suppose other-wise, he gave over the very next lines of his story to a striking contrast of his carriage with that of his chief rival, David Harry. Harry was a fellow apprentice similarly seeking to set himself up as a printer. He had patrons more able and influential than Franklin's. But he had none of Franklin's awareness of the importance of his "credit and character as a tradesman," and he had none of Franklin's commitment to his calling, either. He "was very proud, dressed like a gentleman, lived expensively, [and] took much diversion and pleasure abroad." More than all that, he "ran in debt, and neglected his business." It was because he misman-aged his interest as well as his image that "all business left him."[14]

The issue Franklin intended in this contrast was not simply an issue of industry and application, or even of success and self-advancement. It was, rather, an issue of a certain sort of integrity. Poor Richard intimated it when he pronounced honesty the best policy. It was also an issue of a certain sort of utility. Franklin acknowledged it when he remembered, more than half a century later, the rebuke he received from his father for a youthful "scrape." Franklin and a few "playfellows" had stolen stones set aside for a new house to build themselves a fishing wharf. They were "discovered," "complained of," and "corrected by [their] fathers," and though Franklin "pleaded the usefulness of the work," his father convinced him "that nothing was useful which was not honest." Franklin chose to recall the contretemps as a cautionary tale. He meant his father's injunction to mark the boundary between unalloyed self-interest, how-ever rationalized, and what Tocqueville would one day call self-interest rightly understood. He meant his boyish violation of that boundary to teach others as it taught him that a "projecting public spirit" had to be "justly conducted." Honesty and utility alike had to be measured not by self-serving but by authentic community service.[15]

Franklin did not doubt that he could do well while doing good, and neither did Barnum. Indeed, both men maintained that, rightly under-stood, benevolence and interest were inseparable. Franklin's most essential insight was, as John Updike has said, his recognition of "the close rela-tion between virtue and happiness." Franklin himself averred his "design to explain and enforce [the] doctrine" that it was "everyone's interest to be virtuous, who wished to be happy" in this world as in the next. He had Poor Richard put it even more pithily: "When you're good to others, you are best to yourself."[16]

Upon such premises, it was virtually impossible to set any sharp dis-tinction between private interest and public welfare. In Esmond Wright's apt assessment, "the line between self-help and social service was elu-sive." Franklin simply did not see the self as a solitary entity. Individuals did not act alone, and they did not succeed or even survive on their own. Poor Richard spoke for Franklin in his pungent challenge, "he that drinks his cider alone, let him catch his horse alone."[17]

Franklin almost invariably undertook his enterprises in concert with others. The Library Company, the Union Fire Company, the Pennsyl-vania Hospital, the College of Philadelphia, and a multitude of other civic improvements that he organized were cooperative ventures, delib-erately formed to diffuse credit for their accomplishments. They were all patterned on his first "club for mutual improvement," the Junto.[18]

The Junto was an association of his "ingenious acquaintance," but it was much more than a mere convenience to him at a time when he had neither wealth nor influence and consequently began, as Carl Van Doren said, "where he could." It was his "benevolent lobby for the benefit of Philadelphia, and now and then for the advantage of Benjamin Franklin." It embodied a melding of good works and personal gain which he sought steadfastly from first to last. And exactly because it did, he kept it alive long after he had outgrown his original need to promote his "interests in business by more extensive recommendation." A decade and more after he had given up his printing business entirely, he still prized the Junto's "power of doing good" for the public by collective action and its "atmosphere of camaraderie and companionship" as well. Indeed, a decade and more after he had given up the Junto itself, he still held it close to his heart. When he brought his autobiography to its culmination and conclusion, as he supposed, in 1771, he ended not with his marriage to Deborah Read, an essentially private enterprise, but with the Junto and its launching of the Library Company, his "first project of a public nature."[19]

Barnum was comparably keen to be seen as—and truly to be—public-spirited. He often expressed his scorn for mere money-making. He generally disdained the lucrative schemes and speculations set before him. He consistently conceived his own civic promotions in East Bridgeport as "profitable philanthropy."[20]

He was grateful to the small towns of Connecticut that had taught him to be wary of gullibility and to take advantage of opportunity, but he never sentimentalized those towns and he never for a moment supposed them ideal societies. He recognized that their inchoate capitalism would make some men rich but would never make humanity happy. He understood that their undilute individualism served private ambition better than it promoted social sympathy, and that without such social sympathy Americans were indeed condemned to lives of quiet desperation. "With the most universal means of happiness ever known among any people," he insisted, "we are unhappy."[21]

He saw his own benevolence primarily in the alleviation of such evident unhappiness, through his East Bridgeport enterprises, his charities, and, above all, his museums and circuses. Those spectacles provided masses of Americans with the "relaxations and enjoyments" they required as respite from the "severe and drudging practicalness," the "dry and technical ideas of duty," and the "sordid love of acquisition" so prevalent in mid-Victorian America.[22]

Indeed, exactly like Franklin, Barnum proclaimed happiness rather than accumulation "the true aim of life." Against the grain of official American values, Barnum advanced an acceptance of hedonic gratification. His very entertainments were, on his own account of them, his profoundest philanthropies. They ministered, as did nothing else in nineteenth-century America, to deep human needs for fun and frolic.[23]

Franklin was, if anything, more attached to benevolence than Barnum, in principle and in practice. In his beloved Junto, new members undergoing initiation "had to stand up with their hands on their breasts and say they loved mankind in general." In the Creed that Franklin composed, he maintained that "the most acceptable service of God is doing good to man." In a more ascerbic version of the same sentiment, he had Poor Richard observe that "serving God is doing good to man, but praying is thought an easier service, and therefore more generally chosen."[24]

Benevolence was the divine thing, even if the more difficult. Franklin was enough of a realist to accept indulgently the ways of ordinary men and women. At the same time, he was enough of a humanitarian to hold himself to a more strenuous standard. He simply believed himself a better man than most of his brethren, though he recognized readily that there were others as concerned for the common weal as he. When he set down his observations on his reading of history in 1731, he did declare that parties were impelled by their general interests, and individuals within those parties by their particular private ambitions, but he did not on that account subside into cynicism. On the contrary, he held that even if most people could not rise above partisan perspectives, a "good and wise" minority could. He therefore proposed a "United Party for Virtue," which would form "the virtuous and good men of all nations" into "a regular body" which would "act for the good of mankind." His analysis of human nature pointed to the prevalence of selfish pride; his project pointed to the mobilization of mutuality. And in that project, he did not so much fuse private gain with public good as accord an actual priority to the claims of public life.[25]

Ultimately, Franklin and Barnum both gave themselves so utterly to the public that commentators have questioned whether they had any interior existence at all. Neil Harris wondered if Barnum even "had a notion of privacy, so completely did he define his own needs and reactions in public terms." Harris admitted the possibility that Barnum simply kept his private side "carefully shielded," but beyond that he would not go. When he spoke of Barnum's "inner life," he added the cautious qualification, "if it existed." Constance Rourke was not so archly circumspect. "In a strict sense," she asserted, Barnum "had no private life." He lived "in the midst of crowds, in public; at times it seemed he was the public."[26]

Students of Franklin spoke of similar suspicions and drew comparable conclusions. Herbert Leibowitz noticed that Franklin's *Autobiography* "contains no intimations of neurotic behavior, no dreams or nightmares, no crises of spirit, scarcely any inwardness." Leibowitz found himself "tempted to say that [Franklin] appears to be the only person in American history without an unconscious." Esmond Wright was also struck by Franklin's impenetrable exteriority, and indeed by his "root . . . conviction that the individual is only truly himself in a gregarious, not a solitary, setting." Ormond Seavey concurred that if we would "understand Franklin's self we cannot separate him from the larger public," and he went an essential step farther: "If we accept the premise that the strongest feelings point to the deepest parts of the self, we must look for them in Franklin's public rather than his private life."[27]

Franklin simply "had no intimate friend" to whom he exposed his "inner spirit." He did make a few attempts, in his youth, to maintain close ties with select companions, such as Collins and Ralph, but in the half-dozen decades after he returned from London and lost his patron, the merchant Thomas Denham, to "distemper," he had not a single soulmate nor even any steady circle of comrades in whom he could confide. As Seavey saw, his *Autobiography* presented him in a succession of introductions to people he had not previously known—governors, employers, merchants, and many more—rather than in a recurrence of conditions in which he was long and well known. Franklin meant to be a benefactor to his community and indeed to all mankind, but he meant to do his good works at a distance, in the aggregate and in the abstract. He held himself aloof from extended familiarities with his associates, his "gregariousness notwithstanding." He could still recall, at a half-century remove, his father's comment that "nothing was more common than for those who loved one another at a distance, to find many causes of dislike when they came together." And he echoed his father's observation in Poor Richard's blunt maxim, "Fish and visitors stink in three days."[28]

Franklin would not entangle himself abidingly with others. He abandoned Boston and all his American kindred without ever betraying "a sense of something lost or left behind." Unencumbered by his past, he was free to invent himself anew, again and again. Untrammeled by any enduring commitments, he was at liberty to be always the disengaged spectator of his social relations. He could recall without evident anger and, in truth, with wry amusement the disappointments he had suffered at the hands of people he presumed his friends, because he was never unduly involved emotionally in his attachments to others to begin with.[29]

Barnum too held himself apart from those with whom he worked and, necessarily, lived. In his museum he saw his employees every day. On the road, touring, he saw them incessantly, day and night. Yet he made no effort to come close to them. He described them as "the South African savages" or "those dirty, lazy, and lousy Gipseys." He encapsulated his attitude to any number of the men and women who made his acts in a little outburst against some "d—n Indians": "they are a lazy, shiftless set of brutes—though they will draw." And he did not confine his attitude to foreigners, either. He talked of Tom Thumb's Yankee parents as "crazy" and "absolutely deranged with [their] golden success." He rebuked them when they had the temerity to be "inquisitive about the business" and brought them back "down to the old level," where he vowed to "keep them." As he expostulated to another showman, he could "do business with blockheads and brutes when there [was] money enough to be made by it," but he could not "be tempted by money to associate with them or allow them to rule."[30]

With his fellow showmen, Barnum rarely deigned to reveal more of his feelings than he did with the performers he hired. He wrote letters by the thousands, but he exposed nearly nothing of his personal sentiments in any of them. When he wrote to Moses Kimball, his closest confidant among the impresarios and adventurers in the mass entertainment melée of his day, he wrote almost entirely about gate receipts, contracts, and the latest scams. Even when he wrote to his own partners, he marked his letters "Private," though he trusted nothing to them but entrepreneurial affairs. Just because he effaced his emotions, he quite collapsed the distinction between the private and the public realm. He could bid a college president campaigning for a major contribution from him, "In lower corner of all envelopes addressed to me, always please write *strictly personal*," yet after that ingratiating invitation exchange dozens of letters with the man and never discuss anything but business. Virtually nothing moved Barnum to open himself in strictly personal ways. "His life was," as Rourke remarked, "in the circus."[31]

Neither Barnum nor Franklin was markedly more intimate with family than with friends. Both men were away from home as often as they were there. Both plainly put their business and their public ambitions before their wives and children. And both were actually off in Europe, pursuing that business and those ambitions, while their wives lay dying at home.

Little as Franklin engaged his family devotedly or delineated it lovingly, he did still see his father, his brother, and his wife sharply enough to render them in sketches in his *Autobiography* that at least intimated their individuality. Barnum never perceived any of his kinfolk, except perhaps his grandfather, with any comparable clarity. His wives, his parents, his brothers and sisters, and his own children were all "indistinct" figures in his personal narrative. As Neil Harris said, the only thing we know about a number of them are their dates of birth and death. And almost the only things we know about the rest are the "conventional pieties" in which he swathed them, obscuring whatever personality they possessed.[32]

Barnum did produce a series of panegyrics to "home sweet home" in his autobiography. But every time he did, he told of taking off once more for a year or two on the road. He did introduce the concluding chapter of his memoirs with pledges that he felt "more deeply interested" in his family and homestead "than in all other things combined," that his wife and children were "dearer to him than all things else in the world," and that he would therefore devote his concluding chapter to them. But having said all that, he permitted himself a mere two pages of insipid platitudes about domestic pleasures and then returned to the public endeavors that absorbed him for the remaining twenty-five pages of the chapter.[33]

Where other men of that era, under the sway of emergent ideals of domesticity, sought home, servants, and carriage to enhance the amenity of their family life, Barnum sought those things almost solely to enhance the impression he made in public. If they had been gratifying in their own right, he would not have left them so routinely for the enticements of adventure abroad. If they had even mattered to him intrinsically, he would not have been indifferent to their destruction. One after another, his houses burned to the ground. Each time, he learned of his loss without lamentation, and each time he busied himself building a new one quite unlike the ones that had burned before.[34]

The plain truth was that Barnum's houses were not homes. They were, as he himself admitted, devices for display. He confessed openly that he had deliberately designed his first great house, Iranistan, with "an eye for business." He spent $150,000 on its onion spires, its Arabian Nights facade, its soaring fountains, its opulent gardens, and its rosewood and marble interiors, because he thought "that a pile of buildings of a novel order might indirectly serve as an advertisement of [his] various enterprises." Indeed, he defended his extravagance on his Asiatic palace precisely because it would pay for itself as a pro-motion.[35]

Rather than resent or resist the absorption of his personal residence into his public representation, Barnum abetted it, by reproducing the minareted pleasure dome of Iranistan on his business stationary. Rather than seek domestic seclusion, he went out of his way to augument the invasion of his private life by publicity. When he disbanded a wild animal caravan, he kept one elephant from the enterprise as "a capital advertisement for [his] American Museum." He put it to work on his farm in Bridgeport, in a field where he knew it could be seen from the railroad tracks. And lest anyone miss the outlandish spectacle, he fur-nished the creature's keeper "with a time-table of the road, with special instructions to be busily engaged in his work whenever passanger trains . . . were passing through."[36]

Such staging was, of course, what Barnum did for a living. But a similar sort of facework, as Erving Goffman called it, was what Franklin did all his life as well. When he discovered the Socratic method, he was so "charmed with it" that he "dropped" his argumentative demeanor and "put on the humble enquirer and doubter." Beliefs and the rhetori-cal modes in which they were embodied were like fashions in which to strike "poses" for Franklin. They could be "tried out" and tossed off (as, soon enough, he tossed off his Socratic style). They were, in Seavey's fine phrase, "attire for a self which [had] no required dress."[37]

As if instinctively, Franklin knew that "one does not dress for pri-vate company as for a public ball." He donned guises and doffed them, as circumstances demanded. He put manners on and took them off, according to the situation in which he found himself, and he did the same with morals as he did with manners. His celebrated project for moral perfection made ethical action "a style of dress which the self must put on to make its way in the world." It was, as its author understood from the first, as much an affectation as an aspiration. And just because it was, it could be abandoned "as a kind of foppery" as soon as it threatened to "make [him] ridiculous" in other people's eyes.[38]

Many commentators have worried over Franklin's consciousness of costume and delight in dramatic management of effects. Many have wondered if there was "a more real man behind the myriad personae" and if "the man himself" existed "independently of his images of him-self." Like Esmond Wright, they have feared that we might never find out "what [was] fact and what [was] fiction" in Franklin's multitudinous representations of himself.[39]

But Franklin himself was never bothered by his proliferating public images. If anything, he contributed to their compounding. He sat for more portraits than any other person of his period, and he composed himself differently for almost every one of them. Like Lord Chesterfield in his time, he conceived the management of masks as "both a pleasure and a necessity for the continuance of civil harmony." Like a number of novelists and social scientists of our time—Musil and Mead and Goffman, for just a few examples—he presumed that we are the roles we play and the style with which we play them.[40]

Wright was reaching for such a presumption when he concluded that Franklin finally "became the parts he played." But Franklin did not *become* those parts. He *was* his roles. Wright clung to an ontology that still predicated a reality behind appearances. Franklin let it go. His life and his account of his life alike affirmed the reality of appearances. The very independence he prized was predicated on "society and the concealment of identity it required." The self-consciousness he sought was won in dramatic encounters in public places, not in isolation from such civic contexts. At a time when Jean-Jacques Rousseau, his brilliant Continental contemporary, was imploring readers to fly from the superficialities of social conventions to the deeper realities of the self in solitude, Franklin insisted on the significance of such conventions and the sufficiency of appearances adroitly managed.[41]

Franklin rarely resisted "his histrionic talent for trying on and discarding selves." He "relished playing a repertoire of roles," and he drew sustenance from the range of roles he played. As Poor Richard said, "What one relishes, nourishes." Carl Van Doren was correct when he pronounced Franklin less a unitary personality than a veritable committee, "a harmonious human multitude" (just as Constance Rourke was right when she called Barnum "an amused conglomerate"). Franklin's extended apprenticeship in the crafts of common experience enabled him to adapt fluently to disparate situations, and his overflowing intelligence obliged him to treat such disparate situations as challenges to be joyfully mastered. As Herman Melville put it, Franklin had "carefully weighed the world" and could consequently "act any part in it."[42]

Just as small-town Connecticut could not contain Barnum, so Boston simply could not bring out the best in Franklin. It was too earnest, too plodding, and too homogeneous. Philadelphia afforded Franklin a far more expansive field of play, though it was significantly smaller than the older settlement when he arrived in 1723. The Quaker city had been founded on pluralistic principles rather than under authoritarian, intolerant Puritan auspices. It had from its earliest days a diversity of ethnic, religious, and economic groups that demanded acute attentiveness to difference rather than an overriding regard to orthodoxy. Boston was hospitable to a certain species of hedgehog, Philadelphia to all sorts of foxes. Boston was about integrity, Philadelphia about style. One could not be a cultural anthropologist in Boston.

Franklin reveled in testing himself, in attempting postures and personae he had never tried, in creating himself and recreating himself again and again. Wright did catch this quicksilver quality when he saw that "what makes Franklin so compelling to study . . . is his almost total freedom from the limits of his own environment." Franklin was never as John Woolman was, "single to the truth." He never even aimed at a semblance of such singleness of sensibility.[43]

On the contrary, he experimented with everything: with callings and careers, with beliefs and values, with old women and new nations, with words and deeds, with his identity, and indeed with his very name. He was by turns a "Water-American" who would not touch "muddling liquor" and who considered "sotting with beer all day" a "detestable custom," and a bon vivant who wrote drinking songs and kept five different kinds of champagne in his wine cellar. He could by turns set temperance above all other virtues and rely on rum to induce Indians to negotiate, advise against drinking "to elevation" and toast to intoxication to get a reluctant governor to supply his province's defense. He could follow a "vegetable diet" for years, convinced that eating "animal food" was "a kind of unprovoked murder," and then give it all up in an instant on the trifling enticement of an aroma of cod "hot out of the frying pan." He could counsel thrift and frugality, dispensing maxims to the masses about pennies saved and pennies earned, and then succumb to the temptations of "luxury," first with a 23-shilling silver spoon and China bowl, soon enough with "several hundred pounds'" worth of plate and porcelain. More than that, he could accustom himself to such amenities of elegance for decades and then all at once in Paris fulfill the French legend of the "good Quaker" by ostentatiously putting on "the plain dress of Friends."[44]

It was no accident that Franklin wrote so routinely in styles that were not his own and under names that were not his own. He was, in John Updike's words, "an inveterate impersonator." His very earliest surviving writings were submitted under the pseudonym Silence Dogood, the widow of a country minister. His most widely read works were published under the pseudonym Richard Saunders, the Poor Richard of the almanacs. Franklin delighted in such simulations of other identities. He wrote so casually and so constantly in such characters that, to this day, scholars still quarrel over the extent of his canon. He wrote so frequently in personae remote from his own that their disputes may never be definitively resolved.[45]

When he was a stripling of sixteen, Franklin wrote as an aging widow. When he was a respectable pillar of his community, he wrote as a disreputable woman facing trial for bearing her fifth illegitimate child. When he was middle-aged, he wrote in the modes of youthful folly and elderly wisdom. When he was an impetuous youth, he wrote of restraint, and when (presumably) too old to be in earnest, he wrote of passion. Always, he could get outside himself. Always, he could imagine the other. Updike was struck by "the androgyny of [his] imagination, from the speech of Polly Baker to his literary gallantries among the ladies of Paris." Leibowitz found it equally telling that, when he described his delayed marriage to Deborah Read, Franklin "imagine[d] *her* perspective."[46]

These abilities to assume roles without being consumed in or by them, to fit his psyche to his circumstances with flair and fine humor, to try the other's point of view and allow the other's ethical authenticity, made Franklin more than merely unique in eighteenth-century America. They made him whole, in one special sense. They enabled him to connect his convictions about public life with his perspectives on personal relations. They allowed him to integrate his conceptions of political economy with his predilections in private affairs.

In effect, these capacities to maintain a measure of disengagement from immediate personal interests extended the dominion of benevolence beyond the civil sphere into more personal realms. Those competences to disavow a degree of enmeshment in present passions made disinterestedness a central category of social as well as political experience. People who could get inside the skin if not the soul of others were not people for whom private concerns were pervasive or even primary.

Barnum similarly set the opinions of others before his own. So far from seeing the lone individual as a source of cultural authority, he "insisted again and again" that aggregates were the appropriate arbiters of American taste and that "what pleased the American masses was, by definition, good." The advertising that was the crux of his every operation precluded all possibility of prideful self-assertion. It presupposed that popular wishes were always right. It obliged the showman to abdicate his own judgments and preferences in deep and genuine deference to the desires of his audiences. And it found its justification exactly in the satisfaction of those democratic needs and desires. Barnum "never made the mistake of assuming that all men reflected his tastes and proclivities." He understood himself to be a servant of the public, not a molder of mass opinion, and assuredly not his own man.[47]

Both Franklin and Barnum have been taken for salesmen of the self and of selfishness. Nothing could be farther from the truth, at least in the simplistic and ahistorical sense ordinarily asserted. In actuality, both men set civic and public obligations before private entitlements. Both understood themselves as disinterested and indeed benevolent. More than that, both these putative paragons of privatism were utterly public men. Both these assumptive avatars of individualism were people without any evident inner life. Perhaps, like Moses, they pointed to a promised land of private priorities. They never themselves entered it. Perhaps, like the prophets of old, they forecast the future. They never themselves knew it.

## Notes

1. Ormond Seavey, *Becoming Benjamin Franklin: The Autobiography and the Life* (University Park, Penn., 1988), pp. 180, 76, 217; Gilbert Chinard, "The Apotheosis of Benjamin Franklin, Paris, 1790–1791," *Proceedings of the American Philosophical Society*, 99 (1955): 440–73.

2. Neil Harris, *Humbug: The Art of P. T. Barnum* (Boston, 1973), inside jacket and pp. 281, 280.

3. *Benjamin Franklin: A Profile*, ed. Esmond Wright (New York, 1970), p. ix; Phineas T. Barnum, *The Life of P. T. Barnum* (New York, 1855), p. ii; Esmond Wright, *Franklin of Philadelphia* (Cambridge, Mass., 1986), pp. 12, 355; Harris, *Humbug*, p. 280.

4. Frank Luther Mott, *Golden Multitudes: The Story of Best-Sellers in the United States* (New York, 1947); William Carlos Williams, *In the American Grain* (1925; rep. New York, 1956), p. 156; *Selected Letters of P. T. Barnum*, ed. A. H. Saxon (New York, 1983), p. xiii; Constance Rourke, *Trumpets of Jubilee* (New York, 1927), p. 369.

5. For BF, see almost any of the recent accounts: e.g., Wright, *Franklin of Philadelphia*; Seavey, *Becoming Benjamin Franklin*; Herbert Leibowitz, *Fabricating Lives: Explorations in American Autobiography* (New York, 1989); and R. Jackson Wilson, *Figures of Speech: American Writers and the Literary Marketplace, from Benjamin Franklin to Emily Dickinson* (New York, 1989). For Barnum, see Harris, *Humbug*, pp. 79, 229–30, and Rourke, *Trumpets of Jubilee*, p. 393. Such empowerment of the populace and enshrinement of popular opinion set them far apart from the different and distinctly minor tradition of Jonathan Edwards.

6. Seavey, *Becoming Benjamin Franklin*, pp. 116–17; *The Autobiography of Benjamin Franklin*, ed. Leonard Labaree *et al.* (New Haven, 1964), p. 161.

7. John Updike, "Many Bens," *The New Yorker*, February 22, 1988, p. 115; *Autobiography*, ed. Labaree, pp. 64–65.

8. Barnum, *Life*, pp. 21, 29.

9. Harris, *Humbug*, p. 213.

10. Karen Halttunen, *Confidence Men and Painted Women: A Study of Middle-Class Culture in America, 1830–1870* (New Haven, 1982); Harris, *Humbug*, p. 312.

11. Barnum, *Life*, p. 381; *Letters*, ed. Saxon, pp. xviii, 332, 159.

12. *Letters*, ed. Saxon, pp. 103, 332; Barnum, *Life*, pp. 225, 396, 400. See also Harris, *Humbug*, pp. 54–55, 214–15.

13. Leibowitz, *Fabricating Lives*, p. 34; *Autobiography*, ed. Labaree, pp. 125–26, 150, 159; Seavey, *Becoming Benjamin Franklin*, pp. 62–63.

14. *Autobiography*, ed. Labaree, pp. 125–26.

15. *Ibid.*, p. 54.

16. Updike, "Many Bens," pp. 112–13.

17. Wright, *Franklin of Philadelphia*, pp. 80–81.

18. *Autobiography*, ed. Labaree, p. 116.

19. *Ibid.*; Carl Van Doren, *Benjamin Franklin* (New York, 1938), pp. 73, 75, 77; *Autobiography*, ed. Labaree, pp. 170–71, 130–31; *Benjamin Franklin*, ed. Wright, p. xx; Seavey, *Becoming Benjamin Franklin*, pp. 65–66.

20. Barnum, *Life*, pp. 384–85. Cf. Harris, *Humbug*, pp. 150, 180–81; *Letters*, ed. Saxon, pp. xvi–xvii; and Rourke, *Trumpets of Jubilee*, pp. 406–7, 410, 413, 414.

21. Harris, *Humbug*, p. 214; Barnum, *Life*, p. 399.

22. Barnum, *Life*, p. 399. See also Harris, *Humbug*, pp. 79, 170–71, 217, 271, and *Letters*, ed. Saxon, p. xv.

23. Barnum, *Life*, p. 399. See also Harris, *Humbug*, pp. 33, 37–38, 79, 217, and Rourke, *Trumpets of Jubilee*, pp. 407–10.

24. Van Doren, *Franklin*, p. 78; *Autobiography*, ed. Labaree, p. 162; Leibowitz, *Fabricating Lives*, p. 63.

25. *Autobiography*, ed. Labaree, pp. 161–63.

26. Harris, *Humbug*, pp. 4–5; Rourke, *Trumpets of Jubilee*, p. 371.

27. Leibowitz, *Fabricating Lives*, pp. 29–30; Wright, *Franklin of Philadelphia*, p. 80; Seavey, *Becoming Benjamin Franklin*, p. 101.

28. John Griffith, "Franklin's Sanity and the Man Behind the Masks," in *The Oldest Revolutionary: Essays on Benjamin Franklin*, ed. J. A. Leo Lemay (Philadelphia, 1976), p. 126; *Autobiography*, ed. Labaree, p. 107; Seavey, *Becoming Benjamin Franklin*, pp. 10, 118; William Hedges, "From Franklin to Emerson," in *Oldest Revolutionary*, ed. Lemay, p. 151; Kenneth Silverman, "Introduction," in Benjamin Franklin, *The Autobiography and Other Writings*, ed. Kenneth Silverman (New York, 1986), p. xv.

29. Seavey, *Becoming Benjamin Franklin*, p. 27.

30. *Letters*, ed. Saxon, pp. 110, 24, 22, 31.

31. *Ibid.*, pp. 262, 310, 237; Rourke, *Trumpets of Jubilee*, pp. 422–23. For the only exceptions with Kimball—and those paltry enough—see *Letters*, ed. Saxon, pp. 16, 34, 35, 70, 76.

32. Harris, *Humbug*, p. 14.

33. Barnum, *Life*, pp. 203, 379, and ch. 14.

34. Harris, *Humbug*, p. 155.

35. Barnum, *Life*, pp. 401–3; Harris, *Humbug*, p. 104.

36. Harris, *Humbug*, pp. 104, 147. See also p. 192.

37. Erving Goffman, *Interaction Ritual: Essays on Face-to-Face Behavior* (Garden City, N.Y., 1967); *Autobiography*, ed. Labaree, p. 64; Seavey, *Becoming Benjamin Franklin*, p. 26.

38. *Autobiography*, ed. Labaree, pp. 56–57, 156; Seavey, *Becoming Benjamin Franklin*, p. 79.

39. Wright, *Franklin of Philadelphia*, pp. 9–10.

40. Seavey, *Becoming Benjamin Franklin*, p. 43.

41. Wright, *Franklin of Philadelphia*, p. 10; Seavey, *Becoming Benjamin Franklin*, p. 40.

42. Leibowitz, *Fabricating Lives*, pp. 48, 33; Van Doren, *Franklin*, p. 782; Rourke, *Trumpets of Jubilee*, p. 371; Herman Melville, *Israel Potter: His Fifty Years of Exile* (Evanston and Chicago, Ill., 1982), p. 48.

43. Wright, *Franklin of Philadelphia*, p. 13; Leibowitz, *Fabricating Lives*, p. 33. Jonathan Edwards, by contrast, sought not only Woolman's singleness to the truth but also the establishment of a doctrinal orthodoxy.

44. *Autobiography*, ed. Labaree, pp. 63, 87–88, 99–101, 145, 149; Leibowitz, *Fabricating Lives*, pp. 56–57; Frederick Tolles, "Benjamin Franklin's Business Mentors: The Philadelphia Quaker Merchants," *William and Mary Quarterly*, 3d ser., 4 (1947): 67.

45. Updike, "Many Bens," p. 106; J. A. Leo Lemay, *The Canon of Benjamin Franklin, 1722–1776: New Attributions and Reconsiderations* (Newark, Del., 1986).

46. Updike, "Many Bens," p. 114, though, for a treatment of the speech of Polly Baker that emphasizes its closeness to BF's own outlook, see J. A. Leo Lemay, "The Text, Rhetorical Strategies, and Themes of 'The Speech of Miss Polly Baker,'" in *The Oldest Revolutionary*, ed. Lemay, pp. 91–120; Leibowitz, *Fabricating Lives*, p. 43.

47. Harris, *Humbug*, pp. 79, 86.

# LANGUAGE

# 11

# Reason, Rhythm, and Style

### DAVID LEVIN

Portrayals of Benjamin Franklin and Jonathan Edwards as representative men go back at least as far as the historian George Bancroft. In the 1840s Bancroft labeled Franklin "the sublime of common sense" and portrayed Edwards as the transcendently spiritual Protestant who had given Calvinism its "political euthanasia" by identifying virtue with love.[1] Variations on that central contrast have enriched our understanding of Franklin and Edwards in the twentieth century, and I have not come here to question their value. But since my own brief contributions to the colloquy have sought to refine the central contrast by delineating similarities between the two great contemporaries, I trust you to consider letting me extend those lines this evening without forgetting the important differences. My most recent essay on Franklin and Edwards portrayed them and Cotton Mather as energetic writers who strove to reconcile their duty to be humble and their strong, proud wills by acting virtuously in the world for the glory of God or the public good.[2] Tonight I should like to study more closely and hear more clearly the language in which Franklin and Edwards wrote.

Without presuming to sound the theme for all the other speakers, I should like to take the trope of the keynote almost literally. Let us begin with sound and cadence. Before I have the chance to make you drowsy, please listen to one of Benjamin Franklin's most delightful paragraphs, and hear my version of his cadences. Fifty years after the event, he writes about a minor crisis of conscience that he says he faced at sea while sailing from Boston to New York:

> I believe I have omitted mentioning that in my first Voyage from Boston, being becalm'd off Block Island, our People set about catching Cod and hawl'd up a great many. Hitherto I had stuck to my Resolution of not eating animal Food; and on this Occasion, I consider'd with my master Tryon, the taking every Fish as a kind of unprovok'd Murder, since none of them had or ever could do us any Injury that might justify the Slaughter. All this seem'd very reasonable. But I had formerly been a great Lover of Fish, and when this came hot out of the Frying Pan, it smelt admirably well. I balanc'd some time between Principle and Inclination: till I recollected, that when the Fish were opened, I saw smaller Fish taken out of their Stomachs: Then, thought I, if you eat one another, I don't see why we mayn't eat you. So I din'd upon Cod very heartily, and continu'd to eat with other People, returning only now and then occasionally to a vegetable Diet. So convenient a thing it is to be a *reasonable Creature*, since it enables one to find or make a Reason for everything one has a mind to do.[3]

The wise old narrator of this anecdote has a perfect ear. Even when we grant that any sexagenarian is likely to have polished such a tale through decades of retelling before writing it down, Franklin's skill remains extraordinary. Like our best poets, he lets his greatest emphasis fall on syllables most important to his meaning. He begins with a pair of complex, balanced sentences, which establish a judicious tone by setting inaction or reflection against vigorous action. During a calm, his people haul up and slaughter a great many cod, but young Franklin sticks to his vegetarianism, whose rationale the wise old narrator gives us succinctly in a clause that emphasizes both rhetorical parallels and a persuasive, commonsensical justice based on reciprocal, proportional premises: "since none of them had or ever could do us any Injury that might justify the Slaughter." His shortest sentence, then—"All this seemed very reasonable"—reminds us that the reciprocal premise might be unreliable, just before he switches from what seemed reasonable to the even more powerful language of sensory pleasure. Notice that here the emphasis falls unerringly on words of feeling or what Franklin will soon call Inclination: *Lover, hot*, and *smelt*. As I hear the sentence, Franklin's greatest emphasis falls on *smelt*, the word that evokes the delicious aroma and perhaps reminds us of small fish whose very name is attributed to their peculiar smell. "But I had formerly been a great Lover of Fish, and when this came hot out of the Frying Pan, it smelt admirably well."

The young vegetarian balances, here, between the two abstractions that contend in eighteenth-century views of psychology, and the narrator calls attention to that balance by heavily stressing the verb itself, by giving equal weight to "Principle" and "Inclination," and by echoing sounds in those key words: *principle* and *inclination*. The language of balanced reflection takes over again when young Franklin seems to prefer Principle. He recollects persuasive evidence: "that when the Fish were opened, I saw smaller Fish taken out of their Stomachs." Now the conclusion to the reciprocal argument comes on with a rush; the major premise remains unstated, and the minor premise and conclusion echo in compressed form the logic and the parallel structure that had refused to justify the slaughter. The triumphant "Then thought I" not only releases young Franklin from the temporary balance between Principle and Inclination; it also prepares the way rhythmically for the apparent demolition of his vegetarian rationale: "if you eat one another, I don't see why we mayn't eat you." In the rush, perhaps, we follow right along with him, failing to notice that what he *saw* taken out of the stomachs of the cod was not human flesh but smaller fish. Perhaps the canny narrator's rhythm carries us so decisively from what his young persona literally saw to what he rationally did not see, that we overlook both young Franklin's shift to the second person and the shift in his argument: the fish still have not done *us* or young Franklin any injury that might justify the slaughter.

But if we do overlook the considerable difference between doing human beings any injury and eating smaller fish, old Ben Franklin's skillful rhythm and intricate logic will guarantee that we still get his complex meaning. His decisive address to the codfish ("I don't see why we mayn't eat you!") is followed by a line in which the action of an untroubled conscience flows as easily as the opening triple anapest trips from the tongue: "So I dined upon cod very heartily." Notice, too, that continuing "to eat with other People, returning only now and then occasionally to a vegetable Diet," suggests a chastened willingness to join the community rather than insist on sticking to peculiar resolutions. But then the old narrator's intricate punchline, with its complex puns and its subtle control of rhythm and emphasis, raises the passage from the level of amusing anecdote to that of a profound and humane exemplum.

Franklin, like the Puritan preachers in Boston from whose doctrines he thought he had liberated himself, liked to nail down the meaning of anecdotes and parables. His ironic humor gives the lesson a delicious flavor, but his comment on what we now call rationalizing is as unmistakably didactic as any preacher's doctrine. Even those readers who may have failed to recognize young Franklin's reasoning as the target of old Franklin's humor in the anecdote itself must see the point of the concluding sentence. See it, yes. And one can hardly avoid hearing it too, in the italicized phrase *reasonable Creature*; in the concluding pentameters,

> enables one to find or make a reason
> for everything one has a mind to do;

and of course in the brilliantly placed equivocal terms, "find or make a reason" and "has a mind to do."

This is only one of the most delightful of several passages in which Franklin acknowledged the fallibility of human reason. But it is Franklin's reason, and his clever appeal to our own, that perceives and exposes the fallacies. I see in the wise old narrator's tolerant self-criticism, and I hear in his ironically amused voice, a celebration of reason. Reason enables us not only to find or make convenient reasons for what we have a mind to do, but also to see through some of our own rationalizations and, when warmed by Benjamin Franklin's genial temperament, to look tolerantly on human folly—especially on ethical systems and metaphysical arguments into which error has managed to insinuate itself. The canny old narrator sharpens our wits while delighting our ears and tickling our funny bone.

Evidence of such skill and care would deserve attention even if we did not know that Franklin loved to tinker with language. He introduced one of his deliberately clumsy satirical poems in the *Pennsylvania Gazette* by conceding that "some of my Lines are too short in their Number of Feet," but said he had made "ample Amends" by giving "*very good Measure* in most of the others" (310). Scholars have studied his improvements on the rhythm of proverbs he transcribed; his editorial ear heard in a twelve-word Scottish proverb, for example ("Fresh fish and newcome guests smell by they are three days old"), the opportunity to reduce it to a pithy seven: "Fish and visitors stink in three days" (1200). He transformed the meaning of a couplet he misremembered as Alexander Pope's, by changing three little words. He dabbled in prosodic theory in a letter about lyrics in operatic arias, oratorios, and folksongs (783–84). And he amused himself and delighted readers of *The Way to Wealth* by playing the rhythm of one proverb against that of another when he stood old Father Abraham up before an auction to harangue the crowd with an impromptu sermon that consists almost entirely of economic proverbs by Poor Richard. Here the deliberate variation in rhythm becomes obvious, and the repetitions of the name "Poor Richard" (later, "Poor Dick") punctuate the variations so amusingly that no further analysis will be needed. I only remind you that Poor Richard is the alleged author of the framed narrative, that he has begun by complaining that his competitors rarely quote him, and that he pretends he was a member of Father Abraham's audience. Listen then for the variations in rhythm as Father Abraham intones one proverb after another:

> Sloth, by bringing on Diseases, absolutely shortens life. *Sloth, like Rust, consumes faster than Labour wears, while the used Key is always bright,* as Poor Richard says. But *dost thou love Life, then do not squander Time, for that's the Stuff Life is made of,* as Poor Richard says. How much more than is necessary do we spend in Sleep! forgetting that *The sleeping Fox catches no Poultry,* and that *there will be sleeping enough in the Grave,* as Poor Richard says. If Time be of all Things the most precious, *wasting Time* must be, as Poor Richard says, *the greatest Prodigality,* since, as he elsewhere tells us, *Lost Time is never found again;* and what we call *Time-enough, always proves little enough.* Let us then up and be doing, and doing to the Purpose; so by Diligence shall we do more with less Perplexity. *Sloth makes all Things difficult,* but

Industry all easy, as Poor Richard says; and *He that riseth late, must trot all Day, and shall scarce overtake his Business at Night.* While *Laziness travels so slowly, that Poverty soon overtakes him,* as we read in Poor Richard, who adds, *Drive thy Business, let not that drive thee;* and *Early to Bed, and early to rise, makes a Man healthy, wealthy and wise* (1296).

I have begun with Franklin's attention to rhythm because I hope to establish a connection between his emphasis on this aspect of style and his regular insistence on fitness, proportion, understanding, reasonable judgment. When he proposed a curriculum for an English school in Philadelphia in 1751, Franklin insisted that boys must be taught to learn the meaning of the words they read aloud. "They often read as Parrots speak," he protested. "And it is impossible a Reader should give the due Modulation to his Voice, and pronounce properly, unless his Understanding goes before his Tongue, and makes him Master of the Sentiment. Accustoming Boys to read aloud what they do not first understand, is the cause of those even set tones so common among Readers, which when they have once got a Habit of using, they find so difficult to correct" (350). Of almost every surviving utterance of Franklin's we may confidently say, echoing his own pentameters,

> His Understanding goes before his Tongue, (pen?)
> and makes him Master of the Sentiment.

Hearing his voice is especially important in some of his ironically humorous lines, as in the first sentence of his famous account of his self-taught course on "The Art of Virtue": "It was about this time that I conceiv'd the bold and arduous Project of arriving at moral Perfection" (1383). The incongruity among the casual opening ("It was about this time"), the presumptuously understated terminology ("bold and arduous Project"), and the transcendent goal makes us masters of the sentiment before we learn that, while young Franklin did improve his behavior, he never came close to moral perfection.

Now, no line of Franklin's that I have quoted so far would seem to soften the conventional contrast between his religious or moral sensibility and that of Jonathan Edwards. Edwards might have agreed with the central idea, but he would never have written, as Franklin did, "Let us rejoice and bless God, that we are neither Oysters, Hogs, nor Dray-Horses; and not stand repining that He has not made us Angels" (232). Not even when Franklin calls on one of Edwards's books in defending himself against charges of heterodoxy can we miss the large differences in doctrine, emphasis, and tone. Edwards, though capable of excoriating satire when reducing an opponent's philosophical logic to absurdity,[4] never discusses his own sins or those of others with the playful wit that always lurks in Franklin's moral commentaries. Nor does Edwards ever adopt the easy familiarity with which Franklin sometimes presumes to characterize God as a tolerantly domestic father standing at once beyond the need of his children's praise and above the wrath that would severely punish their folly. Every line of Franklin's seems to be drawn firmly in the earth; when the revivalist George Whitefield thanks him for his hospitality "for Christ's sake," Franklin cannot resist replying, "*it was not for Christ's sake, but for your sake*" (1408). Every line of Edwards's seems to be drawn with an awareness of divine sovereignty and glory.

Yet we may still refine our understanding of the differences between these representative figures if we pay further attention to their similarities. Consider first the letter in which Franklin invokes Edwards when defending his own religious faith. For his own purposes in 1735, Franklin has already appealed to a central distinction on which both Thomas Hooker and Jonathan Edwards had insisted. In his dialogue "A Man of Sense," Franklin has argued that being able to *talk* well about virtue has much less moral value than "having *a thorough Sense*" that enables one to reject vice "and embrace Virtue with a hearty and steady Affection" (246). Then, in the heat of the Great Awakening several years later, Franklin's sister Jane Mecom has apparently rebuked him for opposing the worship of God and for believing that a person's "Good Works would merit Heaven." Franklin replies that he has written "a whole Book of Devotions for my own Use"; and here as elsewhere (Letter to Huey, 475) he denies that "the little Good we can do" on earth "can *merit* so vast a reward hereafter" (427). He advises his sister to read nine pages (367–75) of Edwards's *Thoughts concerning the Present Revival of Religion in New England*. There she would presumably be instructed by Edwards's insistence that "moral Duties, such as Acts of Righteousness, Truth, Meekness, Forgiveness and Love towards our Neighbours . . . , are of much greater Importance in the Sight of God, than all the Externals of his Worship."[5] Franklin might well have cited, too, Edwards's declaration that a habit of "censoriousness must be totally rooted out" of new Christians, some of whose minds (Edwards complained) had become bitterly sharp after their conversion, rather than appropriately "meek, lamb-like," and "sweet."[6]

A central passage in Franklin's brief letter to his sister takes us to the heart of the likenesses and differences that I wish to review this evening. "There are some Things in your New England Doctrines and Worship," Franklin admits, "which I do not agree with, but I do not therefore condemn them, or desire to shake your Belief or Practice of them. We may dislike things that are nevertheless right in themselves. I would only have you make me the same Allowances, and have a better Opinion both of Morality and your Brother" (427). Here, without his characteristic humor, Franklin comes close to the exhilarating reciprocity with which Herman Melville's Ishmael (a century later) would observe the golden rule by worshiping Queequeg's wooden idol. Here too, as in his youthful defense and rejection of vegetarianism, the standard to which Franklin appeals elevates proportion, balance, and reciprocal obligations. Edwards, of course, would never go so far as Franklin or Ishmael. He would never agree to refrain from correcting someone's erroneous religious doctrine simply because he expected "the same Allowances" to be made for his own. But he surely would agree that some things we dislike are nevertheless right in themselves. And he habitually invoked standards of fitness, proportion, and reasonable balance, both when celebrating the beauty of the natural world and in theological and moral argument.

You will notice that the passages I have chosen from Edwards are even longer than my selections from Franklin. Franklin's succinct, epigrammatic qualities may give more value to the individual line. I have not chosen the Edwards passages to try your patience, but to demonstrate the persistence with which Edwards spells out reasons, iterates parallels and proportions, and establishes a rhythm moving toward unavoidable conclusions.

Edwards, like Franklin, wrote a narrative in which his youthful reasoning proves erroneous and in which the noble instrument of reason depends on the young protagonist's inclination to see from a particular point of view. Consider this passage in the light of Franklin's anecdote about the codfish:

> From my childhood up [Edwards wrote in his mid-thirties], my mind had been wont to be full of objections against the doctrine of God's sovereignty, in choosing whom He would to eternal life, and rejecting whom He pleased; leaving them eternally to perish, and be everlastingly tormented in hell. It used to appear like a horrible doctrine to me. But I remember the time very well, when I seemed to be convinced, and fully satisfied as to this sovereignty of God, and His justice in thus eternally disposing of men, according to his sovereign pleasure. But never could give an account, how, or by what means, I was thus convinced, not in the least imagining, in the time of it, nor a long time after, that there was any extraordinary influence of God's spirit in it; but only that now I *saw further, and my reason apprehended* [italics added] the justice and reasonableness of it. However, my mind rested in it; and it put an end to all those cavils and objections, that had 'til then abode with me, all the preceding part of my life. And there has been a wonderful alteration in my mind, with respect to the doctrine of God's sovereignty, from that day to this; so that I scarce ever have found so much as the rising of an objection against God's sovereignty, in the most absolute sense, in showing mercy to whom He will show mercy, and hardening and eternally damning whom He will. God's absolute sovereignty, and justice, with respect to salvation and damnation, is what my mind seems to rest assured of, as much as of any thing that I see with my eyes; at least it is so at times. But I have oftentimes since that first conviction had quite another kind of sense of God's sovereignty, than I had then. I have often since, not only had a conviction, but a *delightful* conviction. The doctrine of God's sovereignty has very often appeared, an exceeding pleasant, bright and sweet doctrine to me: and absolute sovereignty is what I love to ascribe to God. But my first conviction was not with this.[7]

Of course, Edwards believes that his new insight and judgment are caused by grace, the new sense that not only sustains his conviction of

God's sovereignty and justice but converts it into "a *delightful* conviction." Yet the similarity to Franklin's anecdote of the codfish is striking.
Although Edwards does not mock either his own earlier objection to
God's sovereignty or the process by which his attitude was reversed, he
plainly describes his reason as dependent on his transformed, gracious
inclination. He does not represent his eyes here as having seen anything
so specific or so startling as the smaller fish that were taken from the
stomachs of Franklin's cod; but even before his mind comes to love the
formerly objectionable doctrine, Edwards has seen further into spiritual
reality, and his mind has come to rest (at least at times) as confidently
in the new belief as in the reality of his literal sight.

Allow me a few words here, too, about the rhythms of Edwards's
prose. The ghost of a loose iambic pentameter haunts the beginning and
end of the paragraph—"against the doctrine of God's sovereignty/ leaving them eternally to perish/ It used to appear like a horrible doctrine
to me/ in showing mercy to whom He will show mercy/ is what my
mind seems to rest assured of/ as much as of any thing that I see with
my eyes/ I have often since not only had a conviction." The rhythms of
this prose stretch out the line, with a less measured and pointed internal
emphasis than we have heard in the passages I have read from Franklin.
Here as elsewhere, moreover, the rhythm of Edwards's prose insistently
extends and spells out meanings, as when Edwards repeatedly specifies
the powers that he resented as horrible but then came to love to ascribe
to God. Many readers have observed that even in some of his most rig-
orously logical argument or analytical description, his repetition of words
and ideas, and the cumulative force of his rhetoric, give some passages
the quality of incantation.

One of the most interesting points of convergence between Edwards's
thought and Franklin's, nonetheless, explicitly underlines the limits of
human reason without ceasing to rely on it. Both men continue to appeal
to the reader's sense of what is reasonable. Franklin believes he will fail
to persuade us to act virtuously unless he shows us that our true interest
will generally coincide with virtue, whereupon our inclination *may* dis-
pose us toward virtuous choices. He says that the "great *Aim* and *End*
of all Learning" should be first "an *Inclination*" and then "an *Ability* to
serve Mankind, one's Country, Friends, and Family" (342). Edwards
believes that until we are granted a new sense of the heart we will not
understand the nature of true virtue, or of saving grace, any better than
someone who has never tasted honey can imagine its sweetness, or a
person born blind can imagine colors.[8] Yet both writers address us *as if*
our reasoning powers alone enabled us to perceive the truth.

(Perhaps—may I digress for a moment?—perhaps this paradox helps
to account for modern scholars' general neglect of the likelihood that
Edwards would consider all our praise for him either insincere or uncom-
prehending so long as we persist in remaining unregenerate. We may
cheerfully belong to the Edwardsean chapter of the club that Morton

White called Atheists for Reinhold Niebuhr, as Franklin may be called a founder of Freethinkers for Edwards and Whitefield, but Edwards would charge our approval to self-love unless we could approve of him as true believers who love his piety and his writings for their expression of God's glorious benevolence.)

Appeals to our reasonable sense of proportion, meetness, or fitness resound throughout the argumentative prose of both Franklin and Edwards. Just as Franklin argues that no finite creature can *"merit"* an infinite reward from the infinitely wise Creator, so Edwards insists that an offense against an infinite Being deserves infinite punishment. He seems to expect our unregenerate sense of reasonable proportion to perceive the fitness of the relationship. He reasons that God's very benevolence, God's *expression* or radiation of Being in the universe, leads God to detest sinners' hostility to Being in general, and therefore to rejoice in their eternal damnation. The balance of the antitheses, and the parallel declarations of proportion, in one passage from Edwards's *Treatise Concerning Religious Affections*, can stand here for scores of other pages in which the style and the habits of thought appeal to every reader's presumably reasonable sense of binary fitness and proportion:

> But certainly our obligation to love and honor any being, is in some proportion to his loveliness and honorableness, or to his worthiness to be loved and honored by us; which is the same thing. We are surely under greater obligation to love a more lovely being, than a less lovely; and if a being be infinitely lovely or worthy to be loved by us, then our obligations to love him, are infinitely great: and therefore, whatever is contrary to this love, has in it infinite iniquity, deformity, and unworthiness. But on the other hand, with respect to our holiness or love to God, there is not an infinite worthiness in that. The sin of the creature against God, is ill-deserving and hateful in proportion to the distance there is between God and the creature: the greatness of the object, and the meanness and inferiority of the subject, aggravates it. But 'tis the reverse with respect to the worthiness of the respect of the creature to God; 'tis worthless, and not worthy, in proportion to the meanness of the subject. So much the greater the distance between God and the creature, so much the less is the creature's respect worthy of God's notice or regard. The great degree of superiority, increases the obligation on the inferior to regard the superior; and so makes the want of regard more hateful: but the great degree of inferiority diminishes the worth of the regard of the inferior; because the more he is inferior, the less is he worthy of notice, the less he is, the less is what he can offer worth; for he can offer no more than himself, in offering his best respect; and therefore as he is little, and little worth, so is his respect little worth. And the more a person has of true grace and spiritual light, the more will it appear thus to him; the more will he appear to himself infinitely deformed by reason of sin, and the less will the goodness that is in his grace, or good experience, appear in proportion to it. For indeed it is nothing to it: it is less than a drop to the ocean: for finite bears no proportion at all to that which is infinite. But the more a person has of spiritual light, the more do things appear to him, in this respect, as they are indeed. Hence it most demonstrably appears, that true

grace is of that nature, that the more a person has of it, with remaining corruption, the less does his goodness and holiness appear, in proportion to his
deformity; and not only to his past deformity, but to his present deformity,
in the sin that now appears in his heart, and in the abominable defects of his
highest and best affections, and brightest experiences.[9]

Those of you who have not recently read the *Treatise Concerning
Religious Affections* or *The Nature of True Virtue* will be relieved to know
that Edwards makes the prospect less bleak by acknowledging the joy
that elected saints experience even in this world; he soon concedes that
sometimes "they may appear to themselves freest [of corruption] and
best when grace is most in exercise, and worst when the actings of grace
are lowest" (328). My purpose in choosing the passage from *Religious
Affections* was to show how relentlessly intense, pervasive, binary, and
sometimes arbitrary Edwards's invocations of proportion characteristically are. Some readers, unregenerate and regenerate alike, might question whether a finite being can have an "infinitely great" obligation, even
to a being who is infinitely lovely. Not only Edwards's quasi-rational
arguments but his repetitive language and varied rhythms appeal to our
*assumptions* about fitness and proportion. He does not tell us why "the
great degree of superiority increases the obligation on the inferior to
regard the superior"; he simply assumes that as we hear the rhythms of
his prose we will consider the proportion axiomatic. Even when he rises
into lyrical eloquence in his account of his own conversion, he will sometimes show us paradoxical pairs or an oxymoron, as when he describes
an overpowering vision he once had of God's majesty and grace:

> I seemed to see them both in a sweet conjunction;
> majesty and meekness joined together;
> it was a sweet and gentle, and holy majesty;
> and also a majestic meekness; an awful sweetness;
> a high, and great, and holy gentleness.[10]

Franklin's sense of proportion did not always balance infinite majesty and creaturely imperfection in precisely the same way as Edwards
did. Although he argued that an imperfect creature could never *merit*
eternal happiness, Franklin would never have agreed with Edwards that
an imperfect creature could deserve infinite punishment. We can see his
preference clearly in the alleged revision of Pope to which I referred some
minutes ago. Franklin's memory attributed to Pope a couplet that had
actually been written by the Earl of Roscommon:

> Immodest Words admit of no Defence;
> For Want of Modesty is Want of Sense.

Franklin preferred to say,

> Immodest Words admit *but this* Defence,
> That Want of Modesty is Want of Sense.

Yet he cast his defense of his revision in the form of a rhetorical question that appeals to our sense of proportion, just as Edwards did when he declared that the great distance between superior and inferior increases the obligation on the inferior. Franklin's rhetorical question reverses Edwards as well as Pope or Roscommon: "Now is not *Want of Sense* (where a Man is so unfortunate as to want it) some Apology for his *Want of Modesty?*" (1322–23).

Franklin's reciprocal arguments range all the way from his most satirically irreverent ridicule of superstition to both his ironic and his serious political letters and essays concerning the issues in the American Revolution. He often used Scriptural arguments seriously, as in his "Dialogue between Two Presbyterians" (written in 1735), but he sometimes delighted in mocking piety with a mischievous use of theological language. When he wrote from Philadelphia to his brother John during the siege of Cape Breton in 1745, he calculated that New England's prayers on a day of fasting and in private families every morning and evening for several months would have given New England troops 45 million prayers for victory—"a vast balance in your favor," he said, over "the prayers of a few priests in the [French] garrison." Failure of the New England expedition, he said, would give him "but an indifferent opinion of Presbyterian prayers in such cases, as long as I live. Indeed, in attacking strong towns I should have more dependence on *works* [that is, the tunnels and trenches and batteries involved in a siege] than on *faith*; for, like the kingdom of heaven, they are to be taken by force and violence; and in a French garrison I suppose there are devils of that kind, that they are not to be cast out by prayers and fasting, unless it be by their own fasting for want of provisions" (428). And in arguments about the Stamp Act and the powers of Parliament twenty-one years later, Franklin made similar fun of the contention that the colonies really were represented in Parliament, because (one defender of Parliament's authority had written) "*New England lies within England,*" and specifically within "the manor of East Greenwich," in Kent. Since the colonies, with Anglo-American claims to western lands, "are perhaps as big as all Europe," Franklin said, he found the disproportion incomprehensible: "I have read that the whale swallowed Jonah," he wrote; "and as that is in Holy Writ, to be sure I ought to believe it. But if I were told, that, in fact, it was Jonah that swallowed the whale, I fancy I could myself as easily swallow the whale as the story" (571). He also insisted on being told what it was that these supposed inhabitants of East Greenwich in Kent had done to provoke the decision "that they, more than any other inhabitants of Kent, should be curbed in their manufactures and commerce" (571). Even in writing to his scientific correspondent Peter Collinson on similar issues, though here the opening biblical allusion is not irreverent, Franklin fits his reciprocal and proportional argument to a balanced antithetical style. Notice how intricately he varies the rhythm of the parallel elements, so that he plays audible variations on his theme

of balanced proportions, reinforcing thereby his authority as a reasonable man who merely perceives the reciprocal harmonies of natural law:

> We are in your Hands as Clay in the Hands of the Potter; and so in one
> more Particular than is generally consider'd: for as the Potter cannot waste
> or spoil his Clay without injuring himself; so I think there is scarce anything
> you can do that may be hurtful to us, but what will be as much or more so
> to you. This must be our chief Security; for Interest with you we have but
> little: The West Indians vastly outweigh us of the Northern Colonies. What
> we get above a Subsistence, we lay out with you for your Manufactures. There-
> fore what you get from us in Taxes you must lose in Trade. The Cat can
> yield but her Skin. And as you must have the whole Hide, if you first cut
> Thongs out of it, 'tis at your own Expence. The same with regard to our
> Trade with the West India Islands: If you restrain it in any Degree, you
> restrain in the same Proportion our Power of making Remittances to you,
> and of course our Demand for your Goods; for you will not clothe us out of
> Charity, tho' to receive 100 per Cent for it, in Heaven. . . . Does no body
> see, that if you confine us in America to your own Sugar Islands for that
> Commodity, it must raise the Price of it upon you in England? Just so much
> as the Price advances, so much is every Englishman tax'd to the West
> Indians [806–7].

Both Franklin and Edwards rely similarly on parallelism and on
assumptions about reciprocity when writing about the natural order.
Franklin's letters about magic circles and squares, mathematical designs
in which all numbers in a given area or a given direction will add up to
the same total, explain the "magic" in prose that is as tidily balanced as
the squares and concentric circles themselves. First Franklin made what
he called a square of 8, and then, challenged by the achievement of a
rival, a square of 16, in which all the vertical, horizontal, and diagonal
rows of numbers add to 2056. We can see the quality of his prose in his
description of one added feature: "that a four square hole being cut in
a piece of paper of such a size as to take in and shew through it, just 16
of the little squares, when laid on the greater square, the sum of the
16 numbers so appearing through the hole, wherever it was placed on
the greater square, should likewise make 2056" (451). Similar emphasis
on proportion in both rhetoric and argument dominates Franklin's
accounts of polar and reciprocal qualities in his electrical experiments;
Edwards's description of spiders that suspend themselves on their silken
filament and then quickly reabsorb the filament as they climb out of
danger,[11] and Franklin's warning against careless attempts "to mend the
scheme of Providence" (469).

The same similarities of technique and argumentative conception
appear when Edwards and Franklin address the one subject that most
emphatically divides them: self-love or self-interest. Franklin agreed with
Edwards that God and angels are necessarily good, that self-denial is not
the essence of virtue, and that a person would deserve to be called "a
Man of Sense" only if he understood that his truest interest "even
in this World" must coincide with virtue. "Vicious Actions," Franklin

concluded, "are not hurtful because they are forbidden, but forbidden because they are hurtful, the Nature of Man alone considered" (1392). Partly because he regretted some of his early writings about determinism and Deism, Franklin contented himself with this doctrine of enlightened self-interest and did not venture far beyond the nature of man alone, or what might lead to happiness in this world. Implicit in his entire discussion of *The Art of Virtue* is a conviction that vicious and virtuous actions do exist; whether or not what Franklin calls "the moral Virtues I had met with in my Reading" (1384) constituted *true* virtue, they sufficed to occupy his literary and (if we believe his account) his moral attention. His qualifying phrases—"even in this world" and "the Nature of Man alone considered"—plainly acknowledge the existence of larger questions, but Franklin apparently felt no need to define the nature of true virtue. His characteristically succinct reversal of "forbidden" and "hurtful" does not even tell us whose wisdom or authority forbade vicious actions. I see no reason to doubt his faith in some kind of posthumous reward, but his emphasis usually returns to himself, as in his refusal (shortly before his death) to write decisively about the divinity of Jesus. He did not volunteer this opinion. It was President Ezra Stiles of Yale who asked explicitly for Franklin's belief. Franklin admitted to having some doubts on the question, but said he did not "dogmatize upon [it], having never studied it, and think it needless to busy myself with it now, when I expect soon an Opportunity of knowing the Truth with less Trouble" (1179).

Edwards often employed his binary, balanced rhetoric not only to display fitness and proportion, but also to clarify distinctions. From his earliest published sermons, such as *A Divine and Supernatural Light*, to *The Nature of True Virtue* near the end of his life, he took care to distinguish between mistaking natural human faculties for a *cause* of supernatural grace and recognizing natural faculties as a participating subject made use of in the transmission of grace, as our eyes normally see objects in this world but do not cause the light that enables us to see those objects.[12] And in *The Nature of True Virtue*, when he conceded that such natural principles as pity, gratitude, and parental affection often "agree with the tendency to general benevolence" but do not necessarily have the essence of true virtue, he conceded too that "self-love is exceeding useful and necessary; and so are the natural appetites of hunger, thirst, etc. Yet nobody will assert that these have the nature of true virtue." Moreover, as natural "pity preserves [us] from cruelty" and "natural conscience tends to restrain sin in general," a merciful God has so ordered this world that "even self-love often restrains [us] from acts of true wickedness; and not only so, but puts men upon seeking true virtue; yet it is not itself true virtue, but is the source of all the wickedness that is in the world."[13]

Enlightened self-interest is one of the chief articles of Franklin's faith, and it is often the highest principle to which he directs his readers. Virtually all his arguments about religious belief, moreover, call our attention back to the judicious mind of Benjamin Franklin, which must decide what it believes and how it will worship. He may not have said with Thomas Paine that his own mind was his church,[14] but Franklin rarely lets readers forget that he himself will decide whether it is important to know the Truth with more or less trouble. His evocation of that judicious self seems to me most admirable when the rhythms of his prose, as in his parable of the codfish, show that self to be at once self-aware, self-critical, and yet pleased with its achievement and resigned to live with its imperfections.

Edwards, however, though surely just as strong-willed, tends to deflect more and more attention away from the judicious self and toward the central source of all being. I find his self most obtrusive when his faith obliges him to speak literally about the Apocalypse, and least intrusively present when he writes about true virtue. I hear his voice most impressively in his measured disposition of parallel pairs, whether in his appeals to our sense of proportion, in his precise distinctions between qualities that it is all too easy to confuse with one another, or in his calm report of his ecstatic vision of God's majestic meekness.

Our willingness to hear the voices of Franklin and Edwards, and to edit their work and celebrate their achievement two centuries after their death, pays tribute to their genius and to the power of their representativeness in our conception of our culture. Their mastery of clarity, their concern with virtue, their commitment to relatively plain language, and their appeals to our sense of reason and proportion mark them as contemporaneous heirs to both Puritanism and the Enlightenment. They might have worked out their applications of reason in language that put much less emphasis on rhythm and proportional balance than do the passages that I have discussed tonight. But I find their rhythms and parallelisms especially appropriate to their ideas. I trust we shall all enjoy hearing more of their prose in the next two days, and that our acute sense of their differences will not shut out the sound of their similarities.

## Notes

1. George Bancroft, *History of the United States from the Discovery of the Continent* (Boston, 1840), 3:377, 378, 396.

2. David Levin, "Edwards, Franklin, and Cotton Mather: A Meditation on Character and Reputation," in *Jonathan Edwards and the American Experience*, ed. Nathan O. Hatch and Harry S. Stout (New York, 1988), pp. 34–49.

3. *Benjamin Franklin: Writings*, ed. J. A. Leo Lemay (New York, 1987), pp. 1338–39. Further citations of this volume appear in parentheses in the text.

4. See, for example, *WJE, 1*: 343–46.

5. See *PBF, 2*: 385n.

6. JE, *Some Thoughts concerning the Revival*, in *WJE*, 4: 481. Cf. p. 416: "And of all kinds of pride, spiritual pride is upon many accounts the most hateful." Also pp. 416–25.

7. The quotation is from JE's spiritual autobiography. See Samuel Hopkins, *The Life and Character of . . . Jonathan Edwards* [1765], in *Jonathan Edwards, a Profile* ed. David Levin (New York, 1969), pp. 25–26.

8. Jonathan Edwards, *A Divine and Supernatural Light*, in *The Works of Jonathan Edwards*, ed. Edward Hickman (Carlisle, Pa., 1834, rep. 1986), 2: 14.

9. *WJE*, 2: 326–27. Further citation of this volume appears in parentheses in the text.

10. *Edwards, a Profile*, ed. Levin, p. 27.

11. JE, "Of Insects," in *WJE*, 6: 156–58.

12. JE, *A Divine and Supernatural Light*, in *Works of Jonathan Edwards*, ed. Hickman, 2: 15.

13. JE, *The Nature of True Virtue*, ed. William K. Frankena (Ann Arbor, Mich., 1960), pp. 94–95.

14. Thomas Paine, *The Age of Reason*, ed. Moncure D. Conway (New York and London, 1896), p. 22.

# 12

# Rhetorical Strategies in *Sinners in the Hands of an Angry God* and *Narrative of the Late Massacres in Lancaster County*

### J. A. LEO LEMAY

Addressed especially to the unregenerate, *Sinners in the Hands of an Angry God* attempts to bring its audience to the conversion experience.[1] It has the usual Puritan sermon structure: Text, Doctrine, Reasons, and Uses.[2] Infamously the most effective imprecatory sermon in American literature, it outdoes (in my opinion) Father Arnall's hellfire-and-damnation sermon in James Joyce's *Portrait of an Artist as a Young Man*.[3] Jonathan Edwards achieves extraordinary tension and suspense by brilliant rhetorical strategies. The increasing immediacy of person, time, and place throughout *Sinners in the Hands of an Angry God* explains much of its escalating emotional appeal.

The personal references in the sermon gradually become more immediate. In the Text (for clarity, I shall refer to the four parts of the sermon with capital letters—Text, Doctrine, Reasons, and Uses),[4] the reference *they* is to "the wicked unbelieving Israelites." In the Doctrine, the subject changes from "the wicked unbelieving Israelites" to "wicked men." The word *they* throughout the first seven Reasons refers to "wicked men." In Reason eight, the reference becomes "Natural men." Thereafter, "natural men" and "wicked men" are used interchangeably for the remaining three Reasons. In the Use or Application section, Edwards abruptly changes from *they* to *you*: "The use of this awful subject may be for awakening unconverted persons in this congregation. This that *you* have heard is the case of every one of *you* that are out of Christ."

Before proceeding with the personal references in the Uses, however, I should point out that Edwards has prepared for the pronominal shift and implicitly enlarged the meaning of *they* in the first Reason. There, for the initial time, he directly referred to the congregation. Using first person plural pronouns, Edwards wrote: "*We* find it easy to tread on and crush a worm that *we* see crawling on the earth; so it is easy for *us* to cut or singe a slender thread that any thing hangs by: thus easy is it for God, when he pleases, to cast His enemies down to hell. What are *we*, that *we* should think to stand before him, at whose rebuke the earth trembles, and before whom the rocks are thrown down?" These personal references begin to involve the congregation in the sermon. A reference in Reason four strengthens the congregation's involvement: "Yea, God is a great deal more angry with great numbers that are now on earth: yea, doubtless, with many that are now *in this congregation*, who it may be are at ease, than He is with many of those who are now in the flames of hell." Thereafter, the *they* references to "wicked men" or to "natural men" include the unregenerate persons in the congregation.

In the Uses or Applications of the sermon, the personal reference *you* is to "unconverted persons in this congregation." Notice that for the first time, the generic *men* is not used. *Persons* more obviously applies to men, women, and children. Just before enumerating four uses, Edwards began a paragraph with a direct address: "*O sinner!* Consider the fearful danger *you* are in." And after the four Uses, Edwards intensified the personal references: "But this is the dismal case of every soul in this congregation that has not been born again, however moral and strict, sober and religious, they may otherwise be. Oh that *you* would consider it, whether *you* be *young or old!*" In the sermon's antepenultimate paragraph, Edwards directly addressed his appeal to the old, to the young men and young women, and to the children. The increasing immediacy of personal reference helps make the sermon a persuasive rhetorical masterpiece.

Edwards also gains increasing immediacy in time and place. In the first two observations on the Text, he referred to wicked Israelites and naturally used the simple past tense: "That they *were* always exposed to destruction; as one that stands or walks in slippery places is always exposed to fall." But in the third comment on the Text, Edwards changed to the present: "3. Another thing implied is, that they *are* liable to fall of themselves." The present tense continues through the fourth comment on the text. The Doctrine is in the present tense: "There *is* nothing that keeps wicked men at any one moment out of hell, but the mere pleasure of God." In the second paragraph of the fourth Reason, Edwards made the present more immediate by adding the word *now* to the verb: "The wrath of God burns against them, their damnation does not slumber; the pit is prepared, the fire is made ready; the furnace *is now* hot, ready to receive them; the flames *do now* rage and glow."

In the last paragraph of the Reasons, Edwards attenuated the immediacy by using the present progressive tense: "The devil *is waiting* for them, hell *is gaping* for them, the flames gather and flash about them, and would fain lay hold on them, and swallow them up; the fire pent up in their own hearts *is struggling* to break out." In the Application, Edwards used the word *now* more frequently. In the middle of the second Use, he wrote: "*Now* God stands ready to pity you; this is a day of mercy; you may cry *now* with some encouragement of obtaining mercy." Use number four makes the immediate even more present: "We know not who they are, or in what seats they sit, or what thoughts they *now* have. It may be they are *now* at ease, and hear all these things without much disturbance, and are *now* flattering themselves that they are not the persons, promising themselves that they shall escape." Similar *now* references are found in the last paragraph of the sermon.

Along with the increasing immediacy of person and time, Edwards also brilliantly made the place more immediate. At first Edwards referred to the Israelites. But gradually Israel becomes any place where wicked men exist, including America. Reason one anticipates (as I have shown above) the specific reference to "this congregation" (Reason four) by its references to "we" and "us." The Application begins by referring to particular individuals who may be "unconverted persons in this congregation." Finally, in Use four, Edwards referred to individuals sitting in the very seats of the church:

> If they [members of the congregation] knew that there was one person, and but one, in the whole congregation, that was to be the subject of this misery, what an awful thing would it be to think of! If we knew who it was, what an awful sight would it be to see such a person! How might all the rest of the congregation lift up a lamentable and bitter cry over him! But, alas! instead of one, how many is it likely will remember this discourse in hell? And it would be a wonder, if some that are now present should not be in hell in a very short time, even before this year is out. And it would be no wonder if some persons, that now sit here, in some seats of this meetinghouse, in health, quiet and secure, should be there before tomorrow morning.

Before I leave the subject of the effects gained by increasing immediacy, I should point out another rhetorical technique that Edwards employs—the use of dialogue. As Franklin remarked in the *Autobiography*, mixing narration and dialogue is "a Method of Writing very engaging to the Reader, who in the most interesting Parts finds himself as

it were brought into the Company, and present at the Discourse."⁵
Edwards, in Reason nine, imagined how persons might explain their
presence in hell:

> No, I never intended to come here: I had laid out matters otherwise in my
> mind; I thought I should contrive well for myself: I thought my scheme good.
> I intended to take effectual care; but it came upon me unexpected; I did not
> look for it at that time, and in that manner; it came as a thief: Death outwit-
> ted me. God's wrath was too quick for me. Oh, my cursed foolishness! I was
> flattering myself, and pleasing myself with vain dreams of what I would do
> hereafter; and when I was saying peace and safety, then suddenly destruction
> came upon me.

I do not claim that Jonathan Edwards deliberately set out to use all
these rhetorical devices of increasing immediacy as he composed *Sinners
in the Hands of an Angry God*, but I do believe that such a verbal genius
as Edwards could hardly be unaware of the effects that he was creating
as he composed and revised the sermon.⁶

Edwards also achieves an extraordinary tension in the sermon by his
logic and his syntax. The sustained pursuit of any narrow, single idea is
a method of achieving tension. There is a psychological truth in the
application of the word *exhaustive* to an exhaustive (i.e., an absolutely
thorough) study. Edwards's sermon is, except for the final conclusion,
the pursuit of a narrow, single idea. Even *reading* Edwards's sermon is
an emotionally exhausting experience: the same point is suspended before
the reader (the perilous situation of sinners), the same point is repeated
(their inevitable death) and driven home (by example and imagery and
increasing immediacy) over and over again; and each time the tension increases. Consider the repetitiousness⁷ and the slight additions as
Edwards draws out four implications of the text: (1) "That they were
always exposed to destruction." (2) "That they were always exposed to
sudden unexpected destruction." (3) "That they are liable to fall of themselves, without being thrown down by the hand of another." And
(4) "That the reason why they are not fallen already, and do not fall
now, is only that God's appointed time is not come." Following these
four slightly different implications of the text, Edwards states the doctrine: "There is nothing that keeps wicked men at any one moment out
of hell, but the mere pleasure of God."

The tension becomes more unbearable partly because, in the Reasons, the situation and doom of the sinner is presented with more detail
in each of the ten enumerated Proofs. The imagery generally increases
in vividness and power. More important, the repetition of the nearly
identical logic and the nearly identical images grates on the auditor's
already exposed nerve with a cumulative effect that vivid and powerful
imagery alone could not achieve.⁸ From the one small point that Edwards
is making, the reader is never allowed to break away. Who ever thought
that life would not end in death? Further, for Edwards's audience, the

real point is as certain, to quote Franklin, as death and taxes.[9] If those Enfield farmers and merchants believed in God, then the logic of Jonathan Edwards was inescapable. In any case, the logic was emotionally exhausting.[10]

A possibility of relief appears, for the first time, in the Application. Finally, the only way to escape from the logically necessitous circle that Edwards has repeatedly led the auditors through—the necessity of death and the doom that must follow for the unregenerate—is offered: the second birth. There is no other way to resolve the incredible logical and emotional tension that Edwards has created.

Edwards also made *Sinners in the Hands of an Angry God* an unbearably tension-filled sermon by the use of a convoluted, negative syntax that calls out for a positive answer but continually withholds the affirmative. Consider the second sentence of the fourth Reason: "And the reason why they do not go down to hell at each moment, is *not* because God, in whose power they are, is *not* then very angry with them." The rhetoric demands and the reader expects, an affirmation to follow that sentence: "It is because. . . ." But Edwards withholds the affirmation, causing the tension ever to increase simply by the negative rhetorical structures he so commonly uses. The second paragraph of the fourth Reason begins: "So that it is *not* because God is unmindful of their wickedness, and does *not* resent it, that he does *not* let loose his hand and cut them off." Again, the natural rhetorical structure to follow would be, "It is because . . ." But Edwards has intensified the rhetorical tension by combining an attenuated presentness and a suspenseful image with a negative construction. Using the same technique, he continued: "The wrath of God burns against them, their damnation does *not* slumber; the pit is prepared, the fire is made ready, the furnace is now hot, ready to receive them; the flames do now rage and glow. The glittering sword is whet, and held over them, and the pit hath opened its mouth under them."

The sermon's imagery has been the subject of several good essays.[11] I might just comment that the images add to the suspense because they are, almost invariably, suspenseful: walking on air, the waters dammed up, the drawn bow and pointed arrow, the spider images, and the falling, slipping, sliding images. The most tension-filled images are found in the Application. "The bow of God's wrath is bent, and the arrow made ready on the string, and justice bends the arrow at your heart, and strains the bow, and it is nothing but the mere pleasure of God, and that of an angry God, without any promise or obligation at all, that keeps the arrow one moment from being made drunk with your blood." The most frequently recurring imagery is archetypal, not because the icy winter New England ground makes older people afraid of slipping and falling, but because one of the first great challenges that everyone confronts is the ability to stand and to walk upright. For months and, in some cases, years, infants try to stand and walk. Arms outstretched, they master a step or two, only to fall into the rejoicing hands of their parents. And the slipping, sliding, falling continues. Edwards's dominant imagery subliminally returns every auditor to infancy. The seventh Reason says: "Unconverted men walk over the pit of hell on a rotten covering, and there are innumerable places in this covering so weak that they will not bear their weight, and these places are not seen."

Because of its extraordinarily increasing immediacy, because of its inexorably increasing tension and suspense, because of its exhaustively and inescapably convincing logic, and because of its suspenseful and archetypal imagery, *Sinners in the Hands of an Angry God* is a masterpiece of rhetorical strategies.

Jonathan Edwards had an easier rhetorical task than Benjamin Franklin. The unregenerate members of the Enfield, Connecticut, church accepted and believed in the fundamental theological truths that Edwards relied upon for their conversion. Edwards had only to present those truths in a more effective form than the unregenerates had ever heard before in order to be successful. But the Paxton Boys and other Pennsylvania frontiersmen whom Franklin confronted in *A Narrative of the Late Massacres in Lancaster County*[12] believed that some of the "Christian" or "Praying" Indians were in fact responsible for killing innocent whites—including women and children. Edwards's audience may have been prejudiced against him personally, but they shared the assumptions upon which he based his sermon. Franklin's audience was prejudiced against him as a spokesperson for the authorities, and they denied the assumptions upon which he based his pamphlet. They thought that the supposed "Praying Indians" were killers—and many of them believed that all Indians were their enemies.

Franklin's pamphlet, which appeared at the end of January 1764, attempted to enlist public opinion against the Paxton Boys, who were then marching on Philadelphia. Describing the *Narrative* in a letter to Henry Home, Lord Kames, on June 2, 1765, Franklin said that in December 1763 "we had two Insurrections of the back Inhabitants of our Province, by whom 20 poor Indians were murdered that had from the first Settlement of the Province lived among us and under the Protection of our Government. This gave me a good deal of Employment, for as the Rioters threatned farther Mischief, and their Actions seem'd to be approv'd by an encreasing Party, I wrote a Pamphlet entitled a *Narrative* . . . to strengthen the Hands of our weak Government, by rendring the Proceedings of the Rioters unpopular and odious" (*W*811).

Franklin organized the *Narrative* on the model of the classical oration.[13] Let me outline the *Narrative*. The introduction or *exordium* has twelve short paragraphs, mainly taken up with brief characterizations of the individual Conestoga Indians (paragraphs four to ten). The second part of a classical oration is a *narratio* or *praecognitio*, a section devoted to setting forth the facts. It presents the *Narrative* proper, a description of the crime at Conestoga (paragraphs thirteen through eighteen) and the later massacre at Lancaster (paragraphs nineteen through twenty-four), including the proclamations published after each crime. The third section of the classical oration is the *explicatio* or *definitio*, a section defining terms and setting forth the issues to be proved. Franklin does so in paragraphs twenty-seven through thirty. The fourth section of a classical oration, the *partitio* or proposition, states what is to be proved. Franklin's thirty-first paragraph sets forth his thesis: "We pretend to be Christians, and, from the superior Light we enjoy, ought to exceed Heathens, Turks, Saracens, Moors, Negroes, and Indians, in the Knowledge and Practice of what is right. I will endeavour to show, by a few Examples from Books and History, the Sense those People have had of such Actions."

The fifth section of a classical oration is the *amplificatio* or proof. Franklin devotes paragraphs thirty-two to forty-six to quotations and anecdotes proving that most other times and countries have held hospitality sacred. The sixth section provides the *refutatio* or *reprehensio*—the refutation of the opponent's arguments or the censure and denunciation of his arguments. Franklin devotes paragraphs forty-seven through forty-nine to his *reprehensio*. And finally, the *peroration* or *epilogus*, the last three paragraphs (fifty through fifty-two), sums up the arguments and stirs up the audience.

I would like also to point out that in the *Narrative of the Late Massacres in Lancaster County*, the fourth, fifth, and sixth parts of the classical oration beautifully coincide with the form of the Puritan sermon. The *partitio*, quoted above, contains Franklin's Text or thesis.[14] The *amplificatio* or Proof contains ten proofs of the text. And the *refutatio* or *reprehensio* contains three Uses. I shall point out below how Franklin employed and enjoyed the irony of his mini-sermon.[15] Franklin made up many of the anecdotes and passages that he cites. At least one opponent realized that Franklin had created some of the scenes he cited. Franklin, however, must have known that many of his anecdotes could be proved false. Why, then, did he use imaginative creations? The reason, I suspect, lies partly in Franklin's theory of human nature. He believed, or at least wanted to believe, that the majority of persons were naturally benevolent. When he tried to prove his theory in a philosophical essay in the *Pennsylvania Gazette* for November 30, 1732, he played upon the reader's own benevolent sympathy with the plight of fictional characters as the best possible evidence (*W*200–203).[16] In writing the *Narrative*, Franklin probably thought the reader's benevolent emotions would be roused by the anecdotes and stories that he made up— and that though an occasional reader might realize that some of the "proofs" of his thesis were actually created, the sympathetic, benevolent feelings even of that perceptive reader would nevertheless overcome any angry or selfish feelings. He may also, as Denis Barone has recently suggested, have been influenced by the recent work of Lord Kames, *Elements of Criticism*. Though Kames's theory of "ideal presence" seems very similar to Franklin's belief in the benevolent emotions, alas, Franklin confessed shortly afterward, he was wrong in his hopes for human nature.[17]

What is even more surprising about the *Narrative* is that it so clearly reveals the relativistic, cosmopolitan, and perhaps even anti-Christian stance of its author. Franklin almost seems like a *naif*—an unworldly, impractical, ivory-tower intellectual, whose mind is filled with Enlightenment and skeptical notions. Such ideals and such a persona were suitable for an Enlightenment essay, written in Paris and aimed especially at French intellectuals. Franklin's *Remarks Concerning the Savages of North America*, directed to a special audience, opens with an echo of Montaigne: "Savages we call them, because their manners differ from ours, which we think the Perfection of Civility; they think the same of theirs" (*W*969). That opening is entirely appropriate for Franklin's 1782 purposes and his abstract philosophical audience. But in a January 1763 pamphlet addressed to Pennsylvania's frontiersmen and to the ordinary citizens of Philadelphia, Franklin's praise of the superior manners and customs of other times and other peoples (including American Indians) was entirely inappropriate—even foolish. The idealistic Franklin was inexcusably insensitive. Franklin allowed his personal beliefs and his ideals to interfere with an effective authorial persona for the piece.

Franklin's *exordium* (¶ 1) claims that the Conestoga or Susquehannah Indians were the remains of a tribe who welcomed William Penn to Pennsylvania, and with whom Penn made his first mythic treaty of friendship, which would last "as long as the Sun should shine, or the Waters run in the Rivers." But Penn's treaty, part of the folklore of the colonial period—given a magnificent embodiment in Benjamin West's painting and in a series of nineteenth-century imitations by Edward Hicks[18]—was supposedly with the Delaware, not the Susquehanna, Indians. Further, by the time Penn tried to negotiate with the Susquehanna Indians, only a few were left. Diseases and various wars with the whites, the most recent being Bacon's Rebellion, had annihilated most of the tribe.[19] Franklin, however, makes it seem as if the Conestoga Indians were a powerful people who outnumbered and befriended the whites when Penn supposedly negotiated with them. Of course Franklin makes up the words that he quotes from the mythic treaty, though he knew all the commonly used formulaic phrases of Indian treaties so well that the quotation appears to be authentic.[20] The mythic and imaginary treaty is an especially apt beginning for the *Narration*, for, as I shall argue, it is fundamentally a work of imaginative literature, with only a brief section actually dealing with the massacre, and even in that brief narration Franklin creates part of the supposed facts he relates. It is especially fitting that in calling up Penn's mythic treaty, Franklin may have been echoing Voltaire, who claimed: "It is the only treaty between these people [the Indians] and Christians which has never been sworn to and never broken."[21]

Franklin says that the remnants of the Conestoga Indians consisted of twenty people: seven men, five women, and eight children, and he characterizes the adults. He makes them a group of comparative saints, whose good qualities he carefully enumerates. After twelve short paragraphs of introduction or *exordium* (*W*540–41), Franklin begins the *narratio*: "On *Wednesday*, the 14th of December, 1763, Fifty-seven men, from some of our Frontier Townships, came, all well-mounted, and armed with Firelocks, Hangers and Hatchets, having travelled through the Country in the Night to *Conestogoe* Manor. There they surrounded the small Village of Indian Huts and just at Break of Day broke into them all at once" (*W*541, ¶ 13). How, one may well wonder, can Franklin know that there were exactly fifty-seven frontiersmen in the assault? At this point, to heighten the suspense, Franklin interrupts the forward pace of the action, to explain why not all twenty Indians were present. Then he describes the massacre, portrays the reaction of the remaining Indians, and narrates the actions of the Lancaster magistrates, who took the remaining Indians to the Lancaster "Workhouse, a strong Building as the Place of greatest Safety" (*W*542, ¶ 15). He reprints Governor John Penn's proclamation of December 22, 1763, against the "Authors and Perpetrators of the said Crime," who noted that a number of other friendly Indians were now housed and protected in Philadelphia (*W*542–43, ¶ 16–18).

Continuing, Franklin reports the actions of the frontiersmen upon learning fourteen Indians from Conestoga were at Lancaster. On December 27, "Fifty of them, armed as before, dismounting, went directly to the Work-house, and by Violence broke upon the Door, and entered with the utmost Fury in their Countenances" (*W*543, ¶ 19). Franklin again interrupts the progress of the narration in order to heighten the suspense. "When the poor Wretches saw they had *no Protection* nigh, nor could possibly escape, and being without the least Weapon for Defence, they divided into their little Families, the Children clinging to the Parents; they fell on their Knees, protested their Innocence, declared their Love to the *English*, and that, in their whole Lives, they had never done them Injury; and in this Posture they all received the Hatchet! Men, Women and little Children—were every one inhumanly murdered!—in cold Blood" (*W*543–44, ¶ 19).

Obviously Franklin made up the scene. Something like that might have happened, and certainly the Paxton Boys killed the Indians, but the Reverend Thomas Barton, in his defense of the frontiersmen, *The Conduct of the Paxton Men, impartially Represented*, pointed out that the whole attack occupied not more than two minutes and that the only persons present were the Indians and those who killed them. The Paxton boys declared that not an Indian said "a word, and that if they had, it would have been impossible to have heard them for the Noise of the shouting of the Multitude."[22]

Franklin described the Paxtonians' triumph afterward and the burial of the Indians. In the first of his echoes of *Macbeth*, he said: "But the

Wickedness cannot be covered, the Guilt will lie on the whole Land, till Justice is done on the Murderers. *The Blood of the Innocent will cry to Heaven for Vengeance*" (*W*544, ¶ 22). In the next paragraph, Franklin repeated an anecdote about the oldest Indian—a statement that he very probably made up: "It is said that *Shehaes*, being before told, that it was to be feared some *English* might come from the Frontier into the Country, and murder him and his People; he replied, 'It is impossible: There are *Indians*, indeed, in the Woods, who would kill me and mine, if they could get at us, for my Friendship to the *English*; but the *English* will wrap me in their Matchcoat, and secure me from all Danger.'" Franklin exclaimed: "How unfortunately was he mistaken!" (*W*544, ¶ 23). Franklin then reprinted Governor John Penn's proclamation of January 2, 1764, against the murderers, offering a reward of two hundred pounds each for information leading to the conviction of the killers. The proclamation completed the historical part of the *Narrative* (*W*554–56, ¶ 24–26).

In the *Explicatio* or definition, the third part of a classical oration, Franklin turned to the present situation and the reasonings by both parties. He noted that the Paxton Boys' threats had silenced the possible informants and that public opinion in the frontier counties sided with the Paxton Boys. To make his case more convincing, Franklin wrote a series of analogies, which become increasingly personal, increasingly relevant, and increasingly immediate to his audience: "If an *Indian* injures me, does it follow that I may revenge that Injury on all *Indians?* It is well known that *Indians* are of different Tribes, Nations and Languages, as well as the White People. In *Europe*, if the *French*, who are White People, should injure the *Dutch*, are they to revenge it on the *English*, because they too are White People? The only Crime of these poor Wretches seems to have been, that they had a reddish brown Skin, and black Hair; and some People of that Sort, it seems, had murdered some of our Relations. If it be right to kill Men for such a Reason, then, should any Man, with a freckled Face and red Hair, kill a Wife or Child of mine, it would be right for me to revenge it, by killing all the freckled red-haired Men, Women and Children, I could afterwards any where meet with" (*W*546, ¶ 29). Since the Paxton Boys were in general Scots-Irish, many with red hair, the last analogy was particularly telling.

Some frontiersmen leaders had justified their actions by citing "the Command given Joshua to destroy the Heathen." Franklin of course refutes the Biblical reference by an appeal to the ten commandments and by citing the kind of New Testament God that he believed his audience would honor. "Horrid Perversion of Scripture and of Religion! to father the worst of Crimes on the God of Peace and Love!" (*W*546–47, ¶ 30).

The fourth section of a classical oration, the *partitio* or thesis, occupied the next paragraph (*W*547, ¶ 31). The cosmopolitan Franklin, who despised ethnocentrism and who had already written on the superiority of the savage state to civilization (*PBF* 4: 482; cf. later, *19*: 6–7), had long been interested in the laws of hospitality among primitive peoples (*PBF 1*: 125; *6*: 123; and, later, *14*: 254). In the following ten proofs (the fifth part of the classical oration), Franklin showed that other primitive peoples and other non-Christian nations all had customs or laws of hospitality. He began with several examples from Homer's *Odyssey* (in Pope's translation; *W*547–49, ¶ 32–35), then progressed from "the sentiments of the ancient Heathens" to the "Turks."

From the life of Mohammed, Franklin cited Mohammed's severe reprimand of Captain Khaled for killing captives who had surrendered. The authentic incident appears in various versions of Mohammed's life. Franklin may well have read it in a translation of Henri Boulainvilliers' *Life of Mahomet* (London: W. Hinchliffe, 1731), which the Library Company of Philadelphia purchased before 1741.[23] Franklin's third authority was Saladin, who refused to drink with a Christian captain, for that would mean, by Arabic custom, that Saladin must preserve his life. This anecdote too is authentic. Franklin's source may have been Voltaire's *History of the Crusades* as translated and published in the *Gentleman's Magazine*, vols. 20–21, from November 1750 through April 1751. The incident concerning Saladin appeared in the *Supplement to the Gentleman's Magazine*, vol. 20, for the year 1750, p. 578.[24] The fourth reason (*W*550, ¶ 38) is from the modern Mahometans, taken, as I have noted (*W*1533), from John Bell's *Travels* (1763), *2*: 465.

The fifth proof (*W*550–51, ¶ 39) supposedly recorded the extraordinary action of a Spanish Moor in giving hospitality to a Spanish cavalier who, it turned out, had just killed the Moor's son. After the Moor learned that the cavalier had killed his son, he nevertheless aided him: "*Fly far while the Night can cover you. You will be safe in the Morning. You are indeed guilty of my Son's Blood, but God is just and good, and I thank him that I am innocent of yours, and that my Faith given is preserved.*" I noted elsewhere (*W*1533), that Franklin probably created the anecdote. A touching story, it aroused the reader's sympathetic feelings.

The sixth proof briefly sketched the practice of the Spanish in caring for the wares of English merchants, even during wars with England. The seventh proof told the story of Captain William Edwards, who was forced by a storm and a leaky ship to seek refuge in Havana in 1746, during a war with Spain. Despite the war, the Spanish Governor treated the distressed English captain with courtesy and care, granting him the right to repair and refit the ship and then to leave. The story contained a touching speech by the Spanish Governor, which concluded: "*If after that you are taken, you will then be a Prize, but now you are only a Stranger, and have a Stranger's Right to Safety and Protection*" (*W*552, ¶ 41). Neither the editors of the *Papers* nor I could find any reference to Captain William Edwards in the newspapers and magazines for 1746. I suggested (*W*1533) that Franklin also created the anecdote.

In Reason eight, Franklin attributed to "Captain Seagrave" a pertinent story. But the *National Union Catalogue of Pre-1956 Publications*, the British Library's printed *Catalogue*, the bibliographies of travel

literature, the *Gentleman's Magazine*, and the *London Magazine* all fail
to mention any Captain Seagrave. The name alone, *Seagrave*, makes me
suspect that Franklin created it. The story itself so resembles the murder
of the Conestoga Indians; and the speech of Cudjoe, the Black who
befriended the sick second mate William Murray from a New England
sloop, so matches Franklin's analogy in the *explicatio* of the *Narration*,
that I am positive that Franklin made up the anecdote.

According to Franklin, a Dutch ship stopped at Guinea, treacher-
ously seized some blacks, and carried them off as slaves. "Their Relations and Friends, transported with sudden Rage, ran to the House of
Cudjoe to take Revenge, by killing Murray." Cudjoe, however, reasoned
with them and defended Murray. Franklin wrote: "*Nay*, said Cudjoe; *the
White Men that carried away your Brothers are bad Men, kill them when
you can catch them; but this White Man is a good Man, and you must not
kill him*. But he is a White Man, they cried; the White Men are all bad;
we will kill them all. *Nay*, says he, *you must not kill a Man, that has
done no Harm, only for being white. This Man is my Friend, my House is
his Fort, and I am his Soldier. I must fight for him, you must kill me, before you can kill him*" (*W*552–53, ¶ 42). Like Edwards, Franklin created an imaginary dialogue in order to make his work more effective.
But everyone knew that Edwards imagined the scene he described,
whereas Franklin passed off his as reality.

The penultimate reason began with a *concessio*: "Now I am about
to mention something of Indians, I beg that I may not be understood as framing apologies for all Indians." Franklin excluded the "Rum-
debauched, Trader-corrupted Vagabonds and Thieves on *Susquehannah*
and the *Ohio*, at present in Arms against us." But he pointed out that
the Six Nations as a group "have kept Faith with the English ever since
we knew them, now near an Hundred Years." He claimed that the leaders
of the Six Nations have strong notions of honor, and cited the speech
of a Mohawk chief to the Catawba Indians, promising them safe conduct back to their own country, concluding "and there take care of
yourselves, for there we intend to come and kill you" (*W*553–54, ¶ 43–
45). The incident happened, though Franklin probably, as the editors
of the *Papers of Benjamin Franklin* suggested, "himself composed in the
Indian style the speech reported here" (*PBF 11*: 63, n. 2).

The tenth and final reason or proof recalled the Pankeshaw Indians'
heroic defense of the English traders who were their guests against the
French and Indians. "A Number of them, with their old chief, lost their
lives in the Cause" (*W*554, ¶ 46).

After the ten proofs, Franklin turned to the penultimate section of
a classical oration, the *refutatio* or *reprehensio*. He argued that even if
Will Soc, "the most obnoxious" of the murdered Indians, were really
guilty of the offenses rumored against him, he should "have been fairly
tried." Franklin said, "He lived under our Laws, and was subject to them;
he was in our Hands, and might easily have been prosecuted; was it

*English Justice* to condemn and execute him unheard?" Franklin provided details of Will Soc's last moments—which of course he must have made up. He then turns to the other Indians, asking what had they done, "little Boys and Girls, Children of a year old, Babes at the Breast." He concluded the paragraph by recriminating: "Do we come to America to learn and practice the Manners of *Barbarians?* But this, *Barbarians* as they are, they practice against their Enemies only, not against their Friends" (*W*554–55, ¶ 47).

He recalled (as the opening had said) that the Indians greeted their forefathers, William Penn and the first settlers, "with Kindness and Hospitality." And Franklin, anticipating John Logan, St. John de Crevecoeur, Washington Irving, James Fenimore Cooper, and others who used the topoi of the lament for the vanishing Indian (the last of his tribe), wrote: "See, in the mangled Corpses of the last remains of the Tribe, how effectually we have afforded it [protection] to them?"

In the last *reprehensio*, Franklin imitated Shakespeare's technique in Mark Anthony's great speech in *Julius Caesar* ("Friends, Romans, Countrymen, lend me your ears" [III, ii, 87]) of gradually discrediting Brutus by turning the words *ambitious* and *honorable man* into satirical epithets. Franklin briefly repeated his catalogue of proofs, contrasting each example of hospitality with the Christian frontiersmen's treatment of the Indians. Thus he said: "We have seen, that they would have been safer among the ancient *Heathens,* with whom the Rites of Hospitality were *sacred.*—They would have been considered as guests of the Publick, and the Religion of the Country would have operated in their Favour. But our Frontier People call themselves *Christians!*" The second contrast concluded, "But what is the Example of *Turks* to Scripture *Christians?*" The third: "But shall we compare *Saracens* to *Christians?*" The fourth: "However, what was Honourable in *Moors,* may not be a Rule to us; for we are *Christians!*" The fifth: "But shall we imitate *idolatrous Papists,* we that are *enlightened Protestants?*" The penultimate comparison read: "They would even have been safer among the *Negroes* of *Africa,* where at least one manly Soul would have been found, with Sense, Spirit, and Humanity enough to stand in their Defence: But shall *Whitemen* and *Christians* act like a *Pagan Negroe?*" In the seventh and final contrast, Franklin closed: "In short it appears, that they would have been safe in any Part of the known World, except in the Neighbourhood of the *Christian White Savages* of Peckstang and Donegall!—" (*W*555–56, ¶ 49).

Thus ends Franklin's mini-sermon (text, reasons, and uses) as well as the conclusion of the penultimate part of the classical oration, the *reprehensio.* No doubt Franklin enjoyed the irony of chastising Christians in a particularly Christian and Protestant genre. But such cosmopolitanism and relativism were hardly likely to appeal to Franklin's primary audience. Indeed, the Reverend Thomas Barton, in replying to Franklin, travestied his hospitality arguments and claimed that Pennsylvania's white frontiersmen would have been safer anywhere in the world, except under the government of the Pacifist Quakers of Pennsylvania. That ethnocentric point of view, and not his own idealistic, relativistic, imaginative, and cosmopolitan world, appealed to the majority of Franklin's contemporaries.

The three paragraphs of peroration concluding the *Narrative* strike its rhetorical high point. For the first paragraph, Franklin returned to *Macbeth* for his model. He opened with a direct address. "O ye unhappy Perpetrators of this horrid Wickedness! Reflect a Moment on the Mischief ye have done, the Disgrace ye have brought on your Country, on your Religion, and your Bible, on your Families and Children." He wrote three sentences urging the Paxton Boys to "Think on" the results of their crime. "For *Justice*, though slow, will come at last. All good People every where detest your Actions." Then came the *Macbeth* echoes: "You have imbrued your Hands in innocent Blood; how will you make them clean? [Cf. *Macbeth*, II, ii, 57]²⁵ The dying Shrieks and Groans of the Murdered, will often sound in your Ears [cf. IV, iii, 168]: Their Spectres will sometimes attend you, and affright even your innocent Children!— Fly where you will, your Consciences will go with you:—Talking in your Sleep shall betray you, in the Delirium of a Fever you yourselves shall make your own Wickedness known." (Cf. *Macbeth* II, ii, 20; II, i, 51.)

The pamphlet's penultimate paragraph called attention to the 140 peaceable Indians now taking refuge in Philadelphia. Franklin described their plight and, with another allusion to Voltaire's *Letters from England*, recalled Pennsylvania's reputation, "once renowned for Kindness to Strangers."²⁶ He called for the Philadelphians to protect and defend the remaining Indians against the Paxton Boys, whom he named "the armed Madmen of your Country" and "Unmanly Men!": "Unmanly Men! who are not ashamed to come with Weapons against the Unarmed, to use the Sword against Women, and the Bayonet against young Children; and who have already given such bloody Proofs of their Inhumanity and Cruelty." He ended the paragraph with an appeal:

> Let us rouze ourselves, for Shame, and redeem the Honour of our Province from the Contempt of its Neighbours; let all good Men join heartily and unanimously in Support of the Laws, and in strengthening the Hands of Government; that *Justice* may be done, the Wicked punished, and the Innocent protected; otherwise we can, as a People expect no Blessing from Heaven, there will be no Security for our Persons or Properties; Anarchy and Confusion will prevail over all, and Violence, without Judgment, dispose of every Thing [*W*557, ¶ 51].²⁷

In the *peroration*, the final paragraph, Franklin turned to the example of the Royal Highlanders, who had fought against the Indians on the frontier but who escorted and protected the 140 Christian Indians in Philadelphia. Franklin indirectly threatened that if the Paxton Boys attacked Philadelphia, they would have to fight not only whatever militia Franklin organized, but also British regular army troops. He closed with one more condemnation of the Paxton Boys: "I shall conclude with observing, that *Cowards* can handle Arms, can strike where they are sure to meet with no Return, can wound, mangle and murder; but it belongs to *brave* Men to spare, and to protect; for, as the Poet says,—*Mercy still sways the Brave*" (W558, ¶ 52).

The concluding quotation from Pope's translation of the *Odyssey* recalled the first proof in the *Narrative* and nicely rounded off the brilliant oratorical form. But, as all Franklinists know, though he succeeded in his immediate purpose of protecting the Christian Indians, Franklin lost the propaganda war and alienated numerous former friends and allies. He conceded in his letter to Lord Kames, "I became a less Man than ever: for I had by these Transactions made myself many Enemies among the Populace." (W811). His idealistic defense of the Indians was the major reason he, Speaker of the House of Representatives, lost in the bitterly contested election on October 1, 1764.

Franklin, one of the greatest masters of personae in the eighteenth century, created hundreds of brilliant personae in his belletristic writings—and he even used different and beautifully adapted personae for almost all of his private letters. As Larzer Ziff wrote, "Franklin's brilliant creation of the appropriate *persona* for the literary task at hand is a feature of almost every piece he wrote."[28] He was a masterful rhetorician. Why, then, did he not create some clever personae for the *Narrative*? Why did he reveal his complete disgust for the frontiersmen? One might explain his rhetorical mistake by saying that he was under enormous pressure, rushed by continuing demands on his time from the governor and the legislature, by the necessity to raise and equip a militia, by the urgency to feed and care for the remaining 140 Indians—and so he did not have the time to select a suitably clever persona. Or one might hypothesize that Franklin's five years in England, from 1757 to 1762, had put him out of touch with the popular feelings in Pennsylvania. But I can't believe either supposition.

Only one good explanation exists for his failure to appeal to his primary audience. Franklin was so outraged by the massacres that he gave vent to his true feelings, ignoring the almost certain consequences. The opposition buried his pamphlet under a deluge of replies.[29] The ordinary citizens in general and the frontiersmen in particular despised Franklin's pamphlet—and especially scorned his skeptical, rationalistic, relativistic, enlightenment point of view. For Franklin, "the Tribune of the People," the pamphlet was a grotesque error.[30] For Franklin the politician, it was a disaster. But Franklin, enraged by the brutality of the frontiersmen, was not going to be cowed by the possible consequences of his act. If he could have foreseen the consequences of his pamphlet—his loss of popularity and his defeat in the election that coming October—I believe he would have been content to lose the election to set forth his cosmopolitan and benevolent ideals. He lost friends and followers, but, in his outrage, Franklin the idealist judged it a world well lost.

## *Notes*

1. For an overview of the scholarship on the sermon and its place in JE's thought, see Robert Lee Stuart, "Jonathan Edwards at Enfield: 'And Oh the Cheerfulness and Pleasantness . . . ,'" *American Literature, 48* (1976): 46–59.

2. Perry Miller, *The New England Mind: The Seventeenth Century* (1939; reprint, Cambridge, Mass., 1953), ch. 12, "The Plain Style," pp. 331–62.

3. James Joyce, *A Portrait of the Artist as a Young Man* (1916; reprint, New York, 1976), pp. 108–35.

4. Since these references are more specific than page references and since the sermon is commonly available in American literature anthologies, I shall not cite page numbers for *Sinners.* I used the text in *An Early American Reader*, ed. J. A. Leo Lemay (Washington, D.C., 1988), pp. 313–23.

5. *The Autobiography of Benjamin Franklin*, ed. J. A. Leo Lemay and P. M. Zall (New York, 1986), p. 18.

6. An earlier version of the sermon (existing in two drafts) was evidently originally preached at Northampton. Ola Elizabeth Winslow, *Jonathan Edwards, 1703–1758* (1940; reprint, New York, 1961), p. 179. Professor Wilson Kimnach plans to study the textual evolution of *Sinners in the Hands of an Angry God.*

7. *Jonathan Edwards: Representative Selections*, ed. Clarence H. Faust and Thomas H. Johnson (1925; rev. ed. New York, 1962), p. cxii, characterizes JE's style by a frequent repetition of words and constructions. Willis J. Buckingham, "Stylistic Artistry in the Sermons of Jonathan Edwards," *Papers in Language and Literature*, *6* (1970): 136–51, esp. p. 145, has noted how JE's repetitions intensify some effects of *Sinners.*

8. Buckingham, "Stylistic Artistry," p. 149, points out: "The tight, formal outline of *Sinners* establishes a sense of progress, but each new argument begins by referring the hearts back to its point of departure, the scriptural text."

9. *The Writings of Benjamin Franklin*, ed. Albert H. Smyth, 10 vols. (1905–7; reprint, New York, 1970), *10:* 69.

10. Rosemary Hearn, "Form as Argument in Edwards' *Sinners in the Hands of an Angry God*," *College Language Association Journal*, *28* (1984–85): 452–59, argues that JE's ten Reasons or Proofs are all versions of a syllogism with a major premise, a minor premise, and a conclusion.

11. Edwin H. Cady, "The Artistry of Jonathan Edwards," *New England Quarterly*, *22* (1949): 61–72, esp. pp. 63–70; Annette Kolodny, "Imagery in the Sermons of Jonathan Edwards," *Early American Literature, 7* (1972): 172–82, esp. pp. 173–76; William J. Scheick, *The Writings of Jonathan Edwards: Theme, Motif, and Style* (College Station, Tex., 1975), pp. 72–79; and Thomas J. Steele, S. J., and Eugene R. Delay, "Vertigo in History: The Threatening Tactility of *Sinners in the Hands*," *Early American Literature, 18* (1983–84): 242–56.

12. My text is from *Benjamin Franklin: Writings*, ed. J. A. Leo Lemay (New York, 1987), pp. 540–58, cited simply as *W* within the text and subsequent notes. *A Narrative* is also available, with an excellent introduction and full notes, in *PBF*, *11:* 42–69.

13. Cicero, *De Inventione*, Book I, is the classic discussion. A good recapitulation may be found in Richard A. Lanham, *A Handlist of Rhetorical Terms* (Berkeley, 1969), pp. 112–13. In "The Text, Rhetorical Strategies, and Themes of 'The Speech of Miss Polly Baker,'" *The Oldest Revolutionary: Essays on Benjamin Franklin*, ed. J. A. Leo Lemay (Philadelphia, 1976), pp. 91–120, I examined BF's use of the oration form in a different (and earlier) work.

14. Though the text or thesis was commonly from the Bible, the text of John Winthrop's famous sermon "A Modell of Christian Charity" proves that such was not necessarily the case.

15. As a writer for the *New England Courant*, the young genius BF had satirically warned the editor (i.e. himself), "In writing your Courants, we advise you carefully to avoid the Form and Method of Sermons, for that is vile and impious in such a Paper as yours" (*W*46). BF had learned to burlesque sermons from Nathaniel Gardner's mock-jeremiads satirizing the Mathers. See Joseph Fireoved, "Nathaniel Gardner and the *New England Courant*," *Early American Literature*, 20 (1985): 214–35, esp. pp. 221–24. Theodore Hornberger, *Benjamin Franklin* (Minneapolis, 1962), pp. 19–20, pointed out that Franklin's *A Modest Enquiry into the Nature and Necessity of a Paper-Currency* (1729) used the Puritan sermon form. Discussing "The Way to Wealth," I pointed out how "Father Abraham's Speech" "parodies the structure and repetitive 'logical proofs' of the typical Puritan sermon." Lemay, "Benjamin Franklin," in *Major Writers of Early American Literature*, ed. Everett Emerson (Madison, Wis., 1972), pp. 205–43, esp. p. 217. One might also note that near the end of his life BF deliberately called attention to the traditional Puritan sermon structure in one of his last satires against the English assumption of superiority to America (*W*1122–30). See also J. A. Leo Lemay, *The Canon of Benjamin Franklin: New Attributions and Reconsiderations* (Newark, Del., 1986), p. 66.

16. For some notes on the intellectual background of the argument and for my argument that BF wrote the piece, see Lemay, *Canon of Franklin*, pp. 74–75.

17. Denis Barone, "A Note on the Influence of Lord Kames's Theory of Narrative on Benjamin Franklin's *A Narrative of the Late Massacres, 1764*," *American Notes and Queries*, n.s., *1*, no. 3 (1988): 93–97. The reaction of the populace proved to BF "the Depravity and Selfishness of human Minds." *PBF*, *11*: 159.

18. Ann Uhry Abrams, "Benjamin West's Documentation of Colonial History: William Penn's Treaty with the Indians," *Art Bulletin*, *64* (1982): 59–75; Charles Coleman Sellers, "The Beginning: A Monument to Probity, Candor and Peace," *Symbols of Peace: William Penn's Treaty with the Indians* (Philadelphia, 1976); Eleanore Price Mather and Dorothy Canning Miller, *Edward Hicks: His Peaceable Kingdoms and Other Paintings* (Newark, Del., 1983).

19. *The Papers of William Penn*, ed. Mary Dunn and Richard Dunn, 2 vols. (Philadelphia, 1981), 2: 422.

20. *Indian Treaties Printed by Benjamin Franklin 1736–1762*, ed. Julian P. Boyd, with an introduction by Carl Van Doren (Philadelphia, 1938).

21. Voltaire, *Letters from England*, trans. Leonard Tancock (New York, 1980), p. 34.

22. *The Conduct of the Paxton Men*, as reprinted in *The Paxton Papers*, ed. John R. Dunbar (The Hague, 1957), p. 286. See also Marvin Russell, "Thomas Barton and Pennsylvania's Colonial Frontier," *Pennsylvania History*, *46* (1979): 313–34.

23. *The Life of Muhammad: A Translation of Ishaq's Sirat Rasul Allah*, trans. and ed. A. Guillaume (London, 1955), p. 561; Benjamin Franklin, comp., *A Catalogue of Books Belonging to the Library Company of Philadelphia* (Philadelphia, 1741), p. 27.

24. For modern texts, see Andrew S. Ehrenkreutz, *Saladin* (Albany, N.Y., 1972), p. 202, or Geoffrey Regan, *Saladin and the Fall of Jerusalem* (London, 1987), p. 129.

25. Marvin Spevack, *A Complete and Systematic Concordance to the Works of Shakespeare*, 9 vols. (Herstellung, 1968–80). Spevack's *Concordance* is keyed to the line numbers in *The Riverside Shakespeare*, ed. G. Blakemore Evans (Boston, 1974).

26. BF probably alludes to Voltaire's *Letters from England*, Letter 4—one more indication of the idealistic and cosmopolitan background that the persona writing the *Narrative* has taken.

27. BF may echo Pope's *Dunciad*'s conclusion.

28. Larzer Ziff, "Introduction," *Benjamin Franklin's Autobiography and Selected Writings* (New York, 1959), pp. xx–xxi. See also Lemay, *Canon of Franklin*, p. 135.

29. For an edition of some of the pamphlets, see John R. Dunbar, *The Paxton Papers*; for a full listing, see the bibliography in David Sloan, "The Paxton Riots: A Study in Violence and Passive Resistance in Colonial Pennsylvania," unpublished Ph.D. dissertation, University of California, Santa Barbara, 1970.

30. *PBF*, 3: 186.

# 13

# Humanizing the Monster: Integral Self Versus Bodied Soul in the Personal Writings of Franklin and Edwards

R. C. DE PROSPO

I should begin by thanking David Shields for reminding me that the ancient Greeks can make a distinction between *pneuma* and *psyche*: between soul proper, which is supreme in the subhierarchy of the creature, and mind, which, no matter how gifted, focused, trained, stands one rank lower. Shields does his best work when alert to the apparently merely curious and anomalous arcana of the past, including the other-than-exclusively American past, as is true, I think, also of the many fine older scholars of seventeenth- and eighteenth-century culture in the British colonies of North America[1] and the early United States, many of whom are here at this conference. The assemblage and preservation of such arcana enables the perception of unanticipated, sometimes even "*extra vagant*" structures—recall Thoreau's philological play in the conclusion of *Walden*.[2] It is fastidious research such as Shields's that enables extravaganzas, like the teratology I'm going to propose here.

What I'm going to propose here is that an absolutely impermeable barrier can be supposed to exist between soul and mind, and that such an absolutely impermeable barrier can be found not only in the ontology of antiquity but also, suprisingly, in the personal writings of eighteenth-century enlightened heterodox secularists, as well as eighteenth-century awakened fundamentalist evangelicals. This, I should confess, is probably far from anything Shields himself may want to arise from his resurrection of the ancient soul/mind dichotomy. Shields mentions the arcane array, *pneuma, psyche, soma* (body), *sarx* (flesh) (But it scans as memorably as the nursery rhyme/Le Carré title, "Tinker, Tailor, Soldier, Spy," doesn't it?) in "The Object of the Text in Early American Literature," an essay designed to counter with some objectivist hermeneutics Michael Clark's subjectivist, phenomenological, literary theoretist "The Subject of the Text in Early American Literature," which appeared in *Early American Literature* in 1985. Shields was told by *Early American Literature* to omit what he calls in a letter to me the "personal testimonia: but since that was the most scandalous part of the essay, I declined and withdrew," and so the object of the text remains unpublished (but maybe not unpublishable, maybe not unreadable, as I will speculate in my conclusions).[3] Although recalling an ancient hierarchizing of the self in the essay, Shields, following the exegesis of Kierkegaard and Rudolph Bultmann, talks of a "complex play" among the four constituents of human identity, and so joins, in my more strictly orthodox view, what God has put asunder.[4] In implicitly reconstituting as a modern humanist integral self what was originally given as a theist monstrous bodied soul, according to the phrasing of the difference in my title, Shields invites in the back door precisely the play-ful, frolicsome guest that he wants, in contesting Clark, to exclude: that is, modern humanist, poststructuralist, theory.

I'm more than sympathetic toward Shields's project—toward our project—which is to save the texts of early American literature. At the end of an essay that Shields has managed to get accepted promptly, in a recent issue of *Early American Literature*, Shields states this aspiration eloquently, a little bit plaintively, in the context of arguing for the recuperation of "Nathaniel Gardner, Jr., and the Literary Culture of Boston in the 1750s":

> To the extent that we find the rites of literary obeisance offensive, we lose the ethos of literary culture in British America. It may be that the songs of liberty sound too resonantly in our hearing as Americans to recover an attunement to the music of British American poetry. Its decorums insist too vehemently on the security of learning and tradition; its voice is too self-deprecating to suit our post-revolutionary confidence and autonomy. Nonetheless, the spirit of British American neoclassicism is not wholly beyond our appreciation. In the works of a proficient poet like Gardner, one encounters a sense of craft, a refined ethos, and a mood of composure that can compensate in some measure for the restriction of scope and lack of invention.[5]

We all share Shields's intuition that to save early American literature we must find a way, in some measure, to set aside presentism—a ringing in the ears of what Shields calls "songs of liberty." This is, of course, in one sense a commonplace, taught, as Henry F. May notes in the inaugural paper of the big Edwards conference held several years ago at Wheaton College, "in our first courses in historiography";[6] scholars of Edwards ought to be particularly wary of presentism, if only because Edwards himself cautions against it, in the passage from *Freedom of the Will* that derides those who would presume to improve upon "ancient and eminent divines,"[7] a passage that May mentions as "a sufficient put-down of liberal presentism"[8] and that once seemed to me so clairvoyant of certain modernist attitudes toward Edwards himself, that I used it as the epigraph for a book on the phenomenon of Edwards in modern American cultural historiography.[9]

But Shields is also resisting another, more insidious, type of presentism. I'm not sure this type can be sufficiently warned against, because it doesn't simply reject but complexly patronizes early American literature, finding there presentiments of its very own, very highly evolved, self, in the manner, for example, of the subjectivist/theoretist essay by Clark to which Shields would oppose "The Object of the Text." I think, however, that in order effectively to guard against this second, more stubborn and pervasive, way of diminishing early American literature, we're going to have to find ways to be less apologetic, and more extremist, than Shields; we're going to have to find ways to read, and to teach, without shame what Shields stigmatizes variously as the "obeisance," "tradition," "self-deprecation," "decorums," "restriction," and "lack of invention" of the discourse of human identity in early American literature; we're going to have to find something interesting and useful in those very nonself-expressions, or self-nonexpressions, that even a partisan like Shields has to confess are uncongenial. I'd like to suggest how a revision of early American literature can be accomplished by following Thoreau (What could be more American? More modern?) in his return to verbal origins; I'm going to try to differentiate the first words of those most canonical texts of Franklin and Edwards, their personal writings, from the song of modern American selfhood, the song that has been made out—beneath the noise of "tradition," "obeisance," "restriction"—by so many early Americanists.

Who worries about first words any more? Franklin writes a "little history," or "a history of my life," or memoirs, that are retroactively, posthumously, transformed into "autobiography," which of course they can't be, because the word, and hence what the word signifies, doesn't exist in English until about forty years after Franklin's death.

Bibliographical and philological pedantry? "Autobiography" is simultaneous with romanticism (And so, even more to complicate the matter, is philology, including Thoreau's philology; beware late-eighteenth-century Germans, and mid nineteenth-century Americans after them, bearing neo-Platonic autonyms). And the romantic literary historiography that would have "autobiography" being written from time immemorial may be tendentious in ways that romantic literary historiography must disguise and conceal in order to maintain its literary historiographical authority; at least this is the suspicion of a host of insistently and powerfully troubled theorists of romanticism—Foucault, Derrida, de Man, Todorov, Said. That so many old texts are recovered and renamed around 1800 may thus be no accident, and their recovery and renaming may signify something more important, and more partial, than romanticism's mere disinterested esteem for and promotion of the past.[10]

Transformations such as the one that turns memoirs—I'm going to stick with "memoirs" for now because I like the unfamiliar sound of the plural, and of the French—into "autobiography" are certainly not isolated, especially not in American literary historiography: Benjamin Rush writes travels through life, not intended for publication beyond the circle of his family; Jefferson writes memoranda, probably not intended for any kind of publication at all; John Adams writes a sketch called "John Adams" and some diary entries, which are later cobbled together to form a text that, as Bernard Bailyn observes, "hardly exists as an integral document";[11] earlier, Rowlandson writes *The Sovereignty and Goodness of God, Together with the Faithfulness of His Promises Delayed: Being a Narrative of the Captivity and Restauration of Mrs. Mary Rowlandson . . . .*, intended to justify certain apparently discouraging works of God in Massachusetts Bay Colony to man;[12] earlier still Thomas Shepard writes records, intended for his son; and then, of course, there's Edwards, Edwards who writes . . .

What? A letter? An account of his conversion addressed to a single fellow Christian, Samuel Hopkins? Because Edwards wouldn't be willing to identify Hopkins, or anybody else, for that matter, as a disciple, an "Edwardsean," given Edwards's opinions on falling into the state of being a disciple of any man, even of Calvin, opinions aired most conspicuously in *Freedom of the Will*, but also elsewhere throughout his controversial writings, Edwards can't be supposed to anticipate, and thus partly to bear responsibility for, a posthumous wider publication, and the eventual canonization, of the account of his conversion. So to call Edwards's . . . whatever . . . a "personal narrative," this is innocent? a matter only of clarity? of convenience? And similarly to call Rush, Jefferson, Adams, and Shepard "autobiographers"? And similarly to ignore—really, to censor—the grammar, the syntax, the style, of Rowlandson's title by shortening it to "captivity narrative"?

The process of humanizing the . . . am I by now permitted to use some word other than "self" without seeming overfinicky? The process of humanizing the entity that produces these texts and is written about in them, a process governed by what John F. Lynen calls "the design of the present,"[13] begins even before the first words of these texts are read, begins by effacing the first words, the original titles or quasi-titles or non-titles, and thereby begins to familiarize, comfort, sedate us even before we begin to read, and conversely tries to foreclose even before we begin to read our opportunity to read these texts otherwise—to make them strange. This is the most subtle and radical kind of modern humanist misprision: most subtle because it is totally unself-conscious, totally unaware of itself, and so incapable of recognizing its tendencies as tendencies, as anything other than common sense, or, even more self-mystifying, as no sense at all, as merely a transcription, a xeroxing, of the text *an sich*; and most radical because it strikes at, even just simply strikes, the very first words, the root of the text, the title.

This subtle and radical misprision continues in modern humanist readings of what comes immediately after the first words as well, the openings of Franklin's memoirs and of Edwards's account of his conversion, openings that are universally, albeit often silently, dismissed, or at least demoted, in the interest of somehow making salient and whole what must necessarily appear to modern humanist readings, at least initially, as the unemphatic and disintegrated entity that writes these texts and is written about in them.

Franklin's memoirs and Edwards's account of his conversion can only seem to modern humanist readings to begin badly. The unpretentiousness of Franklin's title can be corrected with relative ease, and almost invisibly, and Edwards's blank can be filled in even more easily and unobtrusively. But what about the unmistakable, the redundantly declared, narrowness of Franklin's intentions—the epistolary salutation to Franklin's son, the cheerful admission that the few introductory personal recollections and genealogical discoveries are relevant only to Franklin's family, even the broader apology that addresses the memoirs just to ambitious young men who may be in need of a conduct-book, a way to wealth? What about all the informalities, the desultory anecdotes, the bad jokes, that dominate the first few paragraphs of the memoirs? And what about Edwards's more than just vaguely repellant, more than self-effacing, his downright self-despising, his self-annihilating, and his infuriatingly brief, account of youth and adolescence on the Connecticut River Valley frontier—that "fair seed-time" (recall not just Wordsworth but Ola Winslow recalling Wordsworth, putatively in Edwards's behalf)[14] not only of an individual's but of our very own collective national identity, or so at least we have been taught, and taught—three paragraphs that open Edwards's account of his conversion by characterizing what modern humanist retrospect takes to be foundational personalizing and Americanizing experience as a dog returning to its vomit. Various energetic and ingenious restorative efforts, and more than a few simple acts of repression, are inspired by these beginnings, all designed somehow to make these beginnings either disappear or appear to introduce selves to whom we can spontaneously relate. What is taken for granted is that these beginnings deface the "autobiographies" that they are supposed to head.

Let's see how far we can go following William Spengemann's suggestion that Franklin's memoirs are "something of an anachronism, a holdover from a vanished age."[15] Let's take one of the least fetching passages from the opening of Franklin's memoirs, one that seems merely outrageous and irreverent, and only questionably enlightened, and that does not, at least to my knowledge, ever elicit much more than brief comment from any of Franklin's modern commentators. Take what seems to be one of the worst jokes, which seems to have been left carelessly lying around or stuck in, sore-thumb fashion, to conclude what we modern humanist readers of "autobiography" would anticipate to be at least potentially a crucial and fascinating representation of Franklin's researches in England into the lives of his ancestors. How can we take seriously Franklin's indulging what seems to us the frivolous superstition of metempsychosis: Metempsychosis, that is not exactly a key to modern self-consciousness, although Joyce does manage to make a pretty good running gag out of it in *Ulysses,* beginning with Molly's vaguely salacious, ignorant malapropism, "met him pike hoses";[16] metempsychosis, that seems so precisely and egregiously discredited by the human sciences of genealogy, of genetics, of heredity. What are we supposed to call a writer who indulges this superstition so early in his memoirs, and so prominently, in the very first, the very brief, and the single attempt in all of the memoirs to attribute human identity to family background?

"Autobiographer"? Consider this. Franklin scants the importance of lineage: first, by stating that it is of some small interest to his son alone, as a memoir in the very narrowest sense, and is thus ineligible for wider publication, and so Franklin will have of course then subsequently to supersede this address to his son, defending the wider publication of the memoirs with a justification that seems to us modern readers of "autobiography," in descending order of acceptability, disingenuous, gratuitous, beside the point, or philistine, which is that the memoirs may serve as a conduct-book, a way to wealth, for ambitious young men; second, by refusing to do any more than hazard facetiously, and not even in his own stead (Franklin of course blames his son for the comment), an irrational, supernatural, non-explanation of whatever prodigious continuities of human identity may be detected, even in the direct line of descent within a single family. Franklin is surprisingly, maybe to many of us disappointingly, meiotic on the subject of human being here—surprisingly or disappointingly or both because all of the ingredients are present for Franklin to proclaim some proto-evolutionist, or hereditarian, or geneticist, anthropology. And so Franklin's difference is here especially, even painfully, uncovered, because at the very moment when man in his modern humanist guise seems almost inevitably to be about to appear, Franklin attributes quintessential human identity, *pneuma,* to an Other so distant and ineffable as to have no discourse at all, or what is here the equivalent of no discourse at all, that of ancient myth.[17] The quintessential Franklin (and this phrase is oxymoron, the monster of rhetoric, in keeping with the monstrous structure of human identity that I find in the memoirs, because *pneuma* has no family name, is debased by family name) comes from elsewhere, is neither originated nor perpetuated by human agency, neither human volition nor some occulted version of human volition, the involuntary but nonetheless purposive and coherent force that is presupposed in all modern humanist evolutionist, hereditarian, geneticist theory.

So here's Franklin, at the very start of his memoirs on the very subject of human identity exposing himself as a practitioner of what has come to be known since patristic times as occasionalist cosmogony. And thereby repeating not just the Bible or the early Church fathers, but also, closer to home, repeating Jonathan Edwards, and Jonathan Edwards at his most forbiddingly theist, when Edwards uses occasionalist cosmogony to support the doctrine of imputation to justify damning unbaptized infants to hell. Edwards does this in *Original Sin*, the treatise that a prominent contemporary scholar of Edwards condemns as intellectually poverty-stricken, particularly and explicitly in contrast to Edwards's *True Virtue*, which this same scholar deems comparable to that humanist bible of proto-anthropologist, proto-socialist humanism, written around the same time as both *Original Sin* and *True Virtue*: the Social Contract.[18]

And still more. Franklin repeats not just such supposedly, at least in this context, retrograde misanthropes as the biblical prophets, the early Church fathers, and Edwards, but also one of the most celebrated, seemingly forward-looking of revolutionaries in the British Colonies of North America and the early United States. He's not quite a founding father, maybe, but he's a founding godfather, at least, and reduced to this status primarily because he seems to modern humanist retrospect too radical a proponent of human being. He who is so often cast as America's very own Rousseau, or even Marx, or even Kropotkin, but he who, despite these apparent gratifying precocities, alludes to the doctrine of imputation repeatedly and systematically to ground human identity and thus human rights on the onto-theological origin of mankind, "the time when man comes from the hand of his maker."[19] Thus does . . . Thomas Paine, in *The Rights of Man*, join Benjamin Franklin and Jonathan Edwards in accepting at the deepest discursive level, beneath the generic differences separating political, personal, and theological writings, the helpless dependency of mankind for its very existence on the will of an Other.

Beyond the possible recuperation of what I realize may still be easily dismissed as a trivial passage from Franklin's memoirs, what is accomplished by thus defamiliarizing Franklin's resorting to the myth of metempsychosis to account for a resemblance between himself and a great-uncle whom he never met, a resemblance that we would instantly understand and account for differently, as proof of human autogeny, of heredity. Not only don't I have the space to specify how this way of reading can benefit Franklin's memoirs as an individual text; I'm much more interested in the benefits this way of reading has for the study of early American literature as a whole, and beyond even that, in its benefits for the internationalist theorizing of the sciences of man, the world in which I believe all area study, including even that of early American literature, will ultimately and eventually have to find its place, like it or not. So I'll just invite you, teasingly, to imagine what happens when Franklin's memoirs are read as restricting themselves scrupulously, even to the point of appearing perverse or inhumane or unfeeling, to reporting only that thing which is within the power of man as bodied soul certainly to know, the *psyche*, and never even attempting, except in such joking asides as the reference to metempsychosis, to report what is unknowable, not conceived, never controlled, not even reliably experienced by man, *pneuma*. Try to imagine such an entity as Franklin is in the memoirs, a monstrosity containing the disparate and immiscible components, soul and mind, writing in a form that is decidedly other than "autobiography," some other genre entirely; "memoirs" probably doesn't even sound strange enough—try "profane letters," or Horatian "*splendide mendax*," or Platonic "*gennaion pseudos*," these latter two being prominent Roman neoclassical and ancient Greek classical models, largely forgotten today, authorizing vulgar and mendacious rhetoric calculated obliquely to achieve noble and veracious ends.[20]

Or even still-life, some literary equivalent of preromantic *nature morte*, which as practiced by early French and Flemish painters manages both to dwell on quotidia and also to acknowledge not only the ephemerality of quotidia—seventeenth-century Dutch still-lifes often contain medieval death's-heads—but also the potential guilt, and risk, of dwelling on ephemeral quotidia—early *vanitas* still-lifes implicitly warn, for example by placing in almost impossibly precarious situations the very things in which the observer is invited to become absorbed, against the sinister hoaxing or idolatrous potential of their own art, which is originally and remains for some time complicit in *trompe l'oeil*.

And, finally, to those Franklin scholars who are admittedly making good livings these days working variously on how in the memoirs Franklin becomes Benjamin Franklin, how the memoirs textualize the self, or more generally how they adumbrate the modern humanist, poststructuralist theorizing of the self, or even of presence, I extend, mischievously, an invitation to wonder whether the ultimate beneficiary of their work will be Franklin's memoirs or, rather, such fully-fledged problematizings of the self as Melville's *Pierre*, or Melville's *The Confidence-Man*—or does all this talk of Franklin's "becoming" presume to embellish the text that's about as far beyond needing the support of *epigoni* today as Edwards's sovereign God is beyond profiting from puny human worship in the British colonies of North America and the early United States, the evidently ubiquitous, evidently deathless, *Phenomenology* of Hegel.

In conclusion, back to Edwards's vomit. Another, less obviously neglected beginning—this one always mentioned, because very early, very conspicuous, even unusually detailed and so unusually vivid in this otherwise unspecific and discontinuous account, but never concentrated on for very long because it describes an episode that seems even more

unawakened than Franklin's reference to metempsychosis seems unen-
lightened—is Edwards's description of his booth in the swamp.

And doesn't this episode seem actually a little worse than unenlight-
ened—even vaguely suspicious? I once had a girlfriend—she was from
northern New England and so probably knew better than I what boys
up there do alone in the woods—who always insisted that she knew
exactly what Edwards was up to in that booth. I dismissed this at the
time as simple mockery. I should have known better. It was complex mockery, directed at me more than at Edwards, or at me through
Edwards, and, once fully unpacked, it is suggestive of a denial on my
part about which I used to be more than complacent, about which I
used to be unconscious, but which I now realize was crippling to my
project. What's going on in that booth is much worse, is a great deal
more threatening to me as a modern reader of "autobiography," than
merely genital self-abuse.

The account of the erection of the booth in the swamp is a personal
narrative: it's personal, at least potentially, involving little Edwards's
natural association of piety with heroism and adventure, and it has, at
least potentially, a rich narrative structure, involving not only the construction of the thing, little Edwards hauling boards or, more likely, tree-
limbs, but all sorts of social dimensions implicated in the exploit—think
of the opportunities to portray little Edwards trying to hide from, trying to explain to, finally deciding to share with, his playmates his ingenious plaything, think of the hiding, the deceptions needed to get there
and back, think of the opportunities even for humor, even for suspense.
Here are all the raw materials for the story of Tom Sawyer's robber gang.

But of course to big Edwards it's all too personal, all too narrative,
and so it's all scorned as a false awakening, and so none of these personal or these narrative potentials are actualized. I could say here—as
I've said before—just that this proves simply and decisively that Edwards's
account of his conversion is neither personal nor a narrative except in
passing, except when it fails, except when Edwards is unawakened, except
when Edwards's *psyche* is recognized by him in retrospect to gain ascen-
dency over his *pneuma*, when account of conversion degenerates into
Goddamned story.

I want to go farther now. The erection of the booth in the swamp
can be seen to represent an attempt on Edwards's part somewhat, somehow, to reconcile *psyche*—his inventiveness, his resourcefulness, his cour-
age—with *pneuma*—his abstraction, his cloistered, supernatural quintessence. Thus he constructs a monster, a monument of, or to, asceticism,
an idol of, or to, otherworldliness.[21] But what else is the whole account
of Edwards's conversion, no matter how underpublished, no matter how
laboriously qualified, no matter how obsessively policed, either to ban-
ish or to etiolate or clearly to stigmatize its few, rare, personal or narrative passages or insinuations? What I've been repressing is the realiza-
tion that the erection of the booth in the swamp can be read as *mise en*

*abime*, that is to say, as the part of the text that can be read to equal the whole of the text, but *mise en abime* that stages a real abyss, that does not gloriously proclaim the ubiquity of discourse, and thus the ubiquity of human being, as is invariably the case with the discovery of *mises* by contemporary literary theory ever since André Gide, but that invalidates absolutely the capacity of discourse, or of the natural creature who is distinguished among natural creatures by his unique ability to discourse, to give an account of what really matters—his awakening, his quintessence, his *pneuma*. You see, it's all vomit, even the good parts.

Tough talk. You might think that by now—doesn't it seem like a hundred years since Michael Colacurcio announces that Edwards's modernity is a "dead issue"?[22]—there would be little need to stress so brutally Edwards's difference. Let me call your attention to the latest book on Edwards from Princeton, on Edwards's "philosophical theology" to be precise, whose first two words are "Perry Miller" and whose second paragraph begins thus: "My contention in the present volume is that Edwards was actually more radically 'modern' than Miller himself might have realized."[23] And then there's the article in the last issue of *Religious Studies* that *The Chronicle of Higher Education* considers sufficiently groundbreaking to profile in its regular column, "Research Notes," an article that considers—this in *The Chronicle*'s characterization—"the tactile quality of" Edwards's *Images or Shadows of Divine Things* sufficient to qualify as theoerotica, an article that—*The Chronicle*'s characterization again—"suggests the quality of intimacy and *eros* that Edwards's understanding of human-divine love encompassed."[24]

But Colacurcio may be less wrong than, as is so often the case with Colacurcio, ahead of his time. There does seem to be a movement of late among scholars of Edwards to toughen up, to take a "full look at the Worst" in Hardy's phase, appropriately from *In Tenebris* (II), and to face up to the inhumanities and atavisms that seem now to many to have been underplayed by . . .

I tried to get through this essay without mentioning him in my own voice, but now I give up . . . by Perry Miller. Like so much else in scholarship, this doesn't really make it new: it seems forever since Vincent Thomas takes out after Miller's empirical accuracy, and it's been a while, too, since David Levin worries that the Edwards characterized in his seminal Profile "is too sweet to serve as a just representation of the historical actuality."[25] Emphases of Edwards's dark "historical actuality" that are much less balanced and temperate than Levin's are becoming, if not dominant, at least much more insistent lately—look, for example, at the attacks on Miller's proto-humanist portrait of Edwards in many of the essays from the big Edwards conference at Wheaton College. Insofar as this is a matter only of professional positioning, it doesn't mean much and will pass. But there seems to me also a harder, and more regrettable, version of this toughness lately. In a sense this doesn't make it new either; Joseph Haroutunian was recommending Edwards as a tough-minded corrective to modern humanist optimism a hundred years ago.[26] But in today's climate of curricular and theoretical sectarianism, the position contributes to an ominously reactionary program, becomes a sort of crypto-neofundamentalism that would use Edwards to punish bleeding-heart liberalism, as if a sour dose of Edwardsean absolutism may well season what seems to some the current confection of relativism, a few would say even anarchism, in the academy. I'd be sorry if I were mistaken as making common cause with such dangerously sentimental yearnings for a world without theory.

Neither Quixote nor Luddite nor Ayotollah, I would make the personal writings of Franklin and Edwards reader-unfriendly in order, by way of difference, to advance the theorizing of the subject. In the world of theory, which is where the scholarship of early American literature is going someday to have to learn to live, the major project today is the search for the counter-discourse, for what can be said to lie outside of modern humanism, for a discourse that can be read somehow legitimately to inscribe otherness, a discourse whose existence must now be posited in order fully to expose modern humanism itself to the play of difference. Thus there is a pressing need internationally somehow to make legible, *contra* modern humanism, what is always already potentially subjectivized in modern humanist discourse—to make legible what David Shields calls the object of the text. In the study of early American literature we have a great, for the most part unexploited, opportunity to uncover just such an object: not any forgotten or repressed or mystified projection of the subject; not an essentialized or totalized or monumentalized figure; not a signifier hiding its brackets, quotation marks, erasure; but some thing real, given, created by a Power that is actually prior to language and whose truth is therefore con-, rather than decon-, structionist.

But of course it isn't here, it isn't now. It's there, it's then. Here and now we have, rather, "it." I'm not going to ask, along with the opening of the latest book on Edwards from Oxford, "not only, 'Why was Edwards great?' but 'Was Edwards right?'" and, moreover, "not only, 'Was Edwards right?' but 'Is he?'"[27] Is Edwards right? No, Emerson is right, right for us, for here, for now, that is. To differentiate Edwards from Emerson, or to differentiate Franklin from Rousseau or Goethe, or Melville, or Frederick Douglass or Henry Adams for that matter, is fully to realize the force of those slightest of words, those merely infra-linguistic connectors, those prepositions, those "for"s—for us, for here, for now—and thereby fully to realize our integral, not monstrous, human being—us, here, now—to be indistinguishable from language.

## Notes

1. I'm here avoiding the terms "America" and "American," in keeping with William C. Spengemann's critique of the whiggish tendency to establish presentist

continuities in the literary history of the British Colonies of North America and the early United States, a tendency that is implied in the rhetorical totalizing buried in the terms "America" and "American." Spengemann onomastically and from the outset makes stranger the literature of the British Colonies of North America by never referring to it simply as "American." See, in particular, "Discovering the Literature of British America" in *A Mirror for Americanists, Reflections on the Idea of American Literature* (Hanover, N.H., and London, 1989).

2. Henry David Thoreau, *Walden* (Boston, 1960), p. 221.

3. As it turns out, more than a little bit ironically, although the publishability and readability of "The Object of the Text" may at one time have depended somewhat on concluding speculations of mine, they don't any longer. Evidently in some small part because of the prominence I gave "The Object of the Text" when I delivered this paper at the Franklin/Edwards conference in February 1990 at Yale, *Early American Literature*—I don't know whether or not after exacting a few concessions from Shields—reconsidered and published "The Object of the Text." And *Early American Literature* did so before the close of 1990. David S. Shields, "The Object of the Text," *Early American Literature*, 25 (1990): 307–315. Which is to say, considerably before the paper you're reading was published. Not the least of the appeal of "The Object of the Text" to me—as a last-minute replacement at the Yale conference for a long-invited senior conferee suddenly taken ill—was that it represented a somewhat marginal(ized) effort by a relatively marginal(ized) junior scholar in the field. Since "The Object of the Text" has been so prominently published, and since Shields himself promises inevitably, and perhaps momentarily, to become a very prominent member of the field, himself, "The Object of the Text," ironically, no longer serves my original purposes quite so well.

4. Shields, "Object," p. 308.

5. David Shields, "Nathaniel Gardner, Jr., and the Literary Culture of Boston in 1750s," *Early American Literature*, 24, no. 2 (1989): 196–216, p. 207.

6. Henry F. May, "Jonathan Edwards and America," in *Jonathan Edwards and the American Experience*, ed. Norman O. Hatch and Harry S. Stout (New York, 1988), p. 21.

7. *WJE, 1*: 437.

8. May, "Edwards and America," pp. 25–26.

9. R. C. De Prospo, *Theism in the Discourse of Jonathan Edwards* (Newark, Del., 1985), p. 8.

10. Contemporary literary theory frequently problematizes forms of what has come to be known as "life-writing" as part of its project to problematize selfhood and the subject in general. For example, de Man notes both the historicity and the tendentiousness of the invention of "autobiography," in particular and particularly to the point here, as a more prestigious substitute for "memories": "By making autobiography into a genre, one elevates it above the literary status of mere reportage, chronicle, or memories." Paul de Man, *The Rhetoric of Romanticism* (New York, 1984), p. 67. Derrida thinks enough of the passage to quote it as a means of putting into question Derrida's own, modest, reversion to the form of "memories" to commemorate his dead friend. Jacques Derrida, *Memories for Paul de Man*, trans. Cecile Lindsay, Jonathan Culler, and Eduardo Cadava (New York, 1986), pp. 22–23.

11. Bernard Bailyn, "Butterfield's Adams: Notes for a Sketch," *William and Mary Quarterly*, 19 (1962): 238–56, p. 242.

12. Even "*The Sovereignty and Goodness of God . . .*" is not definitively the original title of Rowlandson's account, the remains of the first edition of which being no more than four leaves recycled in the seventeenth century by somebody to serve as endpapers to help preserve Samuel Willard's 1682 sermon "Covenant-Keeping." Because it is known that the first edition of Rowlandson's account was published in combination with her husband Joseph Rowlandson's last sermon, and because it is also known that so-called "captivity narratives," especially the earliest ones, were frequently integrated within, or attached as pendants to, other, more straightforwardly sermonic, works, it is entirely possible that Mary Rowlandson's account was secondary to, and perhaps therefore subsumed under the title of, her husband Joseph's sermon, "The Possibility of God's forsaking a people, that have been visibly near and dear to him, together with the misery of a people thus forsaken." See *National Index of American Imprints Before 1800, The Short Title Evans* (n.p., 1969), entry no. 39221.

13. John F. Lynen, *The Design of the Present* (New Haven, 1969).

14. "On such days, his East Windsor boyhood was indeed 'fair seed-time' for the soul of a philosopher." Ola Elizabeth Winslow, *Jonathan Edwards, 1703–1758* (New York, 1940), p. 43.

15. William C. Spengemann, *The Forms of Autobiography: Episodes in the History of a Literary Genre* (New Haven, 1980), p. 57.

16. James Joyce, *Ulysses* (New York, 1986), p. 126.

17. Disparagement of metempsychosis is very prominent, and very orthodox, in Enlightened circles, having been of course famously expressed by Locke himself in the *Essay Concerning Human Understanding*. So common is the knowledge of Locke's scorn that a Poe scholar can plausibly claim not only that Poe is aware of it, but that Poe's "Morella" can be understood as a kind of fraud or hoax because of the story's apparent willingness, *contra* Locke, to entertain the possibility of the transmigration of souls—in this case implicitly satirized because the recipient of hand-me-down *pneuma* is no relative of the original host-body, no human being at all, but a horse. S. Gerald Sandler, "Poe's Indebtedness to Locke's *An Essay Concerning Human Understanding*," *Boston University Studies in English*, 5 (1961): 107–21, p. 110.

18. Norman Fiering, *Jonathan Edwards's Moral Thought and Its British Context* (Chapel Hill, N.C., 1981), pp. 48, 335.

19. From "The Rights of Man," in *Thomas Paine*, ed. Harry Hayden Clark (New York, 1961), p. 85.

20. I'm in debt to the late Richard Rodino, whose posthumous article educated me about the existence of such apparently perverse para- or quasi-genres in antiquity, as well as about their survival into much later, Augustan, eighteenth-century English satire: "In [George] Faulkner's 1735 edition of *Gulliver's Travels* the first words identify the protagonist as 'splendide mendax,' a liar for the public good. . . . The allusion is not only to Horace but also to Plato's vastly influential statement of the 'noble lie,' in *The Republic*. Plato's term, *gennaion pseudos*, describes a lie at once high-minded and well-bred, the instrument of a privileged social class, of those in power." Richard H. Rodino, "'Splendide Mendax': Authors, Characters, and Readers in *Gulliver's Travels*," *PMLA, 106*, no. 5 (October 1991): 1054–77, p. 1056.

21. The dubiousness of fusing *pneuma*, as *pneuma* is deployed iconographically in the theology and philosophy of the ancient world, with any thing other or less than spiritual, except teratologically, as I'm outlining here, is very powerfully

stated in a very different context by somebody who knows a lot more than I about the ancient languages: "A student of patristics would [not at all necessarily] be . . . justified in saying that since *pneuma* means both 'spirit' and 'breath,' the outlook of the fathers of the Greek church must have been a materialistic one. That might be a heretical reading of Christianity; allow, at least, that easy divisions between such pairs as immanence and transcendence assume that all problems of meaning and truth have been solved"—which is to say, a modern philological conflation that seizes upon an ancient etymological synonym ought no longer to be accepted, blindly, as merely disinterestedly re-searching a historical fact. Haun Saussy, "The Metaphysics of Translation," *PMLA Forum, 105*, no. 5 (October 1990): 1128–29.

22. Michael Colacurcio, "The Example of Edwards: Idealist Imagination and the Metaphysics of Sovereignty," in *Puritan Influences in American Literature,* ed. Emory Elliott (Urbana, Ill., 1979), p. 55.

23. Sang Hyun Lee, *The Philosophical Theology of Jonathan Edwards* (Princeton, N.J., 1988), p. 3.

24. Ellen K. Coughlin, "Research Notes" (profile of Paula M. Cooey's "*Eros and Intimacy in Edwards*," *The Journal of Religion, 69* [October 1989]: 484–501), *The Chronicle of Higher Education*, January 31, 1990, p. 5.

25. Vincent Thomas, "The Modernity of Jonathan Edwards," *New England Quarterly, 25*, no. 1 (March 1952): 60–85; David Levin, ed., *Jonathan Edwards, A Profile* (New York, 1969), p. xvi.

26. Not really quite a hundred years, yet. Joseph Haroutunian, *Piety Versus Moralism* (New York, 1929).

27. Robert Jensen, *America's Theologian: A Recommendation of Jonathan Edwards* (New York, 1988), p. viii.

# Index